JAMES McCAFFREY OCD

CAPTIVE
FLAMES

A BIBLICAL READING OF
THE CARMELITE SAINTS

First published 2005 by
Veritas Publications
7/8 Lower Abbey Street
Dublin 1
Ireland
Email publications@veritas.ie
Website www.veritas.ie

ISBN 1 85390 920 3

A catalogue record for this book
is available from the British Library.

Cover image shows an icon by Sister Mary Grace,
copies of which are available from:
Carmelite Monastery, 59 Allendale, Terre Haute, IN 47802, USA
812-299-1410
heartsawake.org

Cover Design by Bill Bolger
Printed in the Republic of Ireland
by Betaprint Dublin

Veritas books are printed on paper made from the wood pulp of managed
forests. For every tree felled, at least one tree is planted, thereby renewing
natural resources.

IN MEMORIAM

To my parents

Denis and Alice,

who first taught me to pray in the spirit of Carmel.

CONTENTS

NOTE ON EDITIONS USED AND SYMBOLS TO DENOTE THEM

Works by Teresa of Avila

The Collected Works of St. Teresa of Avila, 3 vols, tr. Kieran Kavanaugh, OCD & Otilio Rodriguez, OCD, Washington, DC: ICS Publications, 1987, 1980 & 1985, including:

C	*The Constitutions*
F	*The Book of Her Foundations*
IC	*The Interior Castle*
Life	*The Book of Her Life*
M	*Meditations on the Song of Songs*
Sat Cri	*A Satirical Critique*
Sp Test	*Spiritual Testimonies*
WP	*The Way of Perfection*

Works by John of the Cross

The Collected Works of Saint John of the Cross, tr. Kieran Kavanaugh, OCD & Otilio Rodriguez, OCD, Washington, DC: ICS Publications, 1991, including:

A	*The Ascent of Mount Carmel*
DN	*The Dark Night*
LF	*The Living Flame of Love*
P	*Poetry*
R	*Romances*

| SC | *The Spiritual Canticle* |
| SLL | *The Sayings of Light and Love* |

Works by Elizabeth of the Trinity

Complete Works of Elizabeth of the Trinity, 2 vols, tr. Aletheia Kane, OCD (vol. I) & Anne Englund Nash (vol. 2), Washington, DC: ICS Publications, 1984 & 1995, including:

GV	*The Greatness of our Vocation*
HF	*Heaven in Faith*
L	*Letters from Carmel [L 84-342]*
LR	*Last Retreat*
PT	*Prayer to the Trinity ['O my God, Trinity whom I adore']*

Œuvres complètes d'Élisabeth de la Trinité, vol. II, Paris: Cerf, 1985, including:

D	*Diary*
IN	*Intimate Notes*
L	*Letters from her Youth [L 1-83]*
Pm	*Poems*

Works by Edith Stein

FEB	*Finite and Eternal Being*, tr. Kurt F. Reinhardt, Washington, DC: ICS Publications, 2002
HL	*The Hidden Life*, tr. Waltraut Stein, Washington, DC: ICS Publications, 1992
LJF	*Life in a Jewish Family*, tr. Josephine Koeppel, OCD, Washington, DC: ICS Publications, 1986
MC	*The Mystery of Christmas: Incarnation and Humanity*, tr. Josephine Rucker, SSJ, Darlington Carmel, 1985
Sci Cr	*The Science of the Cross*, tr. Josephine Koeppel, OCD, Washington, DC: ICS Publications, 2002

SEL   *Edith Stein: Selected Writings*, tr. Susanne M Batzdorff, Springfield, IL: Templegate, 1990

SP   *Self-Portrait in Letters 1916-1942*, tr. Josephine Koeppel, OCD, Washington, DC: ICS Publications, 1993

Works by Thérèse of Lisieux

LC   *St. Thérèse of Lisieux: Her Last Conversations*, tr. John Clarke, OCD, Washington, DC: ICS Publications, 1977

LT   *General Correspondence*, 2 vols, tr. John Clarke, OCD, Washington, DC: ICS Publications, 1982 & 1988

PN   *The Poetry of Saint Thérèse of Lisieux*, tr. Donald Kinney, OCD, Washington, DC: ICS Publications, 1996

Pri   *The Prayers of Saint Thérèse of Lisieux*, tr. Aletheia Kane, OCD, Washington, DC: ICS Publications, 1997

SS   *Story of a Soul: The Autobiography of Saint Thérèse of Lisieux*, tr. John Clarke, OCD, Washington, DC: ICS Publications, 1996

Psalms

Numbering and text follow the Grail version, in *The Psalms: A New Translation*, London & Glasgow: Fontana, 1963.

PROLOGUE

Reading and praying with the saints of Carmel over many years, I have discovered the supreme importance of the scriptures for a better understanding of their teaching. It was this experience that urged me, some time ago, to write *The Carmelite Charism: Exploring the Biblical Roots*. In it, I invited the reader to search more deeply with me into the biblical foundations of Carmelite spirituality. The present book is a sequel to that earlier one.

The Carmelite charism is not an abstraction. It takes on flesh and blood in the lived experience of Carmel's saints. To follow their teaching is to become ever more aware of how deeply embedded their wisdom is in the scriptures. However, 'since we are surrounded by so great a cloud of witnesses' (Hb 12:1) in Carmel, a choice had to be made. This book reflects on only a few among many Carmelites – Teresa of Avila, John of the Cross, Elizabeth of the Trinity, Edith Stein and Thérèse of Lisieux. But these are undoubtedly among those who are better known for their teaching and include no fewer than three Doctors of the Church: Teresa, John and Thérèse.

Teresa of Avila is the great reformer of Carmel. So, chapter I is devoted to her. Prayer is nothing else, in her opinion, than 'an intimate sharing between friends'. She is an inspiration for all who are called to follow her in a life of prayer. 'The number of those who owe to her their way to the light,' writes Edith Stein, 'will become clear only on the day of judgment.' Teresa's call to intimate and friendly converse with God evokes immediately the words of Jesus: 'I have called you friends because I have made known to you everything I have heard from my Father' (Jn 15:15).

Inseparable from Teresa is John of the Cross, her great spiritual mentor, 'father of my soul' as she called him, and her companion in the work of reform. Chapter 2 introduces him as an unerring guide for all who wish to journey into an ever-growing friendship and intimacy with God in a close communion of love. His teaching bears its own original slant of an exodus out of slavery into freedom, as he leads us in hope through the darkness of faith, 'with no other light or guide/than the one that burned in my heart'. In the words of a recent Vatican document, this exodus experience is rich in biblical implications as 'the primordial experience of Israel's faith' and 'the symbol of final salvation'.

But Carmel's heritage is not the preserve of these two great sixteenth-century mystics and Doctors of the Church. Their spirit extends right down to our own times and still continues to enrich the Church in the lives and teaching of three more recent Carmelites. Chapter 3 presents the message of Elizabeth of the Trinity who situates us right at the heart of that friendship and intimacy that is Carmelite prayer. Her writings are like an extended commentary on one of her favourite gospel texts from *John*: 'We will come to them and make our home in them' (Jn 14:23) – all beautifully complemented by the teachings of Paul and especially the call of every Christian to be a 'praise of glory' (Eph 1:12).

The life and message of Edith Stein are recalled in chapter 4. With her passion for truth, she points the way for all believers to take up their cross and follow Jesus into the paschal mystery of dying and rising with the One who said, 'I am...the truth' (Jn 14:6). As a Jewish convert, she is a bridge between the Old Testament and the New, and this may well be her most original contribution to the mystery of Christian prayer.

Carmel's most recent Doctor of the Church, Thérèse of Lisieux, continues to exercise a fascination all her own. In chapter 5, we see how she gently draws us into an intimate friendship with the Jesus of the gospels who is 'gentle and humble of heart' (Mt 11:29), a Saviour eminently human, weak and vulnerable, revealing the heart of a God of mercy who is himself in need of our love. She also reminds us of the fragile nature of the Church, which is this same Christ spread out in the world.

Finally, an Epilogue evokes Mary, Mother and Queen of Carmel, the model and inspiration for all who wish to pray in the spirit of Carmel. To live the Carmelite way is to be plunged into the mystery of Mary. Without her, no book on Carmelite spirituality would be complete.

But is the teaching of these five great contemplatives meant only for Carmelites? Quite the contrary. Many of their writings were designed precisely to help laypeople in their struggle to combine a deep life of prayer with the daily demands of a busy and hectic life. Moreover, the three Doctors of the Church speak to us with the approval of the Church for the universal outreach of their message, blazing a trail for others to follow them. True, they have scaled the heights and plumbed the depths of prayer. But their message is no more, no less than pure gospel wisdom born of intimacy with the word of God; and it is no more, no less challenging than the word of God itself. Like scripture, it is a timeless power still at work among all believers (cf. 1Th 2:13).

These saints of Carmel have in common a very practical approach which speaks to everyone. Real persons of flesh and blood, they share with us their own experience of what it means to be frail and fully human. They are reassuring voices with solid and practical advice for all who struggle with difficulties and distractions in precious moments of prayer, often snatched sporadically in the midst of demanding lives. Like other great figures of history, they are children of their own age — in it, but not of it. They are never outdated: their message is for all time. John Paul II reminds us:

> Saints never grow old. They never become figures of the past, men and women of 'yesterday'. On the contrary, they are always men and women of the future, witnesses of the world to come.

The saints of Carmel are no exception. Their message is a word of life. The specialist will find a deep pool of inspiration in their writings. But so, too, will any person who wishes just to pray silently in the 'inner room' of a quiet heart, longing to drink deeply from springs of living water.

I regard all of these five Carmelites as personal friends. What I have written about them is a record of my own ever-deepening love for their spiritual riches, as these gradually unfolded for me in prayerful reading of their works. For years, it has been my custom to reflect and ponder these Carmelite classics with pencil in hand, jotting down on the margin of page after page copious cross-references to the Bible which seemed to clarify, support and confirm their life-giving doctrine. To that extent, these pages record my personal odyssey in pursuit of a deeper understanding and experience of Carmel's heritage so deeply embedded in the scriptures.

These pages are also a tribute to all who have helped me by their encouragement and careful reading of this book, either in whole or in part, with special mention of my colleague and assistant editor of our Carmelite magazine *Mount Carmel*, Dr Joanne Mosley. I would also like to thank the many retreatants with whom I have had the privilege of sharing my love for the Carmelite saints. Their interest and comments have confirmed for me the universal value and appeal of a prayerful reading of the scriptures in the spirit of Carmel and its saints.

CHAPTER ONE

TERESA OF AVILA: KEEPING COMPANY WITH JESUS, OUR FRIEND

God speaks to his friends

'The invisible God,' Vatican II tells us, 'out of the abundance of His love speaks to people as friends and lives among them, so that He may invite and take them into friendship with Himself.'[1] These words would surely have appealed in a special way to Teresa of Avila. Her remarkable genius for friendship was to condition her whole teaching on prayer and her approach to the scriptures. Deeply aware, as though by instinct, that the 'supreme law' and 'the fundamental norm of the religious life is a following of Christ as proposed by the gospel',[2] she turned to the inspired word of God as the sure foundation and support of her charism: 'I would die a thousand deaths for the faith or for any truth of Sacred Scripture' (*Life* 33:5), she said, knowing the word of God to be not only truth but also love. As we read in the reassuring words of Vatican II: 'in the sacred books, the Father who is in heaven meets His children with great love and speaks with them'.[3] The *Rule* of Carmel, which she longed to restore in all its original force and beauty,[4] called on her to remain 'pondering the Lord's law day and night and keeping watch at [her] prayers' (#10) and reminded her also of Paul's exhortation, 'the word of God must abound in your mouths and hearts' (#19; cf. Col 3:16; Rm 10:8). The *Rule* itself is like a mosaic of biblical quotations, resembling a gospel discourse more than a legal document.[5]

Teresa's love for the scriptures was both profound and remarkable in view of the times and culture in which she lived. She probably never had access to a complete Bible, at least not in her native Castilian. She was not a scholar like John of the Cross, and she knew no Latin. Even the Spanish translations to hand were limited and restricted. Her knowledge of the word of God came mainly through means accessible to the ordinary, simple faithful of her day: the liturgy, partial translations and some spiritual books teeming with scriptural quotations like Francisco de Osuna's *Third Spiritual Alphabet* and Ludolph of Saxony's *Life of Christ*. Her writings contain about six hundred biblical quotations,[6] mostly from John, Paul, the *Psalms* and the *Song of Songs* – on this last, one of her favourite books, she has written a commentary: a work which she referred to as 'my meditations' (M I:8) and which is now called *Meditations on the Song of Songs*.[7]

But Teresa is, above all, the great doctor of prayer[8] and it was mostly in quiet communion with God that she explored the riches of his word. She herself was to learn, as Vatican II expresses it, 'by frequent reading of the divine Scriptures the "excelling knowledge of Jesus Christ".'[9] It was revealed to her in prayer that 'all the harm that comes to the world comes from its not knowing the truths of Scripture in clarity and truth; not one iota of Scripture will fall short' (*Life* 40:1). She knew only too well from her own experience that 'prayer should accompany the reading of sacred Scripture, so that God and people may talk together; for "we speak to Him when we pray; we hear Him when we read the divine sayings".'[10] Origen expresses it well: 'It is prayer above all that is necessary for the understanding of divine things'.[11]

A friend of 'learned men'

Teresa was keenly aware of the unfathomable riches concealed in the scriptures: 'O Jesus!' she exclaims. 'Who would know the many things there must be in Scripture' (IC VII:3:13). And again: 'what a great Lord and God we have. For one word of His will contain within itself a thousand mysteries, and thus our understanding is only very elementary' (M 1:2). Of the *Song of Songs* she writes: 'these words must contain great things and mysteries since they are of such value that when I asked learned men… they answered that the doctors wrote many commentaries and yet never finished explaining the words fully' (M 1:8).[12]

But she was also deeply conscious of her own limitations and need for enlightenment by others: 'learning,' she said, 'is a great thing because learned men teach and enlighten us who know little; and, when brought before the truths of Sacred Scripture, we do what we ought' (*Life* 13:16). She constantly turned to these *letrados* whom she regarded with deep affection and held in highest esteem: 'I have consulted many learned men… I've always been a friend of men of learning' (*Life* 13:18; cf. IC V:1:7). Her preference for the learned director rather than the holy one, if a choice between them had to be made, is well known.

However, Teresa was not one to submit easily and blindly to narrow-minded scholars. She had this to say in praise of Mary, who ceased her questioning upon hearing that the Holy Spirit would come upon her and the Most High overshadow her: 'She did not act as do some learned men… for they want to be so rational about things and so precise in their understanding that it doesn't seem anyone else but they with their learning can understand the grandeurs of God' (M 6:7). Like Mary, Teresa had made her own the lesson of the psalmist: 'I have not gone after things too great nor marvels beyond me' (Ps 130:1).

She was likewise unimpressed by the 'half-learned' who 'cost [her] dearly' (IC V:1:8). 'Half-learned confessors have done my soul great harm' (*Life* 5:3), she wrote, having learned painfully, in the words of Alexander Pope, that 'A little learning is a dangerous thing'.[13] She also warned against people who interpret the scriptures with no reference to the humanity of Christ. Reflecting on the words of Jesus, 'anyone who sees me sees the Father' (Jn 14:9), she writes: '[Such people] will say that another meaning is given to these words. I don't know about those other meanings; I have got along very well with this one that my soul always feels to be true' (IC VI:7:6). An independent woman of great common sense, and with a brilliant sense of humour, she did not hesitate to tease playfully even her beloved soul-mate and companion of her reform, John of the Cross, for his interpretation of the Lord's words to her, 'Seek yourself in me'. She found his interpretation too spiritual but consoled him gleefully: 'Nonetheless, we are grateful to him for having explained so well what we did not ask' (Sat Cri 7). In the last analysis, however, the *letrados* she trusted were, for her, 'those who give us light' (*Life* 13:21; cf. IC VI:8:8) and representatives of the Church 'in the place of God' (F 2:2).

A faithful daughter of the Church

It is hardly surprising that the words, 'in conformity with Sacred Scripture', run like a refrain through all Teresa's writings (*Life* 25:13; 34:11; Sp Test 3:13; cf. IC VI:3:4). So, too, did she make clear that a soul of strong, living faith 'always strives to proceed in conformity with what the Church holds' (*Life* 25:12). Like John of the Cross, Teresa was concerned to let herself be carried along by the living stream of the Church's teaching[14] — ancient, vast, rich and ever-deepening under the Spirit's action with the passage of time. She encouraged a great freedom in our approach to the scriptures and supported the right of every believer to interpret the word of God prayerfully. But she always insisted on the necessity of remaining in communion with the Church: 'If I do not satisfy you,' she told her Carmelite sisters while sharing with them her thoughts on the Our Father, 'you can think up other reflections yourselves. Our Master will allow us to make these reflections provided that we submit in all things to what the Church holds' (WP 30:4).

Teresa strongly affirmed the basic necessity of believing in the truth and efficacy of God's word which, she says, 'cannot fail' (WP

27:2). Her faith embraced the whole range of the scriptures, not just the parts that appealed to her. Importantly, this saved her from the fundamentalist view that would translate isolated passages into general rules.[15] Having decided to follow certain advisers, who were using Paul's words on the role of women in the Church (cf. I Cor 14:34) so as to dissuade her from making new foundations, Teresa then received contrary advice direct from Jesus himself: 'Tell them they shouldn't follow just one part of Scripture but that they should look at other parts, and ask them if they can by chance tie my hands' (Sp Test 15). Her surrender to the demands of God's love was the fruit of a 'living faith' (*Life* 19:5) in the *mysteries of the Church*: she had no reason to envy those who had known the earthly Jesus, for 'the Lord had given her such living faith that when she heard some persons saying they would have liked to have lived at the time Christ our Good walked in the world, she used to laugh to herself. She wondered what more they wanted since in the most Blessed Sacrament they had Him just as truly present as He was then' (WP 34:6). Indeed, he is now even more present, by the power of the Spirit who continues to lead the community of believers through the word 'into all truth' (Jn 16:13).

A doer of the word

Eminently practical, Teresa did not regard the Bible as a mere repertoire of sublime ideas and beautiful sentiments. She was never a mere spectator in the story of salvation as it unfolded in the scriptures. Drawn into the drama, an actor in it, she 'wept with the Magdalene, no more nor less than if she were seeing [Jesus] with her bodily eyes in the house of the Pharisee' (WP 34:7). She could identify with Martha and Mary (WP 17:5-6; 15:7), with the Samaritan woman (*Life* 30:19; cf. M 7:6) and with Peter (*Life* 22:11). Little wonder that *John* seems to have been a gospel specially dear to her. In so many subtle ways, the fourth evangelist constantly invites the reader to be one with his protagonists and to enter with them into dialogue with Jesus. Even from her early years, Teresa learned to be 'a doer' not just 'a hearer of the word' (Jas 1:22). She was only sixteen when a nun, María de Briceño y Contreras, 'began to tell me,' she writes, 'how she arrived at the decision to become a nun solely by reading what the Gospel says: *many are the called and few the chosen*' (*Life* 3:1). Teresa also speaks of her schooldays and of 'the strength the words of God – both heard and read – gave my heart' (*Life* 3:5). She affirms her readiness, later in life, to use 'all my strength to carry out the least part of Sacred Scripture' (*Life* 40:2).

The words of God were always, for Teresa, a source and spring of action. They are efficacious, bringing into effect what they signify: they are 'both words and works' (*Life* 25:3), Teresa tells us. It is true that she also heard *interior words* from the Lord, not with her bodily ears but 'with the ears of the soul… in secret' (IC VI:3:12). These words, received 'in such intimate depths', were exceptional favours granted to her later in life but the criterion of their truth was always their fruits: whether of fortitude and gentleness (*Life* 25:13) or light and quiet (*Life* 25:3). But for Teresa, the greatest criterion was that a word from God 'bears the credentials of being from God if it is in conformity with Sacred Scripture' (*Life* 25:13).

Jesus – 'a living book'

For Teresa, the word of God was Jesus, living and present here and now. He was her 'all' – her 'everything'. She recalls the Lord's consoling words to her when the Inquisition deprived her of many of her favourite books: 'Don't be sad, for I shall give you a living book.' She explains: 'His Majesty had become the true book in which I saw the truths' (*Life* 26:5). Teresa was to discover the absolute centrality of Christ in the spiritual life through a painful experience which cost her dearly. She refers to the influence of certain books that played down the central role of the sacred humanity and confesses that she was led astray by them: 'At no time do I recall this opinion I had without feeling pain,' she says; 'it seems to me I became a dreadful traitor – although in ignorance' (*Life* 22:3). Later, she was to redress the imbalance and, evoking the words of Jesus, 'I am the door' (Jn 10:7.9), she wrote:

> I see clearly...that God desires that if we are going to please Him and receive His great favors, we must do so through the most sacred humanity of Christ... Many, many times have I perceived this truth through experience. The Lord has told it to me. I have definitely seen that we must enter by this gate... desire no other path even if you are at the summit of contemplation; on this road you walk safely. This Lord of ours is the one through whom all blessings come to us... In beholding His life we find that He is the best example. (*Life* 22:6-7)

Teresa's earlier mistake was to prove a happy fault. It would have unique significance for her later teaching. Afterwards, she never ceased to warn others against the dangers of withdrawing from the incarnate Word at any stage on the spiritual path. She advised beginners: 'The soul can place itself in the presence of Christ... This is an excellent way of making progress, and in a very short time' (*Life* 12:2). Those more advanced are told that the failure to keep Christ present as a model 'is why many souls...do not advance further or attain a very great freedom of spirit' (*Life* 22:5):

> I assure them that they will not enter these last two dwelling places [the highest states of union with God]. For if they lose the guide, who is the good Jesus, they will not hit upon the right road. It will be quite an accomplishment if they remain safely in the other dwelling places. The Lord Himself says that He is the way; the Lord says also that He is the light and that no

one can go to the Father but through Him... (IC VI:7:6)

As Teresa shows, there is an essential link between the mystery of Christ and the highest form of prayer. Indeed, the great and final grace of the spiritual marriage was given to her through the sacred humanity of Jesus. It is no surprise, then, that one of her favourite gospel texts was: 'I am the way, the truth and the life' (Jn 14:6).

'He emptied himself'
It was through the human face of Jesus that Teresa discovered a God 'lowering' himself to share in her weakness: 'Christ is a very good friend because we behold Him as man and see Him with weaknesses and trials... I saw that He was man, even though He was God; that He wasn't surprised by human weaknesses; that He understands our miserable make-up, subject to many falls... I can speak with Him as with a friend, even though He is Lord' (*Life* 22:10; 37:5). God's self-abasement and his disguise in Jesus never ceased to touch Teresa deeply: 'He came from the bosom of His Father out of obedience to become our slave,' she tells us (F 5:17). She reminds us that we are 'useless servants' (Lk 17:10), fortunate 'to be able to repay [God] something of what we owe Him for His service toward us... I say these words "His service toward us" unwillingly; but the fact is that He did nothing else but serve us all the time He lived in this world' (IC III:1:8). She does not even hesitate to speak of Jesus as our slave: 'there is no slave who would willingly say he is a slave, and yet it seems that Jesus is honored to be one' (WP 33:4).

It was in this same 'living book' of Christ himself that Teresa read the story of God's 'self-emptying' in the passion of his Son. She had to pass through a number of 'conversions', however, before her so-called 'final conversion' in 1554. It was not quite a Damascus experience – a once-for-all lightning transformation. It was, rather, the culmination of a gradual process. She said of her early years: 'so hard was my heart that I could read the entire Passion without shedding a tear' (*Life* 3:1). But one day in the convent chapel of the Incarnation, when she was praying before the *Ecce Homo* statue of the blood-stained figure of Christ, the sight of the 'much wounded Christ' evoked in her 'what He suffered for us' in such a vivid and lifelike way that 'it seems to me,' she said, 'my heart broke' (*Life* 9:1). Teresa's remarks on the self-abasement of God in the life and passion of Jesus are like a commentary on the gospel passage, 'the Son of man came not to be served but to serve, and to give his life as a ransom for many' (Mk 10:45). She also plumbs the depths of these words of Paul: 'He emptied himself, taking the form of a slave, becoming as human beings are; and being in every way like a human being, he was humbler yet, even to accepting death, death on a cross' (Ph 2:7-8).

'An intimate sharing between friends'

At the beginning of *The Way of Perfection*, Teresa says, 'I shall say nothing about what I have not experienced myself or seen in others [or received understanding of from our Lord in prayer]' (WP Prol. 3). Her own experience is crucial to everything that Teresa explains. It is perhaps nowhere more important than when she speaks about prayer. She concentrates the kernel of that teaching into what we might broadly term her 'definition' of prayer. It contains all the essential ingredients of Teresian prayer:

> mental prayer in my opinion is nothing else than an intimate sharing between friends; it means taking time frequently to be alone with Him who we know loves us. (*Life* 8:5)[16]

Teresa's own capacity for friendship[17] provides us with a key to help us unlock the depths, riches and originality of her special understanding of prayer. Her words are a spontaneous outburst which interrupt her previous line of thought to speak about friendship – a kind of parenthesis characteristic of her style. She introduces her explanation with these words: 'I trust then in the mercy of God, who never fails to repay anyone who has taken Him for a friend' (*Life* 8:5); and she concludes it with an exclamation of praise: 'Oh, what a good friend You make, my Lord!' (*Life* 8:6).

This celebrated description of prayer falls easily into two main components: the essence of Teresian prayer, and the conditions needed for it to deepen. Central is the *intimate sharing between friends*, but also integral is the proper atmosphere required for the friendship to persevere and to grow: *time, space, solitude*. What is perhaps most remarkable, however, is the scriptural depth contained in this teaching of Teresa and how firmly rooted it is in the word of God. Indeed, it is like an epitome of the gospel teaching on prayer – a résumé of Jesus' own witness to prayer both by word and by example.

Turned 'towards' the Father

The intimate sharing between Jesus and his Father – 'who he knows loves him' – is the perfect model of the friendship and companionship to which Teresa invites everyone in prayer. In the story of her life, she speaks of a vision showing her 'that the humanity [of Jesus] was taken into the bosom of the Father' (*Life* 38:17). It was a privileged insight into the truth of John's words: 'The only Son, who is in the bosom of the Father, he has made him known' (Jn 1:18). This image is used of the closest and most tender of human relationships: that of mother and child (Ps 130:2; cf. Nb 11:12), of husband and wife (Dt 13:6), and also of friends, like the beloved disciple reclining on the 'breast' of Jesus at the last supper (Jn 13:23).[18] It describes an intimate friendship of love. The exact form of John's original words (1:18) is quite stunning. The phrase is not strictly '*in* the bosom' but '*into* the bosom' (*eis*), combining as it were both rest and motion, a timeless relationship between Father and Son already accomplished, and at the same time a ceaseless and dynamic thrust between the two.[19] The Aramaic address on the lips of Jesus in Gethsemane, 'Abba, Father' (Mk 14:36), projects onto the stage of time this eternal relationship between Son and Father in the inner life of God – an intimate exchange and filial relationship of friendship unheard of in prayer until the coming of Jesus. Every believer is called to this same intimacy, for God sends 'the Spirit of his Son into our hearts, crying, "Abba! Father!"' (Gal 4:6; cf. Rm 8:15).[20]

This deep relationship within the mystery of God finds expression throughout the gospel in various, complementary ways. They all help to expand, in biblical terms, the meaning of gospel friendship for a better understanding of Teresian prayer. The companionship between Father and Son is *uninterrupted*: 'I am not alone, for the Father is with me' (Jn 16:32). In fact, it is a unique fellowship, involving perfect *oneness*: 'I and the Father are one' (Jn 10:30; cf. 17:11). It is a union of minds and hearts, a deep *mutual knowledge and love*: 'the Father knows me and I know the Father' (Jn 10:15). This is a *reciprocal self-disclosure*: 'no one knows the Son except the Father, and no one knows the Father except the Son' (Mt 11:27). It is ultimately a question of *love*, one for the other: 'the Father loves the Son' (Jn 3:35; 5:20); 'I love the Father' (Jn 14:31). This love expresses itself in a *harmony of wills*: 'I seek not my own will but the will of him who sent me' (Jn 5:30; cf. 4:34; 6:38; Mt 26:39; Hb 10:7). Teresa herself writes, immediately after her description of prayer: 'In order that love be true and the friendship endure, the wills of the friends must be in accord' (*Life* 8:5). Indeed, John explains the purpose of the Christian calling precisely in terms of this perfect friendship which makes God and his people completely one: 'so that you may have fellowship with us; and our fellowship is with the Father and with his Son Jesus Christ' (1Jn 1:3). Here, fellowship, companionship and friendship are one.

'He first loved us'

All through the scriptures, we are reminded that God constantly takes the initiative with the free gift of his love. At the dawn of creation, the Maker of all things drew order and beauty out of chaos while 'Earth was still an empty waste, and darkness hung over the deep' (Gn 1:2, Knox translation). Aquinas describes this action of God as 'the love of God infusing and creating goodness in things'.[21] The Almighty contemplated his own masterpiece and 'saw that it was good' (Gn 1, *passim*). But the Creator did not love the universe *because* it was good: it was good because he *first loved it* into being. So, too, the God of Israel took the initiative in love and created for himself a people to be his own possession: 'It was not because you were more in number than any other people that the Lord set his love upon you and chose you, for you were the fewest of all peoples; but it is because the Lord loves you' (Dt 7:7-8). He led them in love through the desert into the promised land 'for his great love is without end' (Ps 135:10-23; cf. Hos 11:1-4).

In the gospel, Jesus 'went up onto the mountain and summoned those he wanted…and he appointed twelve to be with him' (Mk 3:13-14). This is a free choice of his love: 'he appointed twelve'. Again, God's love is creative: literally, 'he *made* twelve' (*epoíēsen*) in order 'to be *with* him'; that is, he 'summoned' or called them into a close, personal fellowship with himself as his *companions*. God has transformed us, too, into his friends by the power of his love. This choice is God's initiative – an advance of love centred on Christ: 'The God and Father of our Lord Jesus Christ…chose us in [Christ] before the foundation of the world… He destined us in love to be his sons through Jesus Christ' (Eph 1:3-5).

At the last supper, Jesus speaks to his disciples as 'friends': ' I have called you friends… You did not choose me, but I chose you' (Jn 15:15-16). For love and friendship go hand in hand: 'No one has greater love than this, to lay down one's life for one's friends' (Jn 15:13). Jesus is about to lay down his life for his disciples, *not because* they are *already* his friends, but *in order that* all might *become* his friends. Paul expresses the idea well: 'God shows his love for us in that while we were yet sinners Christ died for us' (Rm 5:8). Jesus is offering us a closeness and intimacy with himself, and an invitation to respond: 'We know and believe the love God has for us. God is love... We love, because he first loved us' (1Jn 4:16.19). This is the God Teresa invites us to share with in prayer – a Friend, 'Him who we know loves us'.

A true friend

When Teresa describes prayer as 'an intimate sharing', she is repeating in her own way the lesson of Jesus in the gospels: 'When you pray, go into your room and shut the door and pray to your Father who is in secret; and your Father who sees in secret will reward you' (Mt 6:6). Teresa calls this inner 'room' the 'little heaven of our soul'. It is there, in the depths of the human heart, that she, like Jesus, invites us to share with God in prayer:

> Those who... can enclose themselves within this little heaven of our soul, where the Maker of heaven and earth is present, and grow accustomed to refusing to be where the exterior senses in their distraction have gone or look in that direction should believe they are following an excellent path and that they will not fail to drink water from the fount; for they will journey far in a short time. Their situation is like that of a person who travels by ship; with a little wind he reaches the end of his journey in a few days. But those who go by land take longer. (WP 28:5)

This secret communion with God 'does not lie in thinking much,' Teresa tells us, 'but in loving much' (F 5:2; cf. IC IV:1:7). It releases God's love 'poured out in our hearts by the Holy Spirit who has been given to us' (Rm 5:5), a love already promised as a 'law within' (Jer 31:33), as 'a new heart' and 'a new spirit' (Ez 36:26), 'written...with the Spirit of the living God...on tablets of human hearts' (2Cor 3:3). It is a God-given love in response to the prayer of Jesus, 'that the love with which you [Father] have loved me may be in them' (Jn 17:26). Jesus invites his disciples at the last supper to 'abide' in this love (Jn 15:9-10) – permanently, intimately, and closely united to himself in a covenant of friendship that is deeper even than the love of Jonathan for David: 'The soul of Jonathan was knit to the soul of David... Then Jonathan made a covenant with David, because he loved him as his own soul' (1Sm 18:1.3).

When Jesus calls his disciples 'friends', he explains: 'for all that I have heard from my Father I have made known to you' (Jn 15:15). This self-disclosure of Jesus is 'an intimate sharing' and it was already foreshadowed in the Old Testament: 'The Lord used to speak to Moses face to face,' we are told, 'as a man speaks to his friend' (Ex 33:11). 'With him,' God said, 'I speak mouth to mouth, clearly and not in dark speech' (Nb 12:8). To speak 'face to face' and 'mouth to mouth' is to communicate person to person in an intimate and deep relationship. True friendship requires this trust and open sharing in close intimacy. Without it, there is no true love; and without love, there is no true friendship: 'When love begins to sicken and decay,/It useth an enforced ceremony./There are no tricks in plain and simple faith'.[22]

An 'intimate sharing' also demands entire surrender in service to the other. Jesus has given an example: 'The Son of man came not to be served but to serve' (Mk 10:45); 'No one has greater love than this, to lay down one's life for one's friends' (Jn 15:13). He requires no less of his disciples: 'You are my friends if you do what I command you' (Jn 15:14). Again, the Old Testament provides a beautiful illustration of the friendship between God and Abraham who surrendered in faith to God's command. He obeyed and was called 'my friend' by God himself (Is 41:8).[23] The *Letter of James* expands: 'the scripture was fulfilled, which says, "Abraham believed in God, and it was reckoned to him as righteousness"; and he was called the friend of God' (Jas 2:23; cf. Gn 15:6).

To discover the God of Carmelite prayer is to meet him as a friend in the person of Jesus. The portrait of a true friend in *Ecclesiasticus* is an inspiring and sensitive foreshadowing of what Jesus' friendship can mean for those who wish to commune with God in the spirit of Teresian prayer:

> A loyal friend is a powerful defence:
> whoever finds one has indeed found a treasure.
> A loyal friend is something beyond price,
> there is no measuring his worth.
> A loyal friend is the elixir of life,
> and those who fear the Lord will find one.
> Whoever fears the Lord makes true friends,
> for as a person is, so is his friend too. (6:14-17)

Alone with the alone

Special conditions are laid down by Teresa for authentic Carmelite prayer: 'taking time frequently to be alone' (*Life* 8:5). Each item is important for the friendship to grow and deepen: *time* and *solitude* to pray; perseverance in order to pray *frequently*. Teresa can call upon the example and teaching of Jesus in support of these requirements.

Teresa speaks of 'taking time'. Indeed, she requires *extended periods* of silent prayer for her communities: an hour daily, morning and evening (C 2.7). Mark reminds us that Jesus withdrew from his disciples and 'went into the hills to pray' and then came to them walking on the water 'about the fourth watch of the night' (Mk 6:46.48): that is, between three and six o'clock in the morning. So, Jesus had prayed long and deep into the night. Luke also refers to this protracted prayer of Jesus when he tells us that on one occasion Jesus 'spent all night in prayer to God' (Lk 6:12); and in

Gethsemane, 'being in agony he prayed more earnestly' (Lk 22:44). We see Jesus alone at prayer just before he teaches his disciples the Our Father (Lk 11:1) and at the great turning-points in the unfolding of the plan of salvation – at the choice of the twelve (Lk 6:12), on his manifestation as Messiah (Lk 9:18), and at the transfiguration (Lk 9:28-29).

Teresa, like all Carmelites, had a great love of seclusion. So, too, we see Jesus frequently *alone* with his Father and sharing with his disciples his preference for solitude, as he invites them to 'come away by [themselves] to a lonely place and rest awhile' (Mk 6:31). Mark's first description of Jesus' silent prayer does not refer to an isolated incident but designates the beginning of a typical day in the ministry of Jesus: 'in the morning, a great while before day, [Jesus] rose and went out to a lonely place, and there he prayed' (Mk 1:35).[24] Luke, too, reminds us that this quiet prayer of Jesus occurred constantly during his life: 'he withdrew to the wilderness and prayed' (Lk 5:16) – literally, 'he used to withdraw', repeatedly, into a remote place for quiet prayer. It was a recurring pattern such as Teresa requires for Carmelite prayer, a solitude not lessened by its being shared in community. So, too, when Luke records the solitary prayer of Jesus on the Mount of Olives, he states explicitly that Jesus went there with his disciples 'as was his custom' (Lk 22:39). He had already prayed in that place frequently with his followers.

To pray *frequently*, as Teresa wishes, we must persevere like the importunate friend who comes at midnight and knocks incessantly until his request is granted (Lk 11:5-8). Jesus reinforces this lesson with another parable, that of a widow pleading incessantly with a judge for redress (Lk 18:1-8; cf. 11:5-13). The evangelist introduces it with these challenging and encouraging words, '[We] ought always to pray and never lose heart' (Lk 18:1). The preference of Jesus for the isolation of mountain and hillside, the lonely desert places and the stillness of the night – for long periods of time, day after day – all lends support to Teresa's explanation of prayer as 'taking time frequently to be alone' with God. It shows her teaching to be deeply embedded in the gospels and confirmed by the example of Jesus himself. It is hardly surprising that she had a preference for the gospel scenes where Jesus was alone at prayer. More exactly, she wished to be *alone* just to be *with* Jesus. So, she represented Christ within her 'in those scenes where I saw Him more alone. It seemed to me that being alone and afflicted, as a person in need, He had to accept me. I had many simple thoughts like these' (*Life* 9:4).

A long and painful struggle

Teresa's life was an adventure in prayer. She does not speculate about it; she communicates her own experience and freely invites us to share it with her. But her prayer journey was not a smooth passage from first fervour to the heights of mystical prayer. Her youthful spontaneity and ease with God and her fascination with 'the truth I knew in childhood' (*Life* 3:5) were soon to disappear. For some time, however, she experienced and enjoyed the stimulation of 'good [spiritual] books' (*Life* 3:7) such as Osuna's *Third Spiritual Alphabet*, and remained faithful to her nightly appointment with Jesus in Gethsemane (*Life* 9:4). But growth in prayer became eventually a long and painful struggle. To speak and converse with God as a friend did not come easily to Teresa as the years passed by. In fact, it was the fruit of nearly two decades of intense dryness – although these years were relieved at intervals by brief periods of deep mystical prayer. Teresa's thoughts wandered uncontrollably 'like little moths at night, bothersome and annoying' (*Life* 17:6) and she was unable to reason, think or meditate, or picture things to herself in God's presence. She felt powerless for 'eighteen years' and writes:

> In all those years, except for the time after Communion, I never dared to begin prayer without a book... For the dryness...was always felt when I was without a book. Then my soul was thrown into confusion and my thoughts ran wild. (*Life* 4:9)

She confessed how, during these years of crisis, she used to wait anxiously 'for the striking of the clock' to end the hour of prayer and how she had to 'force' herself to persevere' (*Life* 8:7).

During this troublesome period, Teresa was to experience an additional crisis. She was becoming ill at ease with some friendships and disturbing infidelities in her life. She realised that her prayer and lifestyle were not in harmony. This discrepancy began to disturb her greatly and discouraged her from praying: 'I was then ashamed to return to the search for God by means of a friendship as special as is that found in the intimate exchange of prayer' (*Life* 7:1). So, at some time in 1543, Teresa fled the battlefield and gave up prayer halfway through her long years of struggle. She did, however, return to wrestle with God in prayer after 'a year and a half' or, at any rate, 'at least ... a year' (*Life* 19:4). She described this infidelity as the beginning of the temptation of Judas (*Life* 19:11). Afterwards, she would continue in her earlier resolve. But her unhappy experience was to leave a lasting impression. She would repeatedly caution others against the dangers of abandoning prayer. Her method for perseverance during her trials was simple but effective. It is also highly beneficial for those who are eager to understand the Teresian way of communing with God and to advance in it.

Re-presenting Christ within

During her long years of wrestling with wandering thoughts, Teresa followed a helpful device: what she calls *representing* Christ as near, or within her, where she could speak to him. It grew out of frustrating beginnings, the inability to represent Christ in the gospels with either her intellect or her imagination:

> I had such little ability to represent things with my intellect that if I hadn't seen the things my imagination was not of use to me, as it is to other

persons who can imagine things and thus recollect
themselves. I could only think of Christ as He was as
man, but never in such a way that I could picture Him
within myself... (*Life* 9:6)

This was a painful experience for Teresa, as she longed to establish
a real personal relationship with Jesus and to commune with him,
near or present within her. She therefore pressed into service every
ruse she could conceive of, such as reading a book or identifying
with gospel scenes and her favourite biblical characters. Eventually,
she discovered the key – she *represented* Christ *within*:

> I tried as hard as I could to keep Jesus Christ, our God
> and our Lord, present within me, and that was my way
> of prayer. If I reflected upon some phrase of His
> Passion, I represented Him to myself interiorly...
> God didn't give me talent for discursive thought or for
> a profitable use of the imagination. In fact, my
> imagination is so dull that I never succeeded even to
> think about and represent in my mind – as hard as I
> tried – the humanity of the Lord... This is the
> method of prayer I then used: since I could not reflect
> discursively with the intellect, I strove to represent
> Christ within me... (*Life* 4:7; 9:4)

The phrase, 'to represent Christ within', can have a twofold meaning.
It denotes either picturing him with the imagination, or *representing* him, in the sense of *making him present again*. At prayer,
Teresa did not 'imagine' Christ, nor could she ever do so. She strove
to 're-present' him to herself, to make him present to herself *in faith*
as Someone both real and concrete within herself:

> I was like those who are blind or in darkness; they
> speak with a person and see that that person is with

them because they know with certainty that the other is there (I mean they understand and *believe* this, but they do not see the other)... (*Life* 9:6; italics mine)

There is nothing here resembling the Ignatian method, however valuable in itself, of setting a scene and imagining what the incarnate Word looked like, for example. Teresa just makes space within herself for Jesus in his sacred humanity and invites him to enter her own 'inner room'. There, she can be 'with him' and 'in him', and he in turn be 'with her' and 'in her', so that they can talk and commune together in that 'intimate sharing between friends' which is Teresian prayer. Teresa's attempt to make Jesus, in his mysteries, present again through faith is one with what Jesus himself describes as the 'recalling' action of the Spirit (Jn 14:26).[25] The Spirit makes Jesus present again, alive and active here and now in the heart of the believer, and relevant to the challenge of living the gospel values in the concrete circumstances of every Christian life.

Teresian asceticism[26]

Teresa tells us that 'prayer and comfortable living are incompatible' (WP 4:2). She was not, in fact, one for excessive mortifications and penances: 'we are not angels but we have a body,' she said. 'To desire to be angels while we are on earth... is foolishness' (*Life* 22:10). However, she still required and recommended certain virtues. Although it 'is about prayer that you asked me to say something,' Teresa tells her sisters, she first begins to treat of the things 'necessary for those who seek to follow the way of prayer' (WP 4:3): true *humility*, sincere *love* for one another and radical *detachment* from all created things.[27] All these prerequisites are inseparably linked: 'I cannot understand how there could be humility without love or love without humility; nor are these two virtues possible without detachment from all creatures' (WP 16:2). Teresa invites us to: humility, love and detachment – this last even to the point of detachment from self, or self-sacrifice. It is no coincidence that these three habits or virtues are intertwined in the teaching of Vatican II, which places them side by side: 'The Church, consequently, equipped with the gifts of her Founder and faithfully guarding His precepts of charity, humility, and self-sacrifice, receives the mission to proclaim and to establish among all peoples the kingdom of Christ and of God.'[28] It is also surely significant, too, that these three foundations singled out by Teresa as essential for contemplation are, as we shall now see, what Christ himself insists on for anyone who wishes to follow him as his close friend.

'Gentle and humble of heart'[29]

Teresa lists humility last of the three virtues but stresses its primary importance, for it 'embraces all the others' (WP 4:4). She could see that the Lord, too, favours the virtue of humility: 'It is because God is supreme Truth,' she explains, 'and to be humble is to walk in truth, for it is a very deep truth that of ourselves we have nothing good but only misery and nothingness. Whoever does not understand this walks in falsehood' (IC VI:10:7). To illustrate the power of humility, she compares it to the queen in the game of chess, for '[there is] no queen like humility for making the King surrender' (WP 16:2). Jesus, too, speaks of humility as in some way special to himself: 'Learn of me for I am gentle and humble of heart' (Mt 11:29). His own mother echoes this gospel teaching: 'He raises the lowly' (Lk 1:52). More than once, the gospel reminds us that 'all who humble themselves will be exalted' (Lk 18:14; Mt 23:12; cf. Jas 4:10; 1Pt 5:5-6) and that 'whoever becomes humble like [a] little child is the greatest in the kingdom of heaven' (Mt 18:4). No wonder Teresa could pen these startling words: 'I consider one day of humble self-knowledge a greater favor from the Lord, even though the day may have cost us numerous afflictions and trials, than many days of prayer' (F 5:16).

'By their fruits'

Teresa also stresses the importance of love for one another as a prerequisite for prayer. To be a friend of Jesus is to be a friend of his friends too.[30] She envisaged each of her communities as a gathering of Christ's friends: 'All my longing was and still is that since He has so many enemies and so few friends that these few friends be good ones' (WP 1:2). So important, for Teresa, is fraternal love that she does not hesitate to devote four chapters to it when she shares informally with her sisters in *The Way of Perfection*. Jesus leaves his precious commandment – of loving others as he has loved them – as his parting gift to his disciples. It is 'a new commandment...my commandment' (Jn 13:34; 15:12), and he explains that there is no greater love than 'to lay down one's life for one's friends' (Jn 15:13).[31] 'By this we know love, that he laid down his life for us,' John writes, 'and we ought to lay down our lives for one another... We know that we have passed out of death into life, because we love one another' (1Jn 3:16.14). This dying to self, for others, out of love, is itself a form of martyrdom. As Teresa says: 'the life of a good religious who desires to be one of God's close friends is a long martyrdom' (WP 12:2).

Significantly, when Teresa speaks of love for one another in community, she dwells at great length on forgiveness. Well did she remark that 'to be forgiving is a virtue difficult for us to attain by ourselves' (WP 36:7). She writes:

> how the Lord must esteem this love we have for one another! Indeed, Jesus could have put other virtues first and said: forgive us, Lord, because we do a great deal of penance or because we pray much and fast or because we have left all for You and love You very much... But He said only, 'forgive us because we forgive'. (WP 36:7)

For Teresa, forgiveness is the acid test of authentic prayer. She explains that if 'there doesn't arise in the soul a very resolute desire to pardon any injury however grave it may be and to pardon it in deed when the occasion arises, do not trust much in that soul's prayer' (WP 36:8). It is remarkable how Jesus, too, links his teaching on prayer with forgiveness: 'When you stand in prayer, forgive' (Mk 11:25). It is there again at the heart of the Lord's prayer: 'forgive us our debts as we also have forgiven our debtors' (Mt 6:12). Jesus reinforces this lesson when teaching the Our Father: 'If you do not forgive others their trespasses, neither will your Father forgive your trespasses' (Mt 6:15). Teresa has known many persons of prayer favoured with the gift of contemplation, but she says tellingly: 'even though I see other faults and imperfections in them, I have never seen anyone [unwilling to forgive]' (WP 36:13). She explains why, in a nutshell: 'I cannot believe that a person who comes so close to Mercy itself, where he realizes what he is and the great deal God has pardoned him of, would fail to pardon his offender immediately' (WP 36:12).

'One alone is good, God'

Teresa's third prerequisite for prayer is detachment. The word embraces a wide variety of meanings. It immediately suggests something negative: withdrawal, separation or removal from things. For Teresa, it is the positive aspect that is primary: surrender, or giving oneself to God. 'He doesn't give Himself completely until we give ourselves completely' (WP 28:12), she writes. Anything that impedes this total gift of self is an attachment; it holds us in bondage, enslaved, and impedes our growth and progress in prayer. Teresa is not, for all this, any less demanding than John of the Cross in her insistence on the need for detachment.[32] The choice of vocabulary will differ strikingly as the stark and inexorable logic of John of the Cross gives way – apparently – to Teresa's less absolute, less rigid approach. But the core reality is identical. Ultimately, both Doctors of the Church are saying the same thing: every obstacle that impedes the friendship and intimacy of a growing relationship in prayer must be left behind; or, as Teresa puts it, there must be 'detachment from every creature' (F 4:5). What she is saying is that '[God] never works in the soul as He does when it is totally His without any obstacle' (WP 28:12).

Teresa's primary concern is with nakedness of spirit. She recalls the gospel story of the 'rich young man', invited by Jesus to give up what is closest to his heart (Mk 10:17-22). This kind of detachment is absolutely necessary if we are to be led further into the deepest friendship with God in prayer. Teresa's comments on this story are addressed mainly to 'well-ordered ... virtuous persons of prayer' (IC III:1:7; 2:1.4.13), but whose 'reason is still very much in control'. The problem, she observes, is that 'Love has not yet reached the point of overwhelming reason' (IC III:2:7). Such people cling to the security of their own self-sufficiency and are unwilling to relinquish control over their lives; Teresa compares them to the rich young man unable to renounce everything and follow Jesus (cf. IC III:1:6). For her, detachment consists 'in striving to practice the virtues, in surrendering our will to God in everything, in bringing our life into accordance with what His Majesty ordains for it, and in desiring that His will not ours be done' (IC III:2:6). It is a question, she tells us, of 'whether or not you are truly stripped of what you have left behind' (IC III:2:6); it is an invitation to embrace the wisdom of the cross (cf. 1Cor 2:1-8).

'If your eye is not sound'

Apart from these three prerequisites for prayer – humility, love of one another and detachment – Teresa makes three further demands as predispositions for those who would persevere faithfully to the end of the prayer journey: a good *conscience*, resolute *determination* and great *desires*. She writes: 'You... know that the cornerstone must be a good conscience and that with all your strength you must strive to free yourselves even from venial sins and seek what is the most perfect' (WP 5:3). Here, Teresa is simply echoing the gospel message, 'You, therefore, must be perfect, as your heavenly Father is perfect' (Mt 5:48), and 'Blessed are the pure of heart, for they shall see God' (Mt 5:8). This gave Teresa an abhorrence for venial sin, even more so for serious sin: 'There is nothing... that deserves this name "evil", except mortal sin' (IC I:2:5); 'there's no darker darkness nor anything more obscure and black' (IC I:2:1); 'beseech [God] earnestly for those who are in this state, who have become total darkness, and whose works have become darkness also' (IC I:2:2). Teresa is repeating again the gospel warning: 'Your eye is the lamp of your body... when it is not sound, your body is full of darkness. Therefore be careful lest the light in you be darkness' (Lk 11:34-35; cf. Mt 6:22-23).

Striving to stay in the light demands a commitment to the spiritual combat. Teresa was only too well aware that Satan constantly transforms himself into an angel of light (cf. IC V:I:5). She warns that, all along the path of prayer, the devil works 'like a noiseless file' (IC I:2:16). Teresa has a keen sense of both the devil's ploys and her own sinfulness. But this does not impede her closeness and intimacy with Jesus. She is like Peter clinging in love to Jesus by the lakeside and at the same time imploring him, 'Depart from me, for I am a sinful man, O Lord' (Lk 5:8). Or like the 'the tax collector [who], standing far off, would not even lift up his eyes to heaven, but beat his breast, saying, "God, be merciful to me a sinner!"' (Lk 18:13). We cannot become holy by our own unaided efforts, and Teresa says everything in one simple prayer: 'Do not look at our sins but behold that Your most blessed Son redeemed us' (WP 3:8).

'Determined determination'[33]

One of Teresa's most insistent requirements for perseverance in prayer is 'determinada determinación' – 'determined determination' or 'resolute determination' (WP 21:2). It is a fundamental firmness of purpose in life such as Teresa herself experienced repeatedly. She was fully aware of her own courage and she writes, perhaps paying lip-service to the conventions of her time: 'God has given me more [courage] than women usually have' (*Life* 8:7). She well knew that perseverance in prayer requires more courage 'than to suffer a quick martyrdom' (*Life* 31:17; cf. 12:2) and devotes two chapters of her *Way of Perfection* (21.23) to spelling out the generous determination required: 'a great and very resolute determination to persevere until reaching the end, come what may, happen what may, whatever work is involved, whatever criticism arises, whether they arrive or whether they die on the road, or even if they don't have courage for the trials that are met, or if the whole world collapses' (WP 21:2).

This is a determined commitment to the Jesus of the gospels who 'has nowhere to lay his head' (Lk 9:58) and who said, 'No one who puts his hand to the plough and looks back is fit for the kingdom of God' (Lk 9:62). This absolute resolve to give oneself to prayer is at the heart of Teresian asceticism and inseparably linked with readiness to carry the cross: 'His Majesty wants this determination, and He is a friend of courageous souls' (*Life* 13:2). Here, we catch an echo of Paul's words, 'God loves a cheerful giver' (2 Cor 9:7).

'Undaunted daughter of desires'

Linked with this emphasis on determination and wholehearted commitment to prayer is Teresa's insistence on the importance of great desires. She has rightly been hailed by the poet Crashaw: 'O thou undaunted daughter of desires!'[34] She was astonished at just how much can be done if only we have the courage to attempt great things for God. An insatiable longing for God had been her desire from childhood as she set off, in vain, with her brother Rodrigo to be martyred by the Moors: 'I went because I want to see God,' she explained to her distraught parents, 'and to see Him we must die.'[35] Teresa was already echoing, unwittingly, the deepest aspirations of every human heart expressed in the gospel scene of the Greeks who came searching for Jesus: 'we wish to see Jesus' (Jn 12:21).

The prayer of Teresa was a response to the invitation of Jesus: 'If anyone thirsts, let that person come to me, and drink' (Jn 7:37). One of her very favourite gospel scenes, from childhood on, was Jesus offering the 'living water' to the woman at Jacob's well (Jn 4:7-26). She comments:

> Oh, how many times do I recall the living water that the Lord told the Samaritan woman about! And so I am very fond of that gospel passage. Thus it is, indeed, that from the time I was a little child, without understanding this good as I do now, I often begged the Lord to give me the water. I always carried with me a painting of this episode of the Lord at the well, with the words, inscribed: *Domine, da mihi aquam*. (*Life* 30:19)

Teresa well knew that her deepest desires came from God who, in inspiring them, gives 'both the will and the action' (Ph 2:13). The psalmist captures the deep and lifelong yearning of Teresa's ardent spirit:

> Like the deer that yearns
> for running streams,
> so my soul is yearning
> for you, my God.
> My soul is thirsting for God,
> the God of my life;
> when can I enter and see
> the face of God?
> (Ps 41:2-3; cf. Sg 3:1-2; Jn 20:1.11-18).

All her life, Teresa was on fire with immortal longings and, as a young girl, loved to repeat the words, 'forever and ever and ever' (*Life* 1:4).

'The Lord God planted a garden'

Teresa's writings are primarily about prayer.[36] This is her great gift to Carmel, to the Church – indeed, to the whole world. She provides many images to illustrate her teaching, especially those from nature, such as fields, water or flowers. 'In these things,' she writes, 'I found a remembrance of the Creator. I mean that they awakened and recollected me and served as a book' (*Life* 9:5). From here, it was an easy step for her to picture her own soul as a *garden*, an image she uses to great effect in the *Life*. She says: 'it was a great delight for me to consider my soul as a garden and reflect that the Lord was taking His walk in it. I begged Him to increase the fragrance of the little flowers of virtue that were beginning to bloom, so it seemed, and that they might give Him glory and He might sustain them' (*Life* 14:9). For Teresa, the flowers in her interior garden are the virtues that grow as prayer deepens, develops and matures.

The image of the Lord walking in a garden and taking delight in the fragrance of the flowers is rich with biblical connotations. It evokes the first stirrings of life in the *Song of Songs*: 'Flowers are appearing on the earth…The fig tree is forming its first figs and the blossoming vines give out their fragrance' (Sg 2:12-13). So, too, this image evokes the story of *Genesis*, where we are told: 'The Lord God planted a garden in Eden… And out of the ground the Lord God made to grow every tree that is pleasant to the sight and good for food… A river flowed out of Eden to water the garden… And they heard the sound of the Lord God walking in the garden in the cool of the day' (Gn 2:8-10; 3:8). John of the Cross also uses the image of the garden when he speaks of the sublime state of transforming union: 'the grove and its living beauty' (SC, stanza 39), he says, and he speaks of intimacy with the Beloved in this way: 'Upon my flowering breast… sleeping… in a breeze from the fanning cedars' (DN, stanza 6). Teresa envisages the Lord walking again, in the inner garden of those who journey with her on the way of prayer towards union with God.

'A spring of water'

Teresa, however, is far too practical ever to become entirely lost in the beauty of her imagery. She devotes twelve chapters of her *Life* to describing how to water the garden of the soul (*Life* 11-22). These are like a small treatise on prayer, and could be called a commentary on Paul's words, 'We are fellow workers for God; you are God's field... but only God... gives the growth' (1Cor 3:9.7). For Teresa, the water is God's grace which Jesus promised would flow 'in torrents' from his own heart to all who believe (Jn 7:38): 'The water that I shall give [to believers] shall become in them a spring of water welling up to eternal life' (Jn 4:14).

There are, Teresa explains, four ways of watering the garden.[37] The first is to draw the water painfully, by means of a bucket. This refers to prayer that develops by our own efforts, with the *ordinary* help of God, given to all alike. The second means of irrigation is to use a water-wheel and so draw more water with less labour. This kind of prayer is only possible with *special* help from God. We must cooperate, of course, but he takes over more and more in our prayer as we surrender ever more fully to his guidance. The third way of tending the garden is to irrigate it with a stream, directing the water with much less effort. We still cooperate, but *God now dominates* even more completely as we yield more fully to his action. The fourth and final way of watering comes from torrential rain: we abandon ourselves entirely to God *and he does everything*.

This is Teresa's first lengthy description of her own experience in prayer. It was not her final word. The *Life* is Teresa's first work, and she was only forty-seven when she wrote it.[38] She had yet to reach greater mystical heights of prayer. She had also to refine her teaching further, providing clearer distinctions and developing at length many other facets of her teaching on prayer. Teresa herself was aware that God had given her not just experience of prayer but also the gift of expressing it more clearly in her later works for the benefit of others (cf. *Life* 17:5).[39]

Praying with words

In *The Way of Perfection*, Teresa clarifies and explores still further the mystery of prayer.[40] At first sight, it may seem strange that such an accomplished teacher of mystical prayer would even feel the need to treat of vocal prayer, more astonishing still that she would not admit any real distinction between vocal and mental prayer. She demands just three essential things: awareness of who we are; awareness of whom we are addressing; and awareness of what we are saying. Without this heightened awareness, there can be no authentic prayer, vocal or otherwise: 'if you are to be speaking, as is right, with so great a Lord,' Teresa tells us with a touch of humour, 'it is good that you consider whom you are speaking with as well as who you are, at least if you want to be polite' (WP 22:1). Then, if we are faithful to her prerequisites – engaging our minds and hearts and not just our lips – she reassures us: 'This is mental prayer' (WP 22:8; cf. IC I:1:7).

Teresa also insists on proper respect and due reverence while reciting our vocal prayers. That is how Jesus prayed (cf. Jn 11:41; 17:1). We can only surmise the respect, awe, admiration and adoration of his followers as they watched Jesus rapt in silent prayer. 'He was praying in a certain place, and when he ceased, one of his disciples said to him, "Lord, teach us to pray"' (Lk 11:1). Enthralled, they did not even dare to interrupt him but waited until he had ceased before they asked him to teach them how to pray. They wanted to pray as he himself prayed. 'When you pray,' Jesus answered his disciples, 'say "Father..."' (Lk 11:2). The word 'Father' on the lips of Jesus is '*Abba*' (Mk 14:36) – the most intimate, loving and filial attitude of a child. When we pray as Jesus did, we relate to God in the same way: 'God has sent the Spirit of his Son into our hearts, crying, "Abba! Father!"' (Gal 4:6; cf. Rm 8:15-16).[41] The Our Father, Teresa reminds us, is always at hand to support us in our prayer; it is of all the more inestimable value 'for it comes from the mouth of Truth itself' (WP 42:5).

Words, words, words... [42]

'My words fly up, my thoughts remain below./Words without thoughts never to heaven go,' says the King at prayer in *Hamlet*. [43] Teresa endorses the lesson: 'no one can take vocal prayer from you or make you recite the Our Father hastily and without understanding it' (WP 42:4). Here she is anticipating the words of Paul VI urging us to pray the rosary with 'a quiet rhythm and a lingering pace'. [44] Yet, we so often rattle off glibly and carelessly these two gospel prayers. It is significant that just before Matthew gives us his version of the Our Father, he warns us of the danger of routine, of repeating prayers parrot-like or babbling them with little attention to their meaning: 'In praying do not heap up empty phrases as the Gentiles do; for they think that they will be heard for their many words' (Mt 6:7).

The prayer of the false prophets of Baal provides a striking example of precisely how not to pray (1Kgs 18:26-29). [45] Howling and shrieking, they hurl empty phrases at the silent heavens, prattling on through noon till evening: 'They raved on... but there was no voice; no one answered, no one heeded' (1Kgs 18:29). Vocal prayer is not about striving to overwhelm God with an avalanche of words and pious formulas. Quite the opposite: it is for *us* to be overwhelmed and changed! Hence, right at the heart of Matthew's version of the Our Father, we have the petition, 'Thy will be done' (Mt 6:10). For Teresa, the purpose of all prayer is to bring our will into harmony with God's will: 'everything I have advised you about in [*The Way of Perfection*] is directed toward the complete gift of ourselves to the Creator, the surrender of our wills to His' (WP 32:9; cf. IC II:1:8). To be alert, in our vocal prayers, to this need for inner transformation is to be conscious of Teresa's three requirements for all authentic prayer: to know who we are, what we desire, and who it is that can change us.

For Teresa, the Our Father provides a kind of springboard or taking-off point when we want to set free the wings of prayer. One phrase, one word, one petition can launch us into silent communion with God, and then the ever-deepening silence can draw us further into the stillness of perfect contemplation. Teresa says that this prayer contains 'the entire spiritual way... from the beginning stages until God engulfs the soul and gives it to drink abundantly from the fount of living water, which He said was to be found at the end of the way' (WP 42:5). Eminently practical as always, she illustrates this teaching from her own experience of 'many persons who while praying vocally... are raised by God to sublime contemplation' (WP 30:7). One such person who could only pray vocally came to her in great distress. Teresa asked her about her prayer and then observed: 'I saw that though she was tied to the Our Father she experienced pure contemplation and that the Lord was raising her up and joining her with Himself in union' (WP 30:7). Teresa then applied the acid test of all authentic prayer – the kind of life she was leading: 'from her deeds it seemed truly that she was receiving such great favors, for she was living a very good life' (WP 30:7). It is the gospel lesson: 'You will know them by their fruits' (Mt 7:16).

'This little heaven of our soul'

'I confess,' Teresa writes, 'that I never knew what it was to pray with satisfaction until the Lord taught me this method' (WP 29:7). She is speaking about the *prayer of recollection*,[46] a kind of silent prayer in the presence of God, often considered independent of – and even superior to – vocal prayer. Yet, as Teresa shows, vocal prayer is intimately linked with recollection: 'With this method,' she assures us, 'we shall pray vocally with much calm, and any difficulty will be removed... get used to praying the Our Father with this recollection, and you will see the benefit before long' (WP 29:6). We can readily understand the importance and value of this prayer for Teresa. As we have seen, she experienced a great obstacle on her long and painful prayer journey: an inability to concentrate. The prayer of recollection provided her with the perfect solution. Teresa gives the essence of her teaching in four chapters of *The Way of Perfection* (WP 26-29). Here, she is perhaps at her most practical and helpful. The prayer involves a double movement on our part: introducing Christ into our prayer and entering into ourselves when we pray. It is a prayer-filled response to the gospel text, 'Where your treasure is, there will your heart be also' (Mt 6:21).

The first movement, then, is what we have met earlier – to *represent* Christ or to make him present within: 'Represent the Lord Himself as close to you and behold how lovingly and humbly He is teaching you. Believe me, you should remain with so good a friend as long as you can' (WP 26:1). All Teresa's advice is designed to simplify the tangle of discursive meditation and calm the distractions of too much thinking. Christ is really present. We have only to look at him or see him looking at us, and to listen to what he has to teach us. To *look at him* with a simple and intuitive gaze of faith is the kernel of Teresa's advice: 'behold Him on the way to the garden... Or behold Him bound to the column... Or behold Him burdened with the cross... He will look at you with those eyes so beautiful and compassionate... merely because... you turn your head to look at Him' (WP 26:5). She is simply repeating her earlier advice to beginners: 'one should... just remain there in His presence with the intellect quiet... occupy ourselves in looking at Christ who is looking at us, and... speak, and petition, and humble ourselves, and delight in the Lord's presence' (*Life* 13:22). Communing like this with Jesus at prayer is rooted in what Teresa has called 'an intimate sharing between friends' (*Life* 8:5).

The second movement is to enter into the 'inner room' of the heart to commune with God 'in secret' (cf. Mt 6:6). This, too, is essential to the prayer of recollection. It means withdrawing from externals that dissipate the energies or, in gospel terms, to 'shut the door' on all unnecessary distractions and idle wanderings of the mind (cf. Mt 6:6). Teresa explains: 'This prayer is called "recollection," because the soul collects its faculties together and enters within itself to be with its God' (WP 28:4). She further assures us that this way of prayer is well suited to those 'who cannot engage in much discursive reflection with the intellect or keep [the] mind from distraction' (WP 26:2) – a description that probably applies to most people at one time or another. This prayer can also be called the 'prayer of presence':[47] a peaceful and simple gazing in love through the eyes of faith at Jesus present within. The place 'within' is, as we have seen, 'this little heaven of our soul':

> Do you think it matters little for a soul with a wandering mind to... see that there is no need to go to heaven in order to speak with one's Eternal Father or find delight in Him? Nor is there any need to shout. However softly we speak, He is near enough to hear us. Neither is there any need for wings to go to find Him. All one need do is go into solitude and look at Him within oneself... Those who... can enclose themselves within this little heaven of our soul, where the Maker of heaven and earth is present... should believe they are following an excellent path and that they will not fail to drink water from the fount; for they will journey far in a short time. (WP 28:2.5)

Teresa uses a vivid image to illustrate this centring of the faculties: 'the bees are approaching and entering the beehive to make honey' (WP 28:7). However, she is careful to point out 'that this recollection is not something supernatural, but that it is something we can desire and achieve ourselves with the help of God' (WP 29:4). No *special* grace is required. When such a grace is given, the soul advances to yet higher stages of prayer.

An inner journey[48]

The Interior Castle, also known as *The Mansions*, is generally regarded as Teresa's finest work and was written just five years before her death.

Her powers of expression and understanding of the Carmelite charism have now fully matured. The book was composed amid innumerable distractions, at white heat in just three months. It is like an extended commentary on the gospel text, 'Those who love me will keep my word, and my Father will love them, and we will come to them and make our home in them' (Jn 14:23). Paul expands on this theme of the indwelling of the Blessed Trinity by asking the question: 'Do you not know that you are God's temple and that God's Spirit dwells in you?' (1Cor 3:16; cf. 6:19; 2Cor 6:16). Another gospel text is also basic to an understanding of *The Interior Castle*: 'When you pray, go into your room and shut the door and pray to your Father who is in secret' (Mt 6:6). Teresa speaks of these gospel truths with her image of the soul as a castle where God lives, in the central dwelling place of the human heart. This is surrounded by six other mansions, each with several apartments of its own: 'some up above, others down below, others to the sides; and in the center and middle is the main dwelling place where the very secret exchanges between God and the soul take place' (IC I:1:3; cf. 1:1). Teresa explains how we may embark upon this journey: 'the door of entry to this castle is prayer and reflection' (IC I:1:7). As we advance in prayer, so Teresa directs us ever closer to the innermost room where God dwells. The seven mansions represent stages of prayer from our initial efforts to commune with God, symbolised by the first dwelling places, right through to the seventh ones, representing the deepest union attainable in this life.[49]

'Be still and know'

The first three mansions correspond to Teresa's initial method of watering the garden, outlined in the *Life*: filling a bucket from the well. This is the life of prayer as it develops mainly by our own efforts, with the *ordinary* grace God gives to all who answer the call of Jesus: 'If any want to become my followers, let them deny themselves and take up their cross and follow me' (Mk 8:34). The remaining four mansions correspond to the next three ways of irrigating the garden. Prayer now receives a *special* help from God and develops from passive recollection to the prayer of quiet, union, spiritual betrothal and finally spiritual marriage. The heights of prayer dealt with in *The Interior Castle* reflect and draw on Teresa's own spiritual growth since she first wrote the *Life*:

> It's possible that in dealing with these interior matters I might contradict something of what I said elsewhere. That's no surprise, because in the almost fifteen years since I wrote it the Lord may perhaps have given me clearer understanding in these matters than I had before. (IC IV:2:7)

Even a cursory glance at the general outline of the later stages of prayer in *The Interior Castle* shows how Teresa refines the teaching of her earlier works with significant clarifications and distinctions.

We can take the prayer of recollection, for example. Teresa was careful to point out, in *The Way of Perfection*, that the *active* form of this prayer is 'something we can desire and achieve ourselves with the help of God' (WP 29:4) – something that everyone can practise, with effort, faithfulness and readiness to move beyond words, thoughts and images into silence and listening. But *passive* recollection is not. This is the initial form of *infused prayer* and it cannot be induced by thinking or imagining, or by the use of a mantra or the techniques of what is often called 'centring prayer'.[50] It comes only through a special grace from God. This is an important distinction, which Teresa now clarifies in *The Interior Castle*. However, she is particularly anxious that we should still dispose ourselves for this *special* grace. Indeed, she seems convinced that anyone who perseveres in the habit of recollection *will* receive it. So, with persevering effort to recollect ourselves actively, a deeper awareness of God's presence is born within us. Our attention is somehow 'caught' or 'held captive' by God. As the psalmist says: 'My

soul clings to you; your right hand holds me fast' (Ps 62:9). Teresa
herself evokes the gospel image of the Good Shepherd to explain
this action of God in passive recollection:

> Like a good shepherd, with a whistle so gentle that
> even they themselves almost fail to hear it, He makes
> them recognize His voice and stops them from going
> so far astray so that they will return to their dwelling
> place. And this shepherd's whistle has such power that
> they abandon the exterior things in which they were
> estranged from Him and enter the castle. I don't think
> I've ever explained it as clearly as I have now. (IC
> IV:3:2-3)

'Like a child at rest'
Teresa sees a special advantage for the soul in the prayer of active
recollection preparing it for *passive* prayer: 'its divine Master comes
more quickly to teach it and give it the prayer of quiet than He
would through any other method it might use' (WP 28:4). The
Shepherd's call to 'abandon the exterior things' and 'enter the castle'
(IC IV:3:2) is the first signal that a person is coming into the *prayer
of quiet* which, in Teresa's scheme, follows the prayer of passive
recollection. Earlier, in the *Life*, she had explained this prayer, saying:
'Only the will is occupied in such a way that, without knowing how,
it becomes captive' (*Life* 14:2). Again, in *The Way of Perfection*, she
writes: 'The will is the one that is captive here... [It]... is then
united with its God, and leaves the other faculties free' (WP 31:3.4)
– so, the thoughts and imagination can run wild and sometimes do.
In *The Interior Castle*, Teresa returns to her image of water to clarify
the origin of this prayer: 'the water comes from its own source which
is God... I don't think the experience is something, as I say, that
rises from the heart, but from another part still more interior, as
from something deep. I think this must be the center of the soul, as
I later came to understand' (IC IV:2:4-5).

Teresa goes on to describe the *prayer of union* as 'that prayer in which the entire soul is united with God'– in which there is a 'union of all three faculties' (WP 31:10). She evokes the biblical image of the 'child on its mother's breast' (Ps 130:2) to describe both the prayer of quiet and that of union. But she explains the difference. In the former, 'the mother without her babe's effort to suckle puts the milk in its mouth' (WP 31:9); while in the latter, 'the soul doesn't even go through the process of swallowing this divine food. Without its understanding how, the Lord places the milk within it' (WP 31:10). In *The Interior Castle*, Teresa evokes yet another image, that of silkworms, to describe the transforming effect of this prayer of union: 'with their little mouths they themselves go about spinning the silk and making some very thick little cocoons in which they enclose themselves. The silkworm, which is fat and ugly, then dies, and a little white butterfly, which is very pretty, comes forth from the cocoon' (IC V:2:2). To experience this prayer is to resemble 'one who in every respect has died to the world so as to live more completely in God' (IC V:1:4); 'once this silkworm is grown...it begins to spin the silk and build the house wherein it will die. I would like to point out here,' Teresa adds, 'that this house is Christ' (IC V:2:4). The seed must die (cf. Jn 12:24). Paul's teaching on our identification with Christ takes on profound significance in the prayer of union: 'You have died and your life is hidden with Christ in God... It is no longer I who live, but Christ who lives in me' (Col 3:3; Gal 2:20). 'Somewhere, it seems to me,' comments Teresa, explaining the prayer of union, 'I have read or heard that our life is hidden in Christ or in God (both are the same), or that our life is Christ' (IC V:2:4).

'The bride is for the bridegroom'
Teresa continues to direct the inner journey through the sixth and seventh mansions: *spiritual betrothal* and *spiritual marriage*. The goal is perfect union with Christ, beyond the faculties, in the deepest centre of the soul: 'this secret union takes place,' she explains, 'in the very

interior center of the soul, which must be where God Himself is' (IC VII:2:3).[51] 'This center of our soul, or this spirit,' Teresa confesses, 'is something so difficult to explain... I do not know how to explain [it]' (IC VII:2:10). So, she simply shares her own experience, describing it as best she can. Echoing the words of Paul, 'Whoever is united to the Lord becomes one spirit with him' (1 Cor 6:17), Teresa says: 'the spirit... is made one with God' (IC VII:2:3). Her spousal imagery is deeply embedded in the scriptures and reflects the familiar Old Testament theme of the marriage between God and his people: 'And in that day, says the Lord, you will call me, "My husband"... And I will betroth you to me forever' (Hos 2:16.19; cf. Jer 2:2; Is 61:10). This same imagery recurs in the New Testament, as when the Baptist designates Jesus as the Messianic *bridegroom* of Israel: 'He who has the bride is the bridegroom' (Jn 3:29; cf. Rv 19:7-9; Eph 5:25-32).

While Teresa sees the spiritual marriage as a deepening of union from the spiritual betrothal, she still distinguishes clearly between them: 'the difference is as great as that which exists between two who are betrothed and two who can no longer be separated' (IC VII:2:2). The union of the spiritual betrothal is like the joining of two candles that can still be easily separated, while that of the spiritual marriage is perfect fusion, like rain falling on a river, a stream entering into the sea, or the merging of light beams flooding a room through different windows (IC VII:2:4). In other words, spiritual betrothal is a transient state whereas the spiritual marriage is permanent. In the latter, '[God] has desired to be so joined with the creature that, just as those who are married cannot be separated, He doesn't want to be separated from the soul' (IC VII:2:3). The spiritual marriage is the summit of Teresian prayer; the spiritual betrothal prepares the way for it. There is no closed door between the sixth and seventh dwelling places (IC VI:4:4).

The favours of the spiritual betrothal, recorded at length by Teresa, are like the jewels the Spouse gives to the betrothed and a foretaste of greater blessing yet to come in the spiritual marriage. Repeatedly, Teresa speaks of the 'secrets' generously shared by the Bridegroom with his bride. The meaning of Jesus' words begin to unfold in greater depth: 'I have made known to you everything I have heard from my Father' (Jn 15:15). But Teresa does not hesitate 'to recount some of those trials that I know one will certainly undergo [in the sixth mansions]' (VI:1:2): opposition, severe illnesses, inner sufferings, fears of deception, and even the feeling of rejection by God. Most painful and excruciating of all, however, is what she calls the 'delightful torment' of 'longings' and 'yearnings' in exile for the absent Bridegroom: 'this little butterfly,' Teresa explains, 'is unable to find a lasting place of rest' (IC VI:6:1). The bride is like the Magdalen weeping outside the empty tomb in search of the absent Jesus, or like the distraught lover in the *Song of Songs*: 'On my bed, at night, I sought him whom my heart loves. I sought but did not find him' (Sg 3:1). No respite is possible until the risen Jesus comes finally in the seventh mansions with the reassuring words, 'Peace be with you' (Jn 20:19.21; cf. IC VII:2:3). 'So in this temple of God, in this His dwelling place, He alone and the soul rejoice together in the deepest silence' (IC VII:3:11).

'Good works, good works'[52]

But Teresa's concern is not primarily with stages or degrees of prayer. She is deeply conscious of the diversity of human temperaments and knows that each person is a wonderful and unique creation of God. Her divisions and distinctions help to clarify the freedom of God's action leading each person by their own secret trail to the Father through Jesus in the Spirit (cf. Jn 4:23-24). They are also helpful for spiritual directors entrusted with the extremely delicate task of discerning the diversity of God's action in others. Significantly, each of the mansions has several apartments of its own, where communion with God at each stage of spiritual growth can be lived and experienced in so many different ways by those who pray. Witness the depth, richness and variety of Teresian prayer experienced so fully and with such originality by so many of Carmel's saints – especially by Thérèse of Lisieux, who never once speaks of stages or degrees of prayer!

Much more important for Teresa is what she designates as the fruit of all prayer and especially of the highest union: good works. 'This is the reason for prayer, my daughters,' she says, 'the purpose of this spiritual marriage: the birth always of good works, good works' (IC VII:4:6). Carmelites must 'be occupied in prayer... so as to have... strength to serve' (IC VII:4:12). When she had heard of the havoc wrought by the Lutherans, she confessed, 'It seemed to me that I would have given a thousand lives to save one soul out of the many that were being lost' (WP 1:2). Teresa's sisters must 'be occupied in prayer for those who are the defenders of the Church and for preachers and for learned men who protect her from attack' (WP 1:2). This was her special affirmation of an apostolic dimension to contemplative prayer. On her deathbed, she often repeated full of gratitude: 'I am a daughter of the Church'.[53] She wanted her Carmelite communities of prayer, penance, silence and enclosure to be groups of strong and close friends of one another in the service of their great Friend, his mission and his Church. For Teresa, to love Christ is to love his friends: the whole Christ, body and members – the Church.

A gospel vision of church

There are many models of church in the New Testament.[54] Vatican II devotes an entire chapter to the scriptural image of the Church as the new 'people of God',[55] emphasising the human and communal, rather than the institutional and hierarchical aspect. With the same vision, Teresa would have each of her communities a 'college of Christ' (WP 27:6): a replica, in miniature, of the community of the early church. She stamped her communities with her own delightful and human touch. For her, every community structure is designed primarily to enhance, not to cripple, personal development. Or, as Vatican II reminds us: 'the beginning, the subject and the goal of all social institutions is and must be the human person'.[56]

Teresa exhorts all to holiness and would draw others to Carmel with a winning smile: 'be affable and understanding... that everyone you talk to will love your conversation... and not be frightened and intimidated by virtue... the holier they are the more sociable they are' (WP 41:7). She wanted her communities relaxed and flexible, a real family, a home for her sisters: 'Understand... that I am a friend of intensifying virtue, but not rigour, as will be seen in our houses.'[57] Rigidity is technically the first stage after death! So, Teresa always defended tolerance in applying rules and regulations, since 'a weighed-down soul cannot serve God well'.[58] Her human approach was Teresa's challenge to her sisters always to focus their eyes, in love, on the humanity of Christ and the community that he founded, bonded in love: 'The Lord doesn't look so much at the greatness of our works as at the love with which they are done' (IC VII:4:15). Her challenge to her communities – that their lives may be 'rooted and grounded in love' (Eph 3:17) – is also an invitation to a life of sacrifice, fruitful in union with Christ's love: 'His Majesty will join [our sacrifice] with that which He offered on the cross to the Father for us' (IC VII:4:15).

This kind of sharing between friends is community as we find it in John's gospel, a communion or fellowship described in the allegory of the vine: 'Abide in me, and I in you... I am the vine, you are the branches' (Jn 15:4-5). It is about a fruitfulness which is not possible apart from Jesus: 'Those who abide in me, and I in them, bear much fruit, because apart from me you can do nothing' (Jn 15:5). It is about love: 'Remain in my love' (Jn 15:9). It is an invitation to joy, 'that my joy may be in you, and that your joy may be complete' (Jn 15:11). It is a community all the more apostolic and fruitful in the Church the more it is rooted in love for Christ and for others. It is about a fruit-bearing community that gives glory to God: 'By this my Father is glorified, that you bear much fruit' (Jn 15:8). It is a community of prayer: 'If you abide in me... ask whatever you will and it shall be done for you' (Jn 15:7; cf. 15:16). This marvellously fresh gospel vision of community is recaptured by Teresa, and it heralds a new springtime for the Church of her day and of the future: a communion of love with Jesus and with one another which gives glory to God in a joyful life of prayer; a community with a mission, not primarily to 'go, therefore, and make disciples of all nations' (Mt 28:19) but rather to 'bear fruit' in love and to do so by loving one another as Christ has loved us in his passion and death (cf. Jn 13:34; 15:12). In a word, it is about the friendship at the heart of all Teresa's teaching – and about her longing, 'since He has so many enemies and so few friends that these few friends be good ones' (WP 1:2).

Notes

1   *Dei Verbum* (*Dogmatic Constitution on Divine Revelation*) 2. This opening quotation also contains the following references: Col 1:15; 1Tm 1:17; Ex 33:11; Jn 15:14-15; Bar 3:38.

2   *Perfectae Caritatis* (*Decree on the Appropriate Renewal of the Religious Life*) 2.

3   *Dei Verbum* (*Dogmatic Constitution on Divine Revelation*) 21. These words are quoted by John Paul II in his address when he was presented with the important recent document of the Pontifical Biblical Commission, *The Interpretation of the Bible in the Church*. As the then Cardinal Ratzinger aptly observes, in the 'Preface', '[This document] takes up the paths of the encyclicals of 1893 [*Providentissimus Deus*] and 1943 [*Divino Afflante Spiritu*] and advances them in a fruitful way.': see Pontifical Biblical Commission, *The Interpretation of the Bible in the Church*, Boston, MA: Pauline Books & Media, 1993, pp. 12.29.

4   Significantly, Edith Stein comments: 'Our Holy Mother strenuously denied that she was founding a new Order. She wanted nothing except to reawaken the original spirit of the old Rule [of St. Albert]': see HL, p. 1.

5   For a discussion of the biblical foundations of the Carmelite *Rule*, see the author's *The Carmelite Charism: Exploring the Biblical Roots*, Dublin: Veritas, 2004, ch. 3, pp. 60-81; and also the author's 'The Carmelite Rule: A Gospel Approach', in Eltin Griffin, O Carm (ed.), *Ascending the Mountain: The Carmelite Rule Today*, Dublin: Columba, 2004, pp. 29-48.

6   See Emmanuel Renault, OCD, *Reading the Bible with St Teresa*, Darlington Carmel, [no date], pp. 2-3.

7   This is the standard title used by ICS Publications. The Peers translation has the title, *Conceptions of the Love of God*.

8   On Teresa as Doctor of the Church, see Teresianum, *The Making of a Doctor: A Tribute to St Teresa of Avila by the Discalced Carmelites*, Discalced Carmelite Order, [1970]; *Sancta Teresia a Iesu Doctor Ecclesiae: Historia, Doctrina, Documenta, Ephemerides Carmeliticae*, vol. XXI/1-2, 1970; Otger Steggink, O Carm, 'The Doctorate of Experience', in *Carmelite Studies*, vol. 4, Washington, DC: ICS Publications, 1987, pp. 275-92; Joseph Glynn, OCD, *The Eternal Mystic: St. Teresa of Avila, the First Woman Doctor of the Church*, New York: Vantage Press, 1987, pp. 3-32.

9   *Dei Verbum* (*Dogmatic Constitution on Divine Revelation*) 25.

10   *Ibid.* 25.

11   Origen, in *Patrologia Graeca*, 11:92, quoted in Renault, *Reading the Bible*, op. cit., p. 11.

12   Cf. John of the Cross, SC Prol. 1-2.

13   Alexander Pope, *An Essay on Criticism* (1711), l. 215.

14   This is, in theological terms, *sentire cum Ecclesia*: see Christopher O'Donnell, O Carm, *Ecclesia: A Theological Encyclopedia of the Church*, Collegeville, MN: The Liturgical Press, 1996, p. 423.

15   An excellent treatment of fundamentalism and its dangers can be found in Pontifical Biblical Commission, *The Interpretation, op. cit.*, pp. 72-5.

16   For a discussion of Teresa's description, including a variety of possible translations of the passage quoted above, see Otilio Rodríguez, OCD, *The Teresian Gospel: An Introduction to a Fruitful Reading of the Way of Perfection*, Darlington Carmel, 1993, pp. 44-56. For an exploration of the significance of this passage in its context, see Tomás Álvarez, OCD, *Living with God: St Teresa's Concept of Prayer*, Dublin: Carmelite Centre of Spirituality, 1980, pp. 21-34.

17   On Teresa and friendship, see P Marie-Eugène, OCD, *I Want to See God: A Practical Synthesis of Carmelite Spirituality*, vol. 1, Cork: The Mercier Press, 1953, pp. 250-72; Norah Melia, *St Teresa and Friendship*, Melbourne: Carmelite Communications, 1988; Mary Pia Taylor, OCD, 'Friendship with Christ: Teresa of Avila's Way of Prayer', *Mount Carmel*, vol. 53/4, 2005.

18   See Brooke Foss Westcott, *The Gospel According to St. John*, London: James Clarke & Co, 1958, p. 15.

19   *Ibid.*, p. 15. John also describes Jesus as being 'towards' the Father (*pros*, Jn 1:1.2).

20   See Joachim Jeremias, *The Prayers of Jesus*, London: SCM Press, 1967, pp. 11-65, especially p. 65.

21   '*infundens et creans bonitatem in rebus*': in *Summa Theologica* I q. 20 a. 2.

22   Shakespeare, *Julius Caesar*, Act IV, Scene 2, ll. 2, 20-2.

23   Cf. 'Remember how our father Abraham was tested and became the friend of God after many trials and tribulations' (Jud 8:22), as quoted in *Divine Office*, vol. III, p. [408].

24   'This section [Mk 1:21-34]... is intended to give a typical picture of the early ministry.': see Wilfrid Harrington, OP, *Mark*, Dublin: Veritas (New Testament Message, vol. 4), 1979, p. 15. The reference to prayer in Mk 1:35, which immediately follows this section, is also an integral part of that typical day in Jesus' ministry.

25   See the author's *The Carmelite Charism, op. cit.*, ch. 1, section 'Promptings of the Spirit', pp. 18-20.

26   See Rodríguez, *op. cit.*, pp. 65-79.

27   See Thomas Dubay, SM, *Fire Within: St. Teresa of Avila, St. John of the Cross, and the Gospel – on Prayer*, San Francisco: Ignatius Press, 1989, pp. 111-57.

28   *Lumen Gentium (Dogmatic Constitution on the Church)* 5.

29   For Teresa's treatment of humility, see P Marie-Eugène, *op. cit.*, pp. 377-406.

30   See J Mary Luti, *Teresa of Avila's Way*, Collegeville, MN: The Liturgical Press, 1991, pp. 110-40.

31   See ch. 5, section 'An impossible commandment?'.

32   A point well made in Rodríguez, *op. cit.*, pp. 76-9; see also, for a general treatment of detachment in Teresa and John, Dubay, *op. cit.*, pp. 131-57.

33   For an extensive treatment of this theme, see Luti, *op. cit.*, pp. 61-81.

34   See Cathleen Medwick, *Teresa of Avila: The Progress of a Soul*, London: Duckworth, 2000, p. 254. The appendix (pp. 251-4) contains the third poem of Crashaw's Teresa cycle.

35   P Marie-Eugène, *op. cit.*, p. 16.

36   For an overview of Teresa's writings, see E Allison Peers, *Studies of the Spanish Mystics*, vol. 1, London: The Sheldon Press, 1927, pp. 151-91 and his *Mother of Carmel: A Portrait of St. Teresa of Jesus*, London: SCM Press, 1945, pp. 46-164; Eugene McCaffrey, OCD, *Introduction to the Writings of St Teresa of Avila*, Dublin: Carmelite Centre of Spirituality, 1981; Rowan Williams, *Teresa of Avila*, London & New York: Continuum, 1991, pp. 42-142.

37   For a concise analytical treatment of the four ways, see Louis Bouyer, *Women Mystics: Hadewijch of Antwerp, Teresa of Avila, Thérèse of Lisieux, Elizabeth of the Trinity, Edith Stein*, San Francisco: Ignatius Press, 1993, pp. 101-3.

38   This date refers to Teresa's first version of the *Life* (1562), now lost. The second version, the one which has come down to us, was written at the end of 1565: for a detailed explanation of the various stages of composition, see Tomás Álvarez, *Diccionario de Santa Teresa: Doctrina e Historia*, Burgos: Editorial Monte Carmelo, 2002, pp. 648-50.

39   For treatments of Teresa as a writer, see E Allison Peers, *Studies of the Spanish Mystics*, vol. 1, *op. cit.*, pp. 202-25 and his *Mother of Carmel*, *op. cit.*, pp. 165-79; Joseph Chorpenning, 'St Teresa's Presentation of her Religious Experience', in *Carmelite Studies*, vol. 3, Washington, DC: ICS Publications, 1984, pp. 152-88; Eugene McCaffrey, OCD, *Introduction to the Writings*, *op. cit.*, pp. 15-21 and his 'A Woman for all Ages: Teresa of

Avila', *Spirituality*, vol. 6, 2000, pp. 284-7; Gillian T W Ahlgren, *Teresa of Avila and the Politics of Sanctity*, Ithaca, NY & London: Cornell University Press, 1996, pp. 67-84.

40   For an excellent introduction to *The Way of Perfection*, see Jerome Lantry, OCD, *Saint Teresa on Prayer*, Dublin: Carmelite Centre of Spirituality, 1981; also, Rodríguez, *op. cit.*

41   See note 20.

42   For a good introduction to vocal and mental prayer, see E W Trueman Dicken, *The Crucible of Love: A Study of the Mysticism of St Teresa of Jesus and St John of the Cross*, Longman: Darton, Longman & Todd, 1963, pp. 80-115.

43   Shakespeare, *Hamlet*, Act III, Scene 3, ll. 97-8.

44   *Marialis Cultus (Devotion to the Blessed Virgin Mary)* 47.

45   See the author's *The Carmelite Charism, op. cit.*, pp. 41-3.

46   On the prayer of recollection, see P Marie-Eugène, *op. cit.*, pp. 198-213; Eugene McCaffrey, OCD, 'Praying with St Teresa – 3: The Prayer of Companionship', *Mount Carmel*, vol. 46/4, 1999, pp. 9-14.

47   Also called the 'prayer of companionship': see note 46.

48   For works on the spiritual journey as seen in Teresa's life and writings, see Trueman Dicken, *op. cit.*, pp. 170-214; Deirdre Green, *Gold in the Crucible: Teresa of Avila and the Western Mystical Tradition*, Shaftesbury: Element Books, 1989, pp. 36-76; John Grennan, OCD, *The Inner Journey*, Dublin: Carmelite Centre of Spirituality, 1977.

49   There have recently been a number of commentaries on *The Interior Castle* from a variety of perspectives. See, for example, Julienne McLean, *Towards Mystical Union: A Modern Commentary on the Mystical Text The Interior Castle by St Teresa of Avila*, London & Staten Island, NY: St Pauls, 2003; Peter Tyler, *The Way of Ecstasy: Praying with Teresa of Avila*, Norwich: Canterbury Press, 1997; Ruth Burrows, *Interior Castle Explored: St. Teresa's Teaching on the Life of Deep Union with God*, London: Sheed & Ward/Dublin: Veritas, 1982; Peter Bourne, HMC, *St. Teresa's Castle of the Soul: A Study of the Interior Castle*, Long Beach, CA: Wenzel Press, 1995; Mary Frohlich, *The Intersubjectivity of the Mystic: A Study of Teresa of Avila's Interior Castle*, Atlanta, Georgia: Scholars Press, 1993; Shirley Darcus Sullivan, *Transformed by Love: The Soul's Journey to God in Teresa of Avila, Mother Aloysius of the Blessed Sacrament & Elizabeth of the Trinity*, Hyde Park, NY: New City Press, 2002, pp. 23-73.

50   This does not mean that centring prayer is incompatible with the earlier stages of Carmelite prayer: see Ernest E Larkin, O Carm, 'St

Teresa of Avila and Centering Prayer', in *Carmelite Studies*, vol. 3, *op. cit.*, pp. 191-211 and his 'The Carmelite Tradition and Centering Prayer/Christian Meditation', in Keith J Egan (ed.), *Carmelite Prayer: A Tradition for the 21st Century*, New York & Mahwah, NJ: Paulist Press, 2003, pp. 202-22.

51 John of the Cross refers to this place as 'the intimate center of the substance of the soul' (LF 2:8).

52 For a discussion of the issues of the apostolate of enclosed Carmelite nuns and the nature of 'Teresian works', see Emmanuel Renault, OCD, *The Apostolate of Contemplatives according to St Teresa of Avila*, Darlington Carmel, [no date].

53 See Tomás Álvarez, OCD, *Estudios Teresianos*, vol. 3, Burgos: Editorial Monte Carmelo, 1996, ch. 6, 'Santa Teresa y la Iglesia: Sentirse Hija de la Iglesia', pp. 211-86, especially pp. 285-6.

54 See *Lumen Gentium* (*Dogmatic Constitution on the Church*) 6-7.

55 *Ibid.*, ch. 2 (#9-17). On the importance of this image of the Church as 'people of God', see the explanation by Avery Dulles, SJ, in *The Documents of Vatican II*, London, Dublin & Melbourne: Geoffrey Chapman, 1966, pp. 24-5, note 27.

56 *Gaudium et Spes* (*Pastoral Constitution on the Church in the Modern World*) 25.

57 Letter to Fr Ambrosio Mariano de San Benito Azzaro, December 12th, 1576.

58 Letter to Fr Jerónimo Gracián, February 21st, 1581.

CHAPTER TWO

JOHN OF THE CROSS: GUIDE IN OUR SEARCH FOR GOD

'Things both new and old'

In his doctoral study, John Paul II comments: 'St. John of the Cross did not write his works with a view to the investigations of scholars or those engaged in higher studies'.[1] Nowhere, perhaps, is this more true than in John's use of the scriptures.[2]

The treasure of God's word is inexhaustible, so 'every scribe who becomes a disciple of the kingdom of heaven is like a householder who brings out from his storeroom things both new and old' (Mt 13:52). As Newman observes so well: 'the whole Bible... is written on the principle of development. As the Revelation proceeds, it is ever new, yet ever old.'[3] We are privileged to have our understanding of the Bible enormously enriched by a variety of new approaches and ways of penetrating the depths of the sacred text.[4] But these were largely unknown to John. All indications, however, are that he would have been completely at ease with the developments of recent biblical research in the wake of Vatican II. In his own day, John was familiar with the lively controversy about the interpretation of scripture in the University of Salamanca where he studied. Gaspar Grajal was a prominent figure among the so-called 'scripturists', who sought the literal sense of scripture through scientific methods and the study of languages.[5] He was probably John's professor and was later imprisoned by the Inquisition for these ideas. John, however, did not have a general theory or method of explaining the scriptures.[6] He had a thorough familiarity with the Bible, he had reason, and he had faith.

It might come as a surprise to some that John, who affirms that faith is 'the only proximate and proportionate means to union with God' (2A 9:1), would insistently extol the value and importance of human reason. For him, there is no opposition between faith and reason. His is the celebrated maxim: 'One human thought alone is worth more than the entire world, hence God alone is worthy of it' (SLL 35; cf. 116). He is an uncompromising champion of the dignity of the human person. 'What a piece of work is a man,' wrote Shakespeare, his contemporary, 'how noble in reason'.[7] And the psalmist: 'you have made [man] little less than a god' (Ps 8:6). These are sentiments affirmed by John himself, as his maxim shows. Still, reason – with its lights and limitations – is at its noblest and best when it remains always open to God in mystery. John insists: 'one can get sufficient guidance from natural reason'. But he qualifies this by continuing: 'and from the law and doctrine of the Gospel' (2A 21:4). This is something we can 'understand' only in faith – and, John might add, through faith in the teachings of the Church.

In communion with the Church
Repeatedly, John affirms that his entire teaching is based on the Bible: 'whether I deduce [some point] from Scripture or not, I will not be intending to deviate from the true meaning of Sacred Scripture or from the doctrine of our Holy Mother the Catholic Church' (A Prol. 2). Again: 'I desire to submit... entirely to Holy Mother the Church,' he says; and he adds: 'I want to explain and confirm at least the more difficult matters through passages from Sacred Scripture' (SC Prol. 4). John will also draw on his own experience and knowledge, but always insists: 'my help in all that, with God's favor, I shall say, will be Sacred Scripture' (A Prol. 2).[8] So, even his incomparable familiarity with the ways of the Spirit and

his own intimate communion with God in prayer remain always secondary to the Bible, together with the teachings of the Church.

John well knew that scripture is 'not the word of any human being, but God's word, a power that is working among believers' (1 Th 2:13). It is ever 'alive and active' (Hb 4:12) through the power of the Spirit. 'Taking Scripture as our guide,' he says, 'we do not err, since the Holy Spirit speaks to us through it' (A Prol. 2) – 'speaks' in the present tense, that is: speaks and is still speaking to us, here and now. John is constantly reminding us that the words of the Bible are the actual words of the Holy Spirit (2A 22:2) or of 'Wisdom' (2A 29:7).

We must always remember that the Bible was born in the heart of the Church, the community of believers.[9] The same Spirit is at work in both the Bible and the Church. So, 'we must be guided humanly and visibly in all by the law of Christ, who is human,' John tells us, 'and that of his Church and of his ministers' (2A 22:7). In his understanding of the scriptures, John remains always in communion with the Church and open to the action of the Spirit. Therein lie the inspiration and the perennial value of all that he has left us in his writings.

A deeper spiritual meaning

John was fully aware of the literal sense of the scriptures which could be grasped by reason. But his preference was clearly for the 'spiritual' sense.[10] This latter is intelligible only in the darkness of faith and it unfolds under the action of the Spirit. It is a deeper meaning which incomparably exceeds the literal sense. John writes: '[This spiritual meaning] is... much richer and more plentiful, very extraordinary and far beyond the boundaries of the letter' (2A 19:5). He further adds by way of explanation: '[God's words] embody an abyss and depth of spirit, and to want to limit them to our interpretation and to what our senses can apprehend is like wanting to grasp a handful of air' (2A 19:10).

This deeper, 'spiritual' sense has a solid basis in the scriptures and John rightly finds support for it in the promise of the Paraclete who will guide the Church into 'all truth':

> God usually affirms, teaches, and promises many things, not so there will be an immediate understanding of them, but so that afterward at the proper time, or when the effect is produced, one may receive light about them. Christ acted this way with his disciples. He told them many parables and maxims the wisdom of which they did not understand until the time for preaching had come, when the Holy Spirit descended on them. The Holy Spirit was to explain to them, as Christ affirmed, all that he had taught them during his life… (2A 20:3; cf. Jn 16:13; 14:26; 2:22; 12:16).[11]

When John writes about 'those comparisons of the divine Song of Solomon and other books of Sacred Scripture', he does not hesitate to explain that 'the Holy Spirit, unable to express the fullness of his meaning in ordinary words, utters mysteries in strange figures and likenesses… the abundant meanings of the Holy Spirit cannot be caught in words' (SC Prol. 1). Here, the Mystical Doctor is in line with an ancient Carmelite tradition. Witness the words of one anonymous thirteenth-century Carmelite writer:

> Within these secret words, held captive beneath images, are hidden meanings that are subtle and mystical, like treasures in the ground. To discover these secrets, by separating the spirit from the letter, is to draw up life, the life of the Spirit. Happy is the person who in the misery of exile devotes all his spirit and all his love to the delights of these mysterious meanings![12]

Lectio – the Carmelite way[13]

John's emphasis on the deeper spiritual meaning of the word of God might easily perplex readers familiar with modern tools of biblical interpretation.[14] His approach to the sacred text is much more akin to *lectio divina* – a way of reading the scriptures prayerfully. It is a method deeply embedded in the monastic tradition.[15] God's word emerged spontaneously in the saint's writings from a retentive memory shaped in large measure by the Bible. His mind was constantly echoing to parallel, contrasting, qualifying and explanatory texts, and his works bristle with scriptural quotations. Yet these works, John Paul II reminds us, 'are written for the purpose of directing contemplatives toward union with God'.[16] The saint therefore urges us to savour the sacred text to the exclusion of all else present: 'leave as well all these other things and attend to one thing alone that brings all these with it (namely, holy solitude, together with prayer and spiritual and divine reading), and persevere there in forgetfulness of all things' (SLL 79). In an expansion of one proverbial gospel text, 'seek and you will find' (Mt 7:7), he invites us to explore the scriptures more deeply in prayer: 'Seek in reading and you will find in meditation; knock in prayer and it will be opened to you in contemplation' (SLL 158).[17] Edith Stein sums up well: 'Our Holy Father John...educates us to read the Scriptures. He is said to have had, at the end, only the New Testament in his cell' (SP, p. 218).

Constant repetition of the biblical text in slow and prayerful *lectio* allows the word of God to seep into the heart 'as the rain and the snow come down from the heavens and do not return without watering the earth' (Is 55:10). We should read the works of John himself in the same way. One of his companions on his journeys, Jerónimo de la Cruz, testifies that the saint used to repeat, quietly and with great devotion, the priestly prayer of Jesus (Jn 17).[18] Here, he was praying in the monastic tradition of reading the word of God aloud or, for greater personal impact, *sotto voce*. The testimony of other witnesses also speaks volumes. John's secretary for many years, Fray Juan Evangelista, testifies that the saint knew almost all of the Bible by heart;[19] 'I am sure he knew the whole Bible,' remarked another friar, Pablo de Santa María.[20] Little wonder that Fray Agustín de los Reyes could confide to a friend how he found the saint one day leaning against a wall, 'with a Bible in his hand, absorbed, as usual,' he said, 'in contemplation'.[21]

Lectio and prayer are inseparably entwined in John's interpretation of the Bible and come to their fulfilment in the saint's own works. His incomparable descriptions of the inner life — whether in magnificent verse[22] or in what he calls his 'awkward style' of prose[23] (A Prol. 8) — draw their substance from the drama of the Bible: the love story between God and his people.

A journey into freedom[24]

John's writings offer us a path into freedom,[25] a way of detachment from all that is not God, to focus on him alone. While his writings are rich in imagery from the scriptures, one image of paramount importance for John's overall 'journey' is that of the exodus: the passage of God's people out of Egypt across the desert and into the promised land, a journey out of slavery into freedom. References to this event, explicit and implicit, recur in John's prose and poetry. He compares the cravings of unruly desires — our slavery to sin and temptation — to the way the Israelites were still hankering, in the wilderness, after the food of their captivity:

> Those whom God begins to lead into these desert solitudes are like the children of Israel. When God began giving them the heavenly food, which contained in itself all savors and changed to whatever taste each one hungered after [Wis. 16:20-21], as is there mentioned, they nonetheless felt a craving for the tastes of the fleshmeats and onions they had eaten in Egypt... (IDN 9:5)

John's words of advice to those who guide contemplatives also contain echoes of the exodus experience and again highlight the aspect of the desert:

> Pacify the soul, draw it out, and liberate it from the yoke and slavery of its own weak operation, which is the captivity of Egypt (amounting to not much more than gathering straws for baking bricks) [Ex. 5:7-19]. And, O spiritual master, guide it to the land of promise flowing with milk and honey [Ex. 3:8, 17]. Behold that for this holy liberty and idleness of the children of God, God calls the soul to the desert...
> (LF 3:38)

John's poetry, too, is enriched by this same imagery of Israel's desert experience and further embellished with a delightful interplay of light and darkness. At the outset of his poem, 'The Dark Night', he writes: 'fired with love's urgent longings.../I went out [salí] unseen,/my house being now all stilled' (DN, stanza 1). He compares the spiritual journey to emerging out of darkness 'with no other light or guide/than the one that burned in my heart' (DN, stanza 3). He then describes coming to transforming union in similar paradoxical terms of light and darkness: 'O night more lovely than the dawn!/O night that has united/the Lover with his beloved' (DN, stanza 5). These lines are reminiscent of the Easter *Exsultet* with its pervading exodus theme: 'This is the night when... you freed the people of Israel from their slavery and led them dry-shod through the sea... when the pillar of fire destroyed the darkness of sin!'[26] John's poem also ends with imagery of departure: 'I went out from myself [dejéme],/leaving my cares/forgotten among the lilies' (DN, stanza 8). In *The Spiritual Canticle*, the restless bride voices an anguished cry for her absent Lover: 'I went out [salí] calling you, but you were gone' (SC, stanza 1; cf. Sg 3:1-2; 5:6). Here, too, the bride longs to journey out – out of this life into glory and the marriage of the beatific vision: 'Let us rejoice, Beloved,/and let us go forth to behold ourselves in your beauty' (SC, stanza 36).

John finds much of his inspiration in the biblical texts on the wanderings of the chosen people. He alters, amplifies and adapts superbly the psalm, 'By the rivers of Babylon...' (Ps 136). The resulting poem (R 10) was written while he was imprisoned in a dark dungeon during his captivity in Toledo. There, his mind and heart could echo more easily to the sobbing music of God's captive people, longing in exile for a second exodus. His words give passionate expression to the thirst of every human heart reaching out in pain and waiting on God to lead them, like his banished people, out of slavery into the freedom of the promised land.

'Listen, Israel'[27]
God constantly summons his wayward people on their desert march to obey his commandments. The first two provide a biblical foundation for a better understanding of the ascetical basis on which John builds his spiritual edifice – that is, the basis we call 'active', which deals with *our* efforts to follow God:

> *First commandment:*
> You shall have no other gods before me. (Ex 20:3; Dt 5:7)
> You shall love the Lord your God with all your heart, and with all your soul, and with all your might. (Dt 6:5)

> *Second commandment:*
> You shall not make for yourself a graven image, or any likeness of anything... (Ex 20:4; Dt 5:8)

These two commandments are central to the whole biblical message and provide the conditions for entering the promised land. They constitute the heart of God's covenant with his people in the desert and contain the radical and absolute demands of a 'jealous' God (Ex 20:5), an 'unrivalled' God (Is 45:5).

This is not to imply that John worked out the basis of his synthesis and its development according to a preconceived plan based on these first two commandments. Perhaps he never explicitly thought of his teaching in this way. But, listening to the Spirit guiding him through the scriptures, he entered deeply into the meaning of the Sinai covenant. The word of God yielded its riches to him with its radical and absolute demands. In this light, John wrote the first three books of the *Ascent*. Newman reminds us of the value of this kind of personal exploration and discovery in the Bible:

> There is no greater mistake, surely, than to suppose that a revealed truth precludes originality in the treatment of it... a reassertion of what is old with a luminousness of explanation which is new, is a gift inferior only to that of revelation itself.[28]

No lesser gods

The way in which the first commandment is introduced is a reminder of the exodus: 'I am the Lord your God, who brought you out of the land of Egypt, out of the house of bondage' (Ex 20:2; Dt 5:6). This is a transcendent God, totally 'Other', unique and incomparable: 'You shall have no other gods before me' (Ex 20:3; Dt 5:7; cf. Is 45:5.6.14.21).[29] There is an infinite distance between the Creator and his creation. As John recognises: 'all the being of creatures compared to the infinite being of God is nothing' (1A 4:4). The uniqueness and transcendence of God demand the 'nothing' of all that is not God. God and worldly attachments, John explains, are 'two contraries' (1A 4:2). As Paul expresses it: 'what we have to do is to give up everything that does not lead to God' (Tit 2:12).

The ill-regulated or irrational drives of the senses direct the affections of the restless human heart to a lesser god: our own pleasure and satisfaction. This is equivalently to violate the first commandment of *total love* for the Creator (Dt 6:5). John identifies this as idolatry.[30] To place anything other than God on a level with him is to worship a false god: 'No one can serve two masters' (Mt 6:24).

The saint constantly teaches about the need to purify the unruly cravings of the senses when they are *voluntary, habitual* and *disordered* – 'appetites' (*apetitos*) as he calls them (IA 3-12).[31] His warnings are epitomised by the lessons of Paul: 'Learn to live and move in the spirit; then there is no danger of your giving way to the impulses of corrupt nature. The impulses of nature and the impulses of the spirit are at war with one another; either is clean contrary to the other, and that is why you cannot do all that your will approves' (Gal 5:16-17). But how are we to renounce the seductions and lure of our passions? That is the problem John has to address. He provides an answer in what he calls 'an enkindling with urgent longings of love' (*inflamada de amor y con ansias*):

> A more intense enkindling of another, better love (love of the soul's Bridegroom) is necessary for the vanquishing of the appetites and the denial of this pleasure. By finding satisfaction and strength in this love, it will have the courage and constancy to readily deny all other appetites. The love of its Bridegroom is not the only requisite for conquering the strength of the sensitive appetites; an enkindling with urgent longings of love is also necessary. (IA 14:2; cf. 2A 1:2; DN, stanza 1)

So, it is not enough to have love for the Bridegroom; one must be *inflamed* in that same love.[32]

The restless heart

The commandment of *total love* is clearly of decisive importance at the level of the senses. On the spiritual level, it is no less so. John writes of the need, for the sake of God, to release the will – that vital region of the human spirit – from clinging to anything that is not God:

> For a treatise on the active night and denudation of [the will], with the aim of forming and perfecting it in this virtue of the charity of God, I have found no more appropriate passage than the one in chapter 6 of Deuteronomy, where Moses commands: *You shall love the Lord, your God, with all your heart, and with all your soul, and with all your strength* [Dt. 6:5]. This passage contains all that spiritual persons must do and all I must teach them here if they are to reach God by union of the will through charity. In it, human beings receive the command to employ all the faculties, appetites, operations, and emotions of their soul in God so that they will use all this ability and strength for nothing else... (3A 16:1)

The total renunciation in the purification, or 'night', of the will is here based on the first commandment as formulated positively, in terms of total and exclusive love for God (Dt 6:5). The whole response of Israel to the God of the covenant throughout its history is summed up in this precept of undivided love. Jesus defines it as 'the greatest and the first commandment' (Mt 22:38). John's recurring antithesis, 'All-Nothing', affirms the radical demands of his ascetical teaching. It is there implicitly in the twofold expression of the first commandment in the Old Testament: 'ALL' evoking the *positive* precept to 'love the Lord your God with all your heart, and with all your soul, and with all your might' (Dt 6:5); 'NOTHING' recalling the *negative* prohibition, 'You shall have no other gods before me' (Ex 20:3; Dt 5:7).

It is not only the ill-regulated 'appetites' of the senses, indulged for the sake of personal gratification or satisfaction, that are a form of idolatry. So, too, is a possessive clinging of the will to anything in place of God. Such possessions are idols. They are rivals to God and enslave the heart: 'those who love something together with God undoubtedly make little of God, for they weigh in the balance with God an object far distant from God' (1A 5:4). And again: 'God allows nothing else to dwell together with him' (1A 5:8). Ultimately, only a God unique and transcendent can completely satisfy all the deepest longings and desires of the human spirit. The human heart can go to the lengths of God in undivided love and unfettered freedom. John affirms the need first to strip it bare of all the disordered affections and possessions that enslave it. His teaching recalls the gospel lesson: 'Only one is good, God alone' (Mk 10:18).

A way of unknowing

There are two other regions of the human spirit, apart from the will, requiring preparation for direct union with God: the intellect and the memory.[33] As John explains: 'no form, figure, image, or idea (whether heavenly or earthly, natural or supernatural) that can be grasped by the memory [or acted on by the intellect] is God or like to him' (3A 11:1). So, John concludes that 'in the measure that individuals dispossess their memory of forms and objects, which are not God, they will fix it on God and preserve it empty, so as to hope for the fullness of their memory from him' (3A 15:1). But John does not minimise in any way the importance of images in themselves and is careful to sound a note of warning:

> There is no delusion or danger in the remembrance, veneration, and esteem of images that the Catholic Church proposes to us in a natural manner, since in

these images nothing else is esteemed than the person represented. The memory of these images will not fail to benefit a person, because this remembrance is accompanied with love for whoever is represented. Images will always help individuals toward union with God, provided that no more attention is paid to them than necessary for this love, and that souls allow themselves to soar – when God bestows the favor – from the painted image to the living God, in forgetfulness of all creatures and things pertaining to creatures. (3A 15:2)

Although John himself does not say so explicitly, the second commandment provides a biblical basis for his explanation of the need to purify these two faculties, intellect and memory. It prohibits the making of any likeness or image of God such as the golden calf that Israel fashioned and worshipped at Sinai (Ex 32:1-6). This was, quite literally, idolatry: 'You shall not make for yourself a graven image, or any likeness of anything...' (Ex 20:4; Dt 5:8).

God is incomprehensible and beyond all comparison. The saint explains well: 'God transcends the intellect and is incomprehensible and inaccessible to it' (LF 3:48). No idea, concept, form or image can adequately express God. There is no essential similarity between him and his creation. John quotes the words of Isaiah, 'To what have you been able to liken God? Or what image will you fashion like to him?' (Is 40:18). He then comments:

It is as if Isaiah had said that the intellect will be unable through its ideas to understand anything like God, the will unable to experience a delight and sweetness resembling him, and the memory unable to place in the imagination remembrances and images representing him. (2A 8:5)

The path to direct union with God for the memory and intellect is consequently a way of 'unknowing'. In the words of T S Eliot: 'In order to possess what you do not possess/You must go by the way of dispossession.'[34] John will link the memory with hope as an indispensable means for direct union with God:

> We must draw [the memory] away from its natural props and boundaries and raise it above itself (above all distinct knowledge and apprehensible possession) to supreme hope for the incomprehensible God. (3A 2:3)

While *hope* alone links the memory directly to God, and *love*, as we have seen, links the will, so the mind reaches him directly only in the darkness of *faith*:

> The Holy Spirit in Deuteronomy clearly manifests that God has no form or likeness:...You heard the voice of his words, and you saw absolutely no form in God [Dt. 4:12]. But he affirms that darkness, the cloud, and obscurity (that vague, dark knowledge... in which the soul is united to God) were present. (2A 16:8)

Faith, hope and love – deeply rooted as they are in the first and second commandments – constitute a profound unity in John's whole ascetical teaching in the three books of *The Ascent of Mount Carmel*. These theological virtues unite the believer directly with God as he is in himself – transcendent, unique, incomparable and incomprehensible – and provide the dynamism that constantly impels the believer to an ever-deeper penetration of his mystery.

Learning to bear the beams of love
John's masterly exposition of the active night, in *The Ascent*, is perfectly complemented by his explanation of the passive night in

The Dark Night. Here, the saint looks at the same process of purification, but now the stress is on God's action and our submission to it. Our response is necessary, indispensable. But God's work is always primary: we merely cooperate. The necessity of this searing and penetrating action of God, with its radical and absolute nature, is well summed up in the words of Jeremiah: 'The heart is more devious than any other thing, perverse, too. Who can pierce its secrets? I the Lord search the heart, and probe the loins' (Jer 17:9-10). And Paul writes: 'It is God, for his own loving purpose, who puts both the will and the action into you' (Ph 2:13). God is the active, ever-creative One, and his action is all-embracing: 'May the God who gives us peace make you completely his and keep your whole being, spirit, soul and body free from all fault, at the coming of our Lord, Jesus Christ' (1Th 5:23). Jesus expresses it quite simply: 'Without me you can do nothing' (Jn 15:5).

'If the Lord does not build the house, in vain do its builders labour' (Ps 126:1). This primacy of God's action is a recurring theme of the exodus. The first two commandments are prefaced with a reminder that *it is God who has led* his people into the wilderness. Faith in this guiding action of God throughout their desert wanderings is built into the Israelite *credo*: 'The Lord brought us out of Egypt with a mighty hand and an outstretched arm... and he brought us into this place, and gave us this land, a land flowing with milk and honey' (Dt 26:8-9). But God also leads his people through the desert to growing intimacy with himself: 'I will allure her, and bring her into the wilderness, and speak tenderly to her' (Hos 2:14). God's desire is to make Israel his 'treasured possession... a priestly kingdom... a holy nation' (Ex 19:5-6). In this way, he fashioned a people for himself during the exodus: teaching, training, guiding, sustaining, shielding them 'as the apple of his eye' (Dt 32:10).

For Israel, the desert is a time of testing, but it is God who does the testing. So, too, John observes that this is what takes place during the passive dark night. In words that are often read as a self-portrait, he describes this absolute and radical action by God:

> [Individuals in this state] resemble one who is imprisoned in a dark dungeon, bound hands and feet, and able neither to move nor see nor feel any favor from heaven or earth. They remain in this condition until their spirit is humbled, softened, and purified, until it becomes so delicate, simple, and refined that it can be one with the Spirit of God, according to the degree of union of love that God, in his mercy, desires to grant. (2DN 7:3)

Here, John almost seems to be explaining his own captivity in the cramped cell of his Toledo prison – an imprisonment from which there was (apparently) no exit, no possibility of escape.[35]

Blessed are the pure of heart

The God of the exodus is a God of love, 'merciful and gracious, slow to anger, and abounding in steadfast love and faithfulness, keeping steadfast love for thousands, forgiving iniquity and transgression and sin' (Ex 34:6-7). Love is the reason for the exodus: 'it is because the Lord loves you... that the Lord has brought you out with a mighty hand' (Dt 7:8; cf. Ps 135). This love is a gift of God, it is the 'new heart' promised by the prophets (Ez 36:26; cf. 11:19; Jer 31:33). As Paul writes: 'God's love has been poured into our hearts through the Holy Spirit who has been given to us' (Rm 5:5). This is the love John speaks of when he describes contemplative prayer as an 'inflow of God, which, if not hampered, fires the soul in the spirit of love' (1DN 10:6).

Two compelling images of the saint reinforce this lesson. God's cleansing is his love in action. For John, it is like a ray of light beating on a stained window. The light cannot pierce and illumine the darkness within. But once the obstacles are removed, the 'inner room' is flooded with light. It is a gospel image: 'Your eye is the lamp of your body; when your eye is sound, your whole body is full of light; but when it is not sound, your body is full of darkness' (Lk 11:34).[36] This purifying 'ray of darkness' (LF 3:49) is also like a fire that must first blacken and char the log of wood until all the water oozes out and it can glow with the living flame of God's love.[37]

This chastening touch of God's love in the night, however painful, opens a way to the deepest possible communion with him. John describes the darkness of faith as 'that glad night' (DN, stanza 3) and final union as transformation in the 'living flame of love' which is a 'delicate touch/that tastes of eternal life/and pays every debt!' (LF, stanza 2). He then adds: 'In killing you changed death to life' (LF, stanza 2). *The Spiritual Canticle* explains that love alone gives meaning to God's action in the night. John describes its benefits:

> Now I occupy my soul
> and all my energy in his service;
> I no longer tend the herd,
> nor have I any other work
> now that my every act is love. (SC, stanza 28)

The Spanish word used here for 'energy' is '*caudal*'. It evokes the image of a river in full spate with all its force, energy and power kept in check by banks that are almost at breaking point. So, too, the potential of the human heart is now purified at all levels and entirely released, channelled, united and concentrated in loving unceasingly. In this verse, John says literally: 'only in loving is my exercise' ('*sólo en amar es mi ejercicio*'). This is truly eternal life – an unending ecstasy of love.

'Seeking my love'
Such is the *end* to which John of the Cross leads believers. The *journey* is a search for God: the faith, the hope and the love are in the searching. This theme pervades the saint's writings. He confesses:

'this seeking is my only hope' (P 6, stanza 4). In his *Spiritual Canticle*, John records the anxious lover's pursuit of the Beloved from the beginning of the search right up to the end of the quest. 'Seeking my love', the soul sets out – until, reaching the goal of all its aspirations, it finally exclaims, 'There you will show me/what my soul has been seeking' (SC, stanzas 3.38).

'What are you seeking?' Jesus asks the first disciples (Jn 1:38).[38] It is a challenge to us, too. This gospel question is for all. It occurs again on the lips of the risen Lord but with a significant variation. He asks the Magdalen, '*Whom* are you seeking?' (Jn 20:15). The disciples are not sure what is the object of their search; the Magdalen is in no doubt. She is searching for the person of Jesus. She is like the bride in the *Song of Songs*, fired with love in pursuit of her absent lover. *The Spiritual Canticle* is inspired by this biblical love song, which is clear from the theme, the rich imagery and style, and even the title. The book itself was known to John as the *Canticle of Canticles* and has become, in fact, part of the Carmelite mystical tradition. Teresa herself wrote a whole commentary on it, her *Meditations on the Song of Songs*; and Thérèse, who quoted frequently from the *Song*, was sadly unable to realise her great desire to explain it in depth. Repeatedly, John finds the intense yearnings for an absent God personified in the unsatisfied and passionate love of the bride in the *Song of Songs*. Commenting on his words, 'Seeking my love', he writes:

> Yet, unless they go in search for God, they will not find him, no matter how much they cry out for him. The bride of the Song of Songs cried after him, but did not find him until she went out looking for him. She affirms: *In my bed by night I sought him whom my soul loves; I sought him and did not find him. I will rise up and go about the city; in the suburbs and the squares I will look for him whom my soul loves* [Sg. 3:1-2]. (SC 3:2)

The Beloved is always 'beyond': beyond the mind and heart, beyond the feelings and thoughts, beyond the expectations and desires, beyond all the events that make up the sum of life's experience. He is the 'ah, I-don't-know-what behind their stammering' (SC, stanza 7), the object of love in his lyrical refrain, the '*I-don't-know-what/which is so gladly found*' (P 12). God transcends everything; he is absolutely free. We cannot confine him to any rigid mould of human thought. The mystery of his name is concealed in an immense silence, inexpressible and unutterable. Believers have to wrestle like Jacob in the dark to discover God (cf. Gn 32:22-32). But he always eludes our grasp – a stranger in the night. So, too, the seeker of the Beloved in *The Spiritual Canticle* exclaims, 'I went out calling you, but you were gone' (SC, stanza 1). Just when she seems to discover him, he disappears into the night; the soul finds him only to lose him again; she searches for his presence in the pain of his absence, while the Beloved disappears again into the darkness of his own mystery.

'The Father spoke one Word'
John sums up his teaching on the centrality of Jesus in one phrase, echoing the '*Logos*' from the prologue of John's gospel: 'The Father spoke one Word, which was his Son, and this Word he speaks always in eternal silence, and in silence must it be heard by the soul' (SLL 100; cf. 2A 22:3; Jn 1:1; Hb 1:2). The saint's advice is brief but telling: 'Fasten your eyes on him alone because in him I have spoken and revealed all' (2A 22:5). One brief phrase, repeating this message, says everything: 'fix your eyes only on him' (2A 22:6). Then we will be 'founded on the rock' (Mt 7:24): 'Well and good if all things change, Lord God, provided we are rooted in you' (SLL 34). John directs us to Jesus as the only true model:

> have habitual desire to imitate Christ in all your deeds
> by bringing your life into conformity with his. You must
> then study his life in order to know how to imitate him
> and behave in all events as he would. (1A 13:3)

Yes, fix our eyes on Jesus, but especially when he speaks these stark words from the cross: 'My God, my God, why have you forsaken me?' (Mt 27:46). In this way, John tells us, 'those who are truly spiritual might understand the mystery of the door and way (which is Christ) leading to union with God' (2A 7:11). To drive home his teaching, John heaps up quotations from the gospels, such as: 'This is my beloved Son... listen to him' (Mt 17:5; cf. 2A 22:5); and from Paul: 'In many and various ways God spoke of old to our fathers by the prophets; but in these last days he has spoken to us by a Son' (Hb 1:1-2; cf. 2A 22:4);[39] 'In [Christ] are hidden all the treasures of the wisdom and knowledge [of God]' (Col 2:3; cf. 2A 22:6; SC 2:7; 37:4); '[In Christ] all the fulness of the divinity dwells bodily' (Col 2:9; cf. 2A 22:6). We might add, in support of the saint's teaching, the climax to the prologue in the fourth gospel, a verse referred to more than once by John: 'No one has ever seen God; the only Son... has made [the Father] known' (Jn 1:18; cf. 2A 8:4; 3A 12:1; SC 1:3). Jesus, and he alone, is the revelation of God in person. There is no other.

'You are his dwelling'
But the seeker's question still remains unanswered. It is a 'Where?' 'Where have you hidden,/Beloved, and left me moaning?' (SC, stanza 1). John explains this line: 'God, then, is hidden in the soul, and there the good contemplative must seek him with love... now we are telling you that you yourself are his dwelling and his secret inner room and hiding place' (SC 1:6.7). John sums it all up, drawing on the experience of Augustine in support of his teaching:

> It should be known that the Word, the Son of God,
> together with the Father and the Holy Spirit, is hidden
> by his essence and his presence in the innermost being
> of the soul. Individuals who want to find him should

leave all things through affection and will, enter within themselves in deepest recollection, and let all things be as though not. St. Augustine, addressing God in the *Soliloquies*, said: *I did not find you without, Lord, because I wrongly sought you without, who were within.* (SC 1:6)[40]

To search for this God within is to embark on an exodus journey of faith: 'Seek him in faith and love… Faith and love are like the blind person's guides. They will lead you along a path unknown to you, to the place where God is hidden' (SC 1:11). Here, we catch an echo of Isaiah's words: 'And I will lead the blind in a way that they know not, in paths that they have not known I will guide them' (Is 42:16).

In the history of his people, God is now present, now absent. The never-ending search for him continues. The search in faith for access to this hidden God finds eloquent expression in the deepest yearnings and longings of the psalmist: 'Like the deer that yearns for running streams… My soul is thirsting for God' (Ps 41:2-3); 'O God, you are my God, for you I long; for you my soul is thirsting' (62:2); 'My soul is longing and yearning… for the courts of the Lord' (83:3). But God 'hides his face' (cf. Ps 29:8) or at times 'turns it away' (cf. Ez 7:22) when he appears to abandon his people, to be absent or even without concern. It is like a death of God, 'the silence of God' (cf. Ps 34:22). So, the psalmist longs to 'see the face of God' (Ps 41:3) and implores the Lord to 'let his face shine' (cf. Ps 30:17), not to 'hide his face' (cf. Ps 26:9) or to 'cast him away from his presence' (cf. Ps 50:13).[41]

Beyond the veils of faith

In the early stanzas of *The Spiritual Canticle*, the seeker is dissatisfied with everything that is not God. Creatures reveal some traces of the divine beauty and grandeur. It was the Creator who 'clothed them in beauty' (SC, stanza 5). But created things, even rational creatures, angels and people, 'All who are free' (SC, stanza 7), only increase the seeker's love for God and sorrow at his absence: 'Ah, who has the power to heal me?... all wound me more' (SC, stanzas 6.7). Still longing for the Beloved, the Maker himself in person, we listen to the heart-rending cry, 'Now wholly surrender yourself!.../ Extinguish these miseries.../ and may my eyes behold you,/because you are their light,/and I would open them to you alone./Reveal your presence' (SC, stanzas 6.10.11). Finding no remedy in any creature, the lover turns towards God in longing for his 'presence and image' (SC, stanza 11) hidden within, behind the veils of faith: 'O spring like crystal!/ If only, on your silvered-over faces,/ you would suddenly form/ the eyes I have desired,/which I bear sketched deep within my heart' (SC, stanza 12). It is there in the heart that union with the Beloved must be consummated. Finally comes the discovery and the encounter with the Beloved: 'the wounded stag/is in sight', captivated by the longings of impatient love and 'cooled by the breeze of [the bride's] flight' (SC, stanza 13).

John directs the seeker towards the goal of union with the Beloved: 'the soul, enamored of the Word, her Bridegroom, the Son of God, longs for union with him' (SC 1:2) and '[God] will bring her to the high perfection of union with the Son of God, her Bridegroom, and transformation in him through love' (SC 1:10). The Mystical Doctor is almost at a loss to describe this deep and mysterious union with God. We can feel his struggle when he writes: 'No knowledge or power can describe how this [union] happens' (SC 39:5). We then sense his relief when, at last, he finds in the priestly prayer of Jesus the words to express it adequately: '*I desire... that they may see the glory you have given me...that they may be one as we are one, I in them and you in me; that they may be perfect in one* [*sic*]' (SC 39:5; cf. Jn 17:24.22-23). It is love that urges us on to this union: 'The love of Christ impels us' (2Cor 5:14).[42]

A burning fire

John tells us that 'love's urgent longings' (DN, stanza 1) fire the seeker to go out in search of the Beloved. There is a guiding light, he says, 'that burned in my heart' (DN, stanza 3). Jeremiah speaks in similar terms of an inner dynamism of love: 'There is in my heart as it were a burning fire shut up in my bones, and I am weary with holding it in, and I cannot' (Jer 20:9). This same priority of love in the search for God is dramatically portrayed in the fourth gospel. On Easter morning, Peter and another disciple ran to the empty tomb in search of the absent Jesus. The evangelist is careful to refer to the 'other disciple' as 'the one whom Jesus loved' (Jn 20:2). 'Simon Peter... went into the tomb; he saw the linen cloths lying... Then the other disciple, who reached the tomb first, also went in' (Jn 20:6.8). The climax comes with the words, '[The beloved disciple] saw and believed' (Jn 20:8). The story embodies a leading theme of the fourth gospel: we discover Christ by loving Christ; or rather, Christ discovers or reveals himself to the searching of the disciple *in response to love*. Again, by the lakeside after the resurrection, 'the disciples did not know that it was Jesus,' we are told (Jn 21:4). It was the beloved disciple who did: 'The disciple whom Jesus loved said to Peter, "It is the Lord!"' (Jn 21:7). *The Cloud of Unknowing* translates this priority of love into practical advice: 'Strike that thick cloud of unknowing with the sharp dart of longing love, and on no account whatever think of giving up'; 'By love [God] can be caught and held, but by thinking never' (ch. 6).[43]

Love beyond all knowledge

Repeatedly, John speaks of 'loving knowledge': 'contemplation,' he explains, means 'knowledge and love together, that is, loving knowledge' (LF 3:32). They belong together and are a gift of God: 'it is God who in this state is the agent... The soul conducts itself only as the receiver and as one in whom something is being done; God is the giver and the one who works in it' (LF 3:32). He further explains that 'properly speaking, God does not communicate himself to the soul through... the knowledge it has of him, but through the love it has from this knowledge' (SC 13:11). Yet in so doing he increases the soul's knowledge of God:[44]

The sweet and living knowledge that [the soul] says he taught her is mystical theology, the secret knowledge of God that spiritual persons call contemplation. This knowledge is very delightful because it is a knowledge through love. Love is the master of this knowledge and what makes it wholly agreeable... God communicates this knowledge and understanding in the love with which he communicates himself to the soul... (SC 27:5)

This teaching of the saint is deeply embedded in the gospel where Jesus tells us that God reveals himself and gives his love in response to love: 'Those who love me will be loved by my Father, and I will love them and reveal myself to them' (Jn 14:21). John comments on these words, saying: 'This manifestation includes the knowledge... that God imparts to a person who has reached him and truly loves him' (2A 26:10). Hence: 'Everyone who loves is born of God and knows God. Whoever does not love does not know God' (1Jn 4:7-8).

This 'loving knowledge' is something that is always growing and deepening; it is a gradual process, a continual discovery. T S Eliot captures the idea perfectly: 'We shall not cease from exploration/And the end of all our exploring/Will be to arrive where we started/And know the place for the first time.'[45] 'What I want is... knowledge of God,' writes Hosea (6:6); and 'the love of Christ,' explains Paul, *is* the supreme knowledge, the knowledge 'beyond all knowledge' (Eph 3:19). John refers to this knowledge as a share in God's wisdom, entering into 'the high caverns in the rock/that are so well concealed' (SC, stanza 37). For him, the 'rock' – this supreme object of our knowledge and love – is Christ (cf. 1Cor 10:4):

The high caverns of this rock are the sublime, exalted, and deep mysteries of God's wisdom in Christ...

These mysteries are so profound that [the bride] very appropriately calls them high caverns: high, because of the height of the sublime mysteries; and caverns, because of the depth of God's wisdom in them. As caverns are deep and have many recesses, so each of the mysteries in Christ is singularly deep in wisdom... (SC 37:3)

A search that never ends

There is a curious feature about the seeking of the disciples in John's gospel that may help to clarify this passage. The disciples in *John* are not told, as they are in the synoptics, 'seek and you will find' (Mt 7:7; Lk 11:9; cf. Mk 11:24). Rather, they themselves tell us that they *have found* Jesus (Jn 1:41.45). Yet, this is only the beginning of the search: they are just starting to discover and penetrate something of his mystery.

On the eve of his passion, Jesus says to his followers, 'You will search for me' (Jn 13:33). They are given no assurance that they will find him. The concern of the fourth evangelist is not so much with the finding as with the searching – a 'knowing', which in the fourth gospel connotes a progressive searching in faith that will finally give way to vision, no longer 'darkly as in a mirror' (1Cor 13:12). 'Eternal life is this: to know you, the only true God, and Jesus Christ whom you have sent' (Jn 17:3). For John of the Cross, the transformed soul longs for this vision: 'let us go forth to behold ourselves in your beauty' (SC, stanza 36).

This final 'face-to-face' experience of God is described in scripture with unmistakable echoes of Israel's desert experience: 'They shall hunger no more, neither thirst any more; the sun shall not strike them, nor any scorching heat. For the Lamb in the midst of the throne will be their shepherd, and he will guide them to springs of living water' (Rv 7:16-17; cf. Is 49:10; Ps 120:6). And so, the possession of eternal life, here in the darkness of faith and hereafter in the clear vision of glory, unfolds as an ever-deeper penetration, guided by the hand of the Lord, into the ineffable mystery of God. In this broad sense, it is a kind of unending search, so to speak, a perpetual and ever-renewed exploration – one surprise after another. The Mystical Doctor explains that this search never ends:

> There is much to fathom in Christ, for he is like an abundant mine with many recesses of treasures, so that however deep individuals may go they never reach the end or bottom, but rather in every recess find new veins with new riches everywhere. On this account St. Paul said of Christ: *In Christ dwell hidden all treasures and wisdom* [Col. 2:3]. (SC 37:4)

No wonder Paul cries out: 'O the depth of the riches and wisdom and knowledge of God! How unsearchable are his judgments and how inscrutable his ways! "For who has known the mind of the Lord, or who has been his counsellor?" "Or who has given a gift to him that he might be repaid?"' (Rm 11:33-35; cf. Is 40:13; Jb 41:11).

Walking the way of the cross

'The gate entering into these riches of his wisdom,' writes John, 'is the cross'; this entrance 'is narrow, and few desire to enter by it' (SC 36:13). To find Jesus is to walk the way of Christ himself. Jesus is on a journey when he calls the first disciples: he is 'walking along' (Jn 1:36). No further detail is given, except that they walk along with him, accepting the invitation to 'Come and see' (Jn 1:39). As the gospel unfolds, however, the journey becomes Jesus' return to his Father through his passion-resurrection. This 'passage' of Jesus to his Father is the new 'passover' (cf. Jn 13:1), the new exodus of the paschal mystery.[46] It is along this route that Jesus invites his disciples to search for, and to follow, him. 'Where I am going you cannot follow me now; but you will follow afterwards' (Jn 13:36) – once Jesus himself has returned to his Father through his passion and death. In their searching, the disciples will walk this same exodus journey of Jesus, his 'passover' or 'crossing' to the Father, and discover God's wisdom unceasingly in the paschal mystery. In the language of *The Spiritual Canticle*, this is a call to journey 'further, deep into the thicket./And then...go on/to the high caverns in the rock' (SC, stanzas 36.37).

'His heart an open wound'

The saint refers to the communication of God's 'loving knowledge' as an 'inflow' or infusion of God. He writes:

> This dark night is an inflow of God into the soul...
> which the contemplatives call infused contemplation
> or mystical theology. Through this contemplation,
> God teaches the soul secretly and instructs it in the
> perfection of love... (2DN 5:1; cf. 1DN 10:6)

But John also likens a communication of God to a 'manifestation' (SC 1:3). God does not disclose the mystery of his inner life through mere abstract ideas. His revelation is a communication of himself, in his knowledge and love. This is how the fourth evangelist expresses it: 'I have made known to them your name, and I will make it known, that the love with which you have loved me may be in them, and I in them' (Jn 17:26).

The saint often refers to the 'Beloved' as 'wounded' (SC 13:9) and explains how it is the wounded One who leads the soul to himself: 'in solitude he guides her,/he alone, who also bears/in solitude the wound of love' (SC, stanza 35). This is a key point: our search for God is in fact *initiated* by God; it is a response to his invitation to seek for him. John comments: '[the Bridegroom] is wounded with love for the bride... he alone guides her, drawing her to and absorbing her in himself' (SC 35:7). The fourth gospel, too, speaks of a God who 'draws' all to himself: 'When I am lifted up from the earth, I shall draw all people to myself' (Jn 12:32). Here, this phrase, 'lifted up', designates the exaltation of Jesus in his passion (cf. Jn 3:14; 8:28). The supreme communication of God and the attraction of his love flow from the Crucified – or, as the saint expresses it in the refrain of his poem known as 'The Little Shepherd Boy' (*Un Pastorcico*): '*his heart an open wound with love*' (P 7). It is through this 'wound' that God reaches out and draws the seeker into transforming union with himself in love.

'The Hound of heaven'

> This flame of love is the Spirit of its Bridegroom, who is the Holy Spirit. The soul feels him within itself not only as a fire that has consumed and transformed it but as a fire that burns and flares within it... that flame, every time it flares up, bathes the soul in glory and refreshes it with the quality of divine life. Such is the activity of the Holy Spirit in the soul transformed in love... (LF 1:3)

These words of the saint are like a commentary on the *Song of Songs*: 'Love is strong as death, a passion relentless as Sheol. The flash of it is a flash of fire, a flame of Yahweh himself' (Sg 8:6). This is the love in which the 'wounded' God communicates himself, and into which the seeker is plunged in a final exchange of love within the Blessed Trinity. Little wonder that the saint admits how no words can adequately express this transformation in love which, as he shows in his writings, is the final goal of all our strivings. The seeker is now burning 'with a flame that is consuming and painless' (SC, stanza 39), 'not oppressive' (LF, stanza I), and cries out in longing for its full perfection: 'now consummate!' (LF, stanza I). At this stage, 'One thing only is left for [the soul] to desire: perfect enjoyment of God in eternal life… this beatific pasture of the manifest vision of God' (SC 36:2).

All of this, however, would be impossible by our own unaided efforts – even in response to God's invitation. For it is not merely a question of *our* search for God. The seeking is mutual. John writes: 'if anyone is seeking God, the Beloved is seeking that person much more' (LF 3:28). He thus echoes these words of scripture: 'In this is love, not that we loved God but that he loved us… We love, because he first loved us' (1Jn 4:10.19). In fact, we would not be searching for God at all if he had not first found us. John writes: 'stricken by love,/I lost myself, and was found' (SC, stanza 29). God seeks with a gaze that searches to the depths of our hearts. The psalmist opens himself to this gaze in prayer: 'O Lord, you search me and you know me… where can I flee from your face? If I climb the heavens, you are there' (Ps 138:1.7-8). John, too, has also experienced these same tender and compassionate eyes of God: 'When you looked at me/your eyes imprinted your grace in me…/now truly you can look at me/since you have looked/and left in me grace and beauty' (SC, stanzas 32.33).

From the cry of God in Eden, 'Where are you?' (Gn 3:9), he has never ceased to seek out his people. He reassured Israel in exile: 'I myself will search for my sheep, and will seek them out. As a shepherd seeks out his flock… so will I seek out my sheep; and I will rescue them' (Ez 34:11-12). We are all in exile, as we sojourn here on earth. But even here, John sees the Good Shepherd as ever-watchful, drawing the seeker into the final embrace of transforming union:

> Like the good shepherd rejoicing and holding on his
> shoulders the lost sheep for which he had searched
> along many winding paths [Lk. 15:4-5], and like the
> woman who, having lit the candle and hunted through

her whole house for the lost drachma, holding it up in her hands with gladness and calling her friends and neighbors to come and celebrate, saying, rejoice with me, and so on [Lk. 15:8-9], now, too, that the soul is liberated, this loving Shepherd and Bridegroom rejoices. And it is wonderful to see his pleasure in carrying the rescued, perfected soul on his shoulders, held there by his hands in this desired union. (SC 22:1)

Notes

1   Karol Wojtyla, *Faith according to St. John of the Cross*, San Francisco: Ignatius Press, 1981, p. 35.

2   For an excellent treatment of John's reading and use of scripture, see Terence O'Reilly, 'St John of the Cross and the Traditions of Monastic Exegesis', in Margaret A Rees (ed.), *Leeds Papers on Saint John of the Cross: Contributions to a Quatercentenary Celebration*, Leeds: Trinity and All Saints College, 1991, pp. 105-26 (also reproduced in *Hallel*, vol. 20, no. 2, 1995, pp. 101-13).

3   John Henry Newman, *Essay on the Development of Christian Doctrine*, London & New York: Sheed & Ward, 1960, p. 48.

4   For an outline and critical assessment of methods of interpretation of the Bible, see Pontifical Biblical Commission, *The Interpretation, op. cit.* and *The Jewish People and their Sacred Scriptures in the Christian Bible*, Vatican: Libreria Editrice Vaticana, 2002, especially #19-22, pp. 42-51.

5   See *The Collected Works of St. John of the Cross*, Washington, DC: ICS Publications, 1979, p. 18.

6   See Federico Ruiz Salvador, OCD, *Introducción a San Juan de la Cruz: El escritor, los escritos, el sistema*, Madrid: Biblioteca de Autores Cristianos, 1968, p. 85.

7   *Hamlet*, Act II, Scene 2.

8   Thomas Merton highlights this same point: 'even though [John] draws upon his experimental knowledge of mysticism, he does not attempt to prove anything by that experience alone. All that he says of the graces of prayer serves him as an occasion to seek out the final theological answer, the true Catholic doctrine on each point, in the revealed word of God. Saint John of the Cross does not merely *illustrate* his doctrine by a literary use of Scripture, he *proves* it by Scripture. More than that, he finds his doctrine in the Bible.': see Thomas Merton, *The Ascent to Truth*, London: Hollis & Carter, 1951, p. 91.

9   For an expansion of this theme of the origin of the gospels in the community of believers, see the author's *The Carmelite Charism, op. cit.*, pp. 60-1 and 'The Carmelite Rule', *op. cit.*, pp. 29-30.

10   'As a general rule, we can define the spiritual sense, as understood by Christian faith, as the meaning expressed by the biblical texts when read, under the influence of the Holy Spirit, in the context of the paschal mystery of Christ and of the new life which flows from it... While there is a distinction between the two senses, the spiritual sense

can never be stripped of its connection with the literal sense. The latter remains the indispensable foundation.": see Pontifical Biblical Commission, *The Interpretation, op. cit.*, p. 85.

11   Ignace de La Potterie, SJ has given a masterly treatment of these Johannine texts on the action of the Spirit: see Ignace de La Potterie, SJ & Stanislaus Lyonnet, SJ, *The Christian Lives by the Spirit*, New York: Alba House, 1971, ch. 3, 'The Paraclete', pp. 57-77.

12   In Henri de Lubac, SJ, *Exégèse médiévale: Les quatre sens de l'Écriture*, vol. 4, Paris: Aubier-Montaigne, 1964, pp. 498-9.

13   For a more extended treatment of *lectio divina* in the Carmelite spirit, see the author's *The Carmelite Charism, op. cit.*, pp. 31-5.

14   See note 4.

15   For an excellent treatment of the subject, see Mariano Magrassi, OSB, *Praying the Bible: An Introduction to Lectio Divina*, Collegeville, MN: The Liturgical Press, 1998.

16   Wojtyla, *op. cit.*, p. 35.

17   This saying comes from the Carthusian Guigo II's *Scala paradisi*, ch. 2, in Migne, *Patrologia Latina*, 40.998.

18   See *The Collected Works of Saint John of the Cross*, Washington, DC: ICS Publications, 1991, p. 624, note 1; cf. Ruiz Salvador, *op. cit.*, p. 82.

19   See Colin P Thompson, *The Poet and the Mystic: A Study of the Cántico Espiritual of San Juan de la Cruz*, Oxford: Oxford University Press, 1977, p. 3.

20   See Crisógono de Jesús, *Vida de San Juan de la Cruz*, Madrid: Biblioteca de Autores Cristianos, 1982, p. 301, note 46.

21   See Ruiz Salvador, *op. cit.*, p. 83.

22   See Hans Urs von Balthasar, *The Glory of the Lord: A Theological Aesthetics*, vol. 3, Edinburgh: T & T Clark, 1986, section 'St John of the Cross', pp. 105-71; Thompson, *The Poet and the Mystic, op. cit.* and his *St John of the Cross: Songs in the Night*, London: SPCK, 2002; George H Tavard, *Poetry and Contemplation in St. John of the Cross*, Athens: Ohio University, 1988.

23   As a helpful introduction to John's writings, see Wilfrid McGreal, O Carm, *John of the Cross*, London: Fount, 1996; Norbert Cummins, OCD, 'Reading St. John of the Cross', *Mount Carmel*, vol. 28/3, 1980, pp. 116-29 and his *Freedom to Rejoice: Understanding St John of the Cross*, London: HarperCollins, 1991, pp. 6-17; Iain Matthew, OCD, *The Impact of God: Soundings from St John of the Cross*, London, Sydney & Auckland: Hodder & Stoughton, 1995, pp. 116-8; Richard P Hardy,

John of the Cross: Man and Mystic, Boston, MA: Pauline Books & Media, 2004, 'Appendix A: How to Read the Works of Fray Juan de la Cruz', pp. 145-8; Thomas Moore, OCDS, 'How to Read St. John of the Cross', *Review for Religious*, vol. 49/6, 1990, pp. 885-90. John's prose style is not only at times 'awkward' but also tends to be dense and tangential. Kieran Kavanaugh remarks, in relation to 2A 33:3, in which John announces his procedure for the subsequent chapters: 'He now so multiplies subdivisions that he allows himself to enter a forest without exit.': see *The Collected Works*, 1991, *op. cit.*, p. 329, note 1.

24 A number of recent works have outlined the stages of the inner journey described by John: Edith Stein, *The Science of the Cross* (see 'Note on Editions Used'); Cummins, *Freedom to Rejoice, op. cit.*; Matthew, *op. cit.*; Kieran Kavanaugh, OCD, *John of the Cross: Doctor of Light and Love*, New York: Crossroad, 1999; Hein Blommestijn, O Carm, Jos Huls, O Carm & Kees Waaijman, O Carm, *The Footprints of Love: John of the Cross as Guide in the Wilderness*, Leuven: Peeters (The Fiery Arrow Collection), 2000; Eileen Lyddon, SLG, *Door through Darkness: St John of the Cross and Mysticism in Everyday Life*, London, Dublin & Edinburgh: New City, 1994.

25 See Cummins, *Freedom to Rejoice, op. cit.*; Matthew Blake, OCD, 'Experiencing Freedom: Journeying with John of the Cross', in *Mount Carmel*, vol. 52/2, 2004, pp. 15-18; Daniel Chowning, OCD, 'Free to Love: Negation in the Doctrine of John of the Cross', in *Carmelite Studies*, vol. 6, Washington, DC: ICS Publications, 1992, pp. 29-47; John Welch, O Carm, *When Gods Die: An Introduction to John of the Cross*, New York & Mahwah, NJ: Paulist Press, 1990, ch. 5, 'Liberation of the Heart', pp. 70-88.

26 For a useful article on this theme, see John Sullivan, OCD, 'Night and Light: The Poet John of the Cross and the "Exsultet" of the Easter Liturgy', *Ephemerides Carmeliticae*, vol. xxx, no. 1, 1979, pp. 52-68.

27 See the discussion of the desert experience in relation to John's teaching, in Fabrizio Foresti, OCD, *Sinai and Carmel: The Biblical Roots of the Spiritual Doctrine of St. John of the Cross and three other Biblical Conferences*, Darlington Carmel, [no date], pp. 1-37.

28 John Henry Newman, *Historical Sketches*, vol. II, London: Pickering & Co, 1881, pp. 475-6.

29 On the utter transcendence of God, see Carmel McCarthy, RSM, 'The God of Israel', *Scripture in Church*, vol. 4, no. 14, 1974, pp. 310-4.

30 'it ought to be kept in mind that an attachment to a creature makes a person equal to that creature; the stronger the attachment, the closer is the likeness to the creature and the greater the equality, for love effects a likeness between the lover and the loved. As a result David said of those who set their hearts on their idols:... Let all who set their hearts on them become like them' (1A 4:3; cf. Ps 113:8).

31 See especially 1A 11. This purification is precisely the means of dying to idols: 'The death of false gods is another way of describing the experience of the night... The pain and sorrow of the night are the grief that accompanies the death of gods.': see Welch, *op. cit.*, p. 113.

32 See Welch, *op. cit.*, section 'A More Intense Enkindling', pp. 85-6.

33 Note that, for John, the memory is not just the receptacle and storehouse of past experiences. As Bonaventure explains (in *The Soul's Journey into God*), drawing on the Augustinian system which John follows in his division of the faculties, 'the memory retains the past by remembrance, the present by reception and the future by foresight': see Bonaventure, *The Soul's Journey into God, The Tree of Life, The Life of St. Francis*, New York, Ramsey & Toronto: Paulist Press (The Classics of Western Spirituality), 1978, p. 80. For a discussion of the role of the memory in John, see Cummins, *Freedom to Rejoice, op. cit.*, pp. 104-16; Ross Collings, OCD, *John of the Cross*, Collegeville, MN: The Liturgical Press, 1990, pp. 122-8; Edward Howells, *John of the Cross and Teresa of Avila: Mystical Knowing and Selfhood*, New York: Crossroad, 2002, pp. 31-4.

34 T S Eliot, 'East Coker', in *Four Quartets*, London: Faber & Faber, 1959, p. 25, ll. 140-1.

35 The Toledo imprisonment and its psychological impact on the saint have been well described in Kevin Culligan, OCD, 'From Imprisonment to Transformation: John of the Cross in Toledo', in *Carmelite Studies*, vol. 8, Washington, DC: ICS Publications, 2000, pp. 209-39; see also Matthew, *op. cit.*, pp. 9-11.

36 Significantly, this text of *Luke* used to be part of the gospel reading for the Mass of the feast of John of the Cross in the liturgy proper to the Carmelite Order.

37 For the image of light, see SC 26:17; for the image of the log of wood, see LF 1:19.

38 On the theme of seeking, see, for example, the author's *Thirsting for God in Scripture*, Locust Valley, NY: Living Flame Press, 1984.

39 Paul is referred to in this chapter as the author of both *Hebrews* and *Ephesians*, which was commonly accepted in John's day.

40   John is in fact quoting from Pseudo-Augustine, *Soliloquiorum animae ad Deum*, ch. 30: see Migne, *Patrologia Latina*, 40.888 ('Non inveni, quia male quaerebam foris, quod erat intus'); see also Teresa (*Life* 40:6; WP 28:2; IC IV:3:3).

41   For further references, see the author's *Thirsting for God*, *op. cit.*, pp. 35-7.

42   The original Greek word for 'impels', *synéchei*, designates here 'constrains' or 'compels': see Max Zerwick, SJ & Mary Grosvenor, *A Grammatical Analysis of the Greek New Testament*, Rome: Editrice Pontificio Istituto Biblico, 1988, p. 544. The *Vulgate* translates this as: 'Charitas enim Christi *urget* nos'.

43   *The Cloud of Unknowing and Other Works*, Harmondsworth: Penguin, 1978, p. 68.

44   Note, however, John's observation that love is the effect of knowledge in the natural order: 'Naturally, it is impossible to love without first understanding what is loved' (SC 26:8). For an in-depth study of the theme of knowledge in John of the Cross, see Marie-Joseph Huguenin, 'Le Thème de la connaissance chez Jean de la Croix', *Teresianum*, vol. liv, no. 1, 2003, pp. 79-116.

45   T S Eliot, 'Little Gidding', in *Four Quartets*, *op. cit.*, p. 48, ll. 239-42.

46   'The Exodus, the primordial experience of Israel's faith (cf. Dt 6:20-25; 26:5-9) becomes the symbol of final salvation. Liberation from the Babylonian Exile and the prospect of an eschatological salvation are described as a new Exodus. Christian interpretation is situated along these lines with this difference, that the fulfilment is already substantially realised in the mystery of Christ.': see Pontifical Biblical Commission, *The Jewish People*, *op. cit.*, #21, p. 47.

CHAPTER THREE

ELIZABETH OF THE TRINITY: PROPHET OF THE PRESENCE OF GOD

A Hidden Mystery

Elizabeth of the Trinity, like Thérèse of Lisieux, distils the essence of her spirituality into one simple prayer.[1] It is addressed to the Trinity and begins with the words, 'O my God, Trinity whom I adore'.[2] For her, this mystery of God, Three in One, is not something abstract, remote or irrelevant. It is at the heart of the gospel message, essential for the complete understanding of the Christian life and for the full flowering of our baptismal grace. It took the Church centuries to hammer out the language of 'nature' and 'person' to express the mystery: three persons in one nature.[3]

The final revelation of this inner life of God, however, needed a long period of preparation. Paul spoke of this same God to the philosophers at Athens: 'In him we live and move and have our being' (Acts 17:28); and John says that 'through him all things came into being' (Jn 1:3). This is the God who keeps all creation suspended, as it were, over non-existence, sustaining the universe as a singer keeps his song in being. 'All things were created through him and for him. He exists before all things and in him all things hold together' (Col 1:16-17). This is also the God of the Old Testament, the God of the burning bush (Ex 3:2-3) who identifies himself to Moses as 'the God of your father, the God of Abraham, the God of Isaac, and the God of Jacob' (Ex 3:6), and freely binds himself on Sinai by covenant in a personal relationship with his people, 'my own possession among all peoples... a kingdom of priests and a holy nation' (Ex 19:5-6).[4] Moses was warned to remove the sandals from his feet: he was treading on 'holy ground' and must not draw closer to the divine presence (Ex 3:5). It is a reminder to Israel's great leader, and through him to the Israelites themselves, of the distance between God and them, something that neither he nor they must ever forget: 'I am God and not man, the Holy One in your midst' (Hos 11:9). This is no God aloof and uncaring, but a God who keeps a close and watchful eye over the unfolding events of salvation history. This is a redeeming God: 'I have seen the affliction of my people... and have heard their cry... I know their sufferings, and I have come down to deliver them out of the hand of the Egyptians... I will send you to Pharaoh that you may bring forth my people, the sons of Israel, out of Egypt' (Ex 3:7-8.10).

The doctrine of the Trinity would be empty and meaningless without this sure foundation of the one Creator and saving God, who is not just a god among other gods. He is the only God: 'I am the Lord your God, who brought you out of the land of Egypt, out of the house of bondage. You shall have no other gods before me' (Ex 20:2-3).

Elizabeth of the Trinity speaks of this same God in the words of the psalmist: 'Adore the Lord, for He is holy... adore Him always because of Himself' (LR 21; cf. Ps 98:9). His glory fills all of creation: 'Holy, holy, holy is the Lord of hosts; the whole earth is full of his glory' (Is 6:3). This glory is God's holiness revealed, the visible manifestation of him who is 'the Holy One' (Is 40:25; Jer 50:29), the transcendent and totally 'Other' who cannot give his glory to another: 'Not to us, Lord, not to us, but to your name give the glory' (Ps 113[B]:1). Elizabeth frequently refers to the Trinity as 'holy', 'immense', 'immutable', 'magnificent', 'majestic' in order to convey God's absolute 'Otherness' or, as she writes in her Trinity prayer, 'the abyss of Your greatness'. She glorifies God with the worship, adoration and praise which are due to him alone, as again she does in her Trinity prayer: 'I wish to cover You with glory'.[5]

In communion with the Trinity[6]
But a whole new vision of God opens up to faith 'in the fulness of time' (Gal 4:4), with the coming of the Word made flesh in 'his glory, glory as of the only Son from the Father' (Jn 1:14) who 'is the reflection of God's glory and bears the impress of God's own being' (Hb 1:3). This Jesus is one of God's family. He is 'the only Son, who is in the bosom of the Father' (Jn 1:18), turned forever 'towards' (*pros*, Jn 1:1.2)[7] his Father in a dynamic thrust of love. The Son is born eternally 'out of the bosom of the Father'.[8]

The intimacy and bond between Father and Son could hardly be more complete. Both embrace each other in a love that is the third person of the Trinity. It is this love, Paul tells us, that 'has been poured into our hearts through the Holy Spirit who has been given to us' (Rm 5:5). It is the fruit of the passion. Jesus prays 'that the love with which you [Father] have loved me may be in them, and I in them' (Jn 17:26). We are called to communion in this love: 'our fellowship is with the Father and with his Son Jesus Christ' (1Jn 1:3).

That is what Elizabeth's prayer to the Trinity is all about: communion in love with the Father, Son and Spirit. Jesus prays 'that those, whom you [Father] have given me, may be with me where I am' (Jn 17:24). In her prayer, Elizabeth draws us into the family of God where Jesus is, in order that with her we might share – already here and now – in an everlasting dialogue with the God who is love (1Jn 4:16). It is a dynamic prayer, full of movement and exchange: 'overwhelm me... possess me... Come into me... Bury Yourself in me that I may bury myself in You...' It is also highly personal, directed to *her* God: 'my God', 'my Unchanging One', 'my Three', 'my All', 'my Beatitude'. It is rightly called her *Prayer to the Trinity*, although she herself did not give it a title. However, it is also her prayer in communion *with* the Trinity. She invites us to enter with her into an unending exchange of love forever flowing between the persons of the Father, Son and Spirit and to make her prayer our own.

A window onto eternity

The well-known icon of the Trinity by the Russian Orthodox monk, Andrei Rublëv, can help us revisit the prayer of Elizabeth with added depth and wonder.[9] It is an icon born, like Elizabeth's prayer, of silence and communion with God. It is not merely to be admired as if by a detached spectator. It is like a window onto eternity and is meant to be read prayerfully, like the gospels themselves. It contains the lesson of the scriptures about the Trinity expressed in visible form through colour, shape and symbol.

It is inspired by the story in *Genesis* (18:1-8), of the three visitors who come to Abraham. The angel on the left is the Father, source of all life; the angel in the centre is the Son, his head bowed gently towards the Father in total surrender to him; the angel on the right is the Spirit, the giver of new life, in a posture which speaks of one who 'proceeds from the Father and the Son'. And so, the inner movement of eternal life comes full circle in a communion of flowing relationships between all three persons.[10] There is an unbroken exchange between them – an eternal to-ing and fro-ing, receiving and giving. This is the Trinity that Elizabeth addresses in her prayer.

A sacrificial meal

The colours are also significant: the blue on the garments of all three symbolises divinity, shared by each of the persons; the red worn only by the Son points to his passion and death; the green on the Spirit's robe evokes the freshness of new life; the yellow on the Father's outer garment reflects the radiance of his glory and allows the blue of his divinity to shimmer through. This same yellow colour of 'the Father's house', or heaven, in the background bathes all three persons in that glory which is the radiance or splendour of their inner holiness.

The table at the centre of the icon, where all three persons sit, symbolises a meal. It implies a community of love. The hands of the Three gesture towards the chalice at the centre of the table. This unites them with the symbol of the Son's suffering, capturing the moment of divine dialogue concerning the work of salvation.[11] The cup itself, with the image of a sacrificial lamb, evokes the Old Testament 'sacrifice and offerings… holocaust and victim' (Ps 39:7; cf. Hb 10:5-6). While absorbed eternally in perfect contemplation of each other, the Three-in-One share with the Son in the pain of the world and his work of redemption. In Elizabeth's Trinity prayer, it is also the crucified Jesus who holds centre stage. Her address to Jesus is the heart of her outpouring: 'O my beloved Christ,' she prays, 'crucified by love… Come into me as Adorer, as Restorer, as Savior.'

Within that sacred space
The empty fourth place at the table invites the spectator into a sacred space of encounter with the Trinity in their silence and energy, repose and movement. There is only one opening into the unending circle of divine life. It goes through the table of sacrifice that speaks of a crucified Saviour at the centre of God's eternal plan. The Rublëv masterpiece invites us to a prayerful experience of God as Three, and to a sharing in the dialogue and ceaseless exchange of love in the inner life of God. Elizabeth does the same in her prayer, and so takes her place within a whole tradition of Carmelite prayer.

John of the Cross compares his experience of God to 'the breathing of the air…/in the serene night,/with a flame that is consuming and painless' (SC, stanza 39). He then comments by way of explanation:

By his divine breath-like spiration, the Holy Spirit elevates the soul sublimely and informs her and makes her capable of breathing in God the same spiration of love that the Father breathes in the Son and the Son in the Father. This spiration of love is the Holy Spirit himself, who in the Father and the Son breathes out to her in this transformation in order to unite her to himself... In the transformation that the soul possesses in this life, the same spiration passes from God to the soul and from the soul to God with notable frequency and blissful love, although not in the open and manifest degree proper to the next life. (SC 39:3-4)

Teresa records a similar experience but with her own original touch. She tells how the mystery of the Trinity was revealed to her 'through a certain representation of the truth' and provides her own explanation of her experience:

Here all three Persons communicate themselves to [the soul], speak to it, and explain those words of the Lord in the Gospel: that He and the Father and the Holy Spirit will come to dwell with the soul that loves Him and keeps His commandments. Oh, God help me! How different is hearing and believing these words from understanding their truth in this way! Each day this soul becomes more amazed, for these Persons never seem to leave it any more, but it clearly beholds, in the way that was mentioned, that they are within it. In the extreme interior, in some place very deep within itself, the nature of which it doesn't know how to explain, because of a lack of learning, it perceives this divine company. (IC VII:1:6-7)

Beauty ever new

The exquisite beauty of Rublëv's icon will also strike a chord in every lover of Elizabeth's spirituality. Her experience of the Trinity attracts and draws us into the mystery of a God who is Beauty itself. She herself was already an accomplished musician at thirteen when she won prizes for her piano recitals at the Dijon Conservatory. Her perception of the beautiful informs her entire teaching.

Elizabeth speaks of 'a soul of silence that remains like a lyre under the mysterious touch of the Holy Spirit so that He may draw from it divine harmonies' (HF 43). Again, she warns anyone who 'scatters its forces' at prayer that: 'Its lyre does not vibrate in unison... it must continually adjust the strings of its instrument which are all a little out of tune' (LR 3). Elizabeth assures us, about the 'praise of glory', that 'Her song is uninterrupted, for she is under the action of the Holy Spirit who effects everything in her' (HF 44), that same Spirit who is 'supreme Beauty!' (Pm 54). She reminds her own sister, also a musician, that the Lord 'is so jealous for the beauty of your soul' that 'the Word will imprint in your soul... the image of His own beauty', and that 'the Holy Spirit will transform you into a mysterious lyre, which, in silence, beneath His divine touch, will produce a magnificent canticle to Love' (L 269).

At times, beauty can take our breath away and leave us silent, lost in awe and wonder at the grandeur of God. 'Adoration, ah!' Elizabeth exclaims. '...It seems to me it can be defined as the ecstasy of love. It is love overcome by the beauty, the strength, the immense grandeur of the Object loved' (LR 21). She will refer to her death as 'my first meeting with Divine Beauty' (L 269), 'this first face-to-face with Divine Beauty' (L 270).

The engaging face of God

In contemporary spiritual writing, there has been a remarkable renewal of interest in the aesthetic.[12] Perhaps this young Carmelite's sense of the beauty of God, at work in her and with her at prayer, may well be one of her most valuable contributions to our confused 'postmodern' world. So many today are often bored with our outmoded and jaded concepts of God and with our archaic and bookish language of faith. Elizabeth can help us to discover the more engaging face of a God who is Beauty itself, 'ever ancient, ever new'. Her teaching can answer to the recent plea of Cardinal Godfried Danneels for a renewed experience of beauty in the Church today:

> I wonder whether we make sufficient use of beauty as the doorway leading to God? God is, indeed, truth, holiness and moral perfection, but also beauty... Truth, beauty and goodness: those are three of God's names and three paths that lead to him. But beauty has hardly been pressed into use by theology or religious teaching up until now. Isn't it time to do so?[13]

The teaching of Elizabeth can certainly help us restore beauty to its rightful place in the life of the Church. Here again, she is in line with a long Carmelite tradition of prayer.[14] John of the Cross provides an important reflection on beauty when he comments, in his *Spiritual Canticle*, on this line of his poem: 'and let us go forth to behold ourselves in your beauty' (SC, stanza 36). He expresses a wish:

> That I be so transformed in your beauty that we may be alike in beauty, and both behold ourselves in your beauty, possessing then your very beauty; this, in such a way that each looking at the other may see in the other their own beauty, since both are your beauty alone, I being absorbed in your beauty... (SC 36:5)

The Mystical Doctor is not directing these words of longing to Carmelites alone. He is addressing the whole Church which, 'when she sees God face to face,' he says, 'will participate in the very beauty of [God]' (SC 36:5).

Into the depths of God

Like the *Rule* of Carmel itself, the Trinity prayer of Elizabeth is a tissue of biblical quotations and allusions.[15] As the prayer unfolds, her mind is constantly echoing to the word of God.[16] It would be almost impossible to unravel all the scriptural connotations that fuse there and complement each other.[17] Indeed, Elizabeth would hardly expect us to do so. Her prayer is, rather, an invitation to enter with her through these inspired texts into the depths of God's self-disclosure and to live with him there, hidden in the life of her beloved Three. The influence of Paul on her writings is commonly acknowledged, but not so readily the impact of John.[18] Yet, she clearly loved John even from an early age, and some of her later writings are at times like a mosaic of texts from his gospel and first letter, with her own words almost a commentary – original variations on his formulas of indwelling: 'You in me and I in you' (Jn 17:21), or 'Remain in me, and I in you' (Jn 15:4). Elizabeth writes:

> 'Remain in me'... not for a few moments, a few hours which must pass away, but '*remain...*' permanently, habitually. Remain in Me, pray in Me, adore in Me, love in Me, suffer in Me, work and act in Me. (HF 3)

Clearly, John also provides a key that helps us unlock the riches of this prayer. Its movement reflects the style of the fourth evangelist.[19] His mind advances in a circular or spiral curve, like a tidal wave. He winds his way gradually into his subject, announcing, developing and expanding it, and then returning to it again at the end. Take, for example, the prologue of his gospel.[20] It begins in eternity: 'In the beginning was the Word, and the Word was with God, and the Word was God' (Jn 1:1); it touches earth when 'the Word became flesh and dwelt among us' (Jn 1:14), and returns again, like the swing of a pendulum, back into the timeless life of God: 'the only Son, who is in the bosom of the Father' (Jn 1:18). Elizabeth's prayer does the same. It begins in eternity with the Trinity, her 'Unchanging One'; it centres on Christ, 'Eternal Word, Word of my God', and concludes with deeper insights into the same mystery: the Trinity now becomes for her 'my All', 'my Beatitude' 'infinite Solitude', 'Immensity in which I lose myself'. We are left at the end, like Elizabeth herself, breathless with adoration 'to contemplate...the abyss' of God's greatness.

Wholly vigilant in faith
Elizabeth longs to be God's 'heaven', 'dwelling', 'resting place'. With these simple terms she translates her much-loved text of *John*, which provided her with the basis for her central message, the indwelling of the Trinity: 'We,' Jesus says, 'will come to them and make our home *in* them' (Jn 14:23). Her prayer also speaks of faith in the same dynamic terms as John does. He never refers to faith as something static, a kind of icing on a cake. For him, faith is something active, always in movement. He speaks of 'believing', never of 'belief'. Neither does he speak of believing 'in', rather it is always 'into'.[21] This is exactly how Elizabeth experiences faith: 'may each minute carry me further into the depths of Your Mystery'. She desires to remain 'wholly present', with her faith 'wholly vigilant', longing to be at rest in the Trinity – ever-still, yet ever-active, as she prays: 'Give peace to my soul'. Again, it is the same peace promised progressively by Jesus in *John* as 'peace... my peace... peace in me' (Jn 14:27; 16:33). Here, we have Elizabeth 'wholly adoring' the Three within her or, in Johannine terms, worshipping the Father 'in spirit and truth' (Jn 4:23-24).

'In spirit and truth'
We might describe the subsequent development of the prayer as an original and highly personal commentary on these words of *John*, 'the

true worshippers will worship the Father in spirit and truth' (Jn 4:23; cf. 4:24). The direction of the prayer now begins to move towards the Father in the Son under the action of the Spirit. The Truth, in *John*, is not an abstract idea, image or concept. It is love – communicating, giving and sharing itself in Jesus who is the Truth in person (cf. Jn 14:6; 1:14).[22] Elizabeth's desire to share that love is intense, even to the point of giving herself entirely to Jesus as he gave himself to her: 'crucified by love'. In John's terms, he loved her 'to the end' (Jn 13:1). Echoing these words again on Calvary, he released the full potential of his love with the cry: 'It is ended' (Jn 19:30). Elizabeth longs to do the same for him: 'I wish to love You...' she says, 'even unto death!' Nor is her weakness an obstacle. The words of John are there to reassure her: 'apart from me you can do nothing' (Jn 15:5). So, she prays: 'substitute Yourself for me... Come into me as Adorer, as Restorer, as Savior.' He is in her and she in him. '"God in me, I in Him", oh! this is my life!' (L 62). The indwelling is her great message. It is reciprocal, and there is a true exchange: her weakness for his strength.

Strength in silence

Elizabeth is primarily a Carmelite – a woman of prayer. She describes her communing with God as *listening* to the Word. For her, Jesus is the 'Eternal Word, Word of my God', to whom she prays: 'I want to spend my life in listening to You'. Again, there are echoes of John. He speaks of Jesus as the Word existing eternally 'in the beginning' before time began (Jn 1:1-2). The followers of Jesus are those who listen: 'the sheep hear his voice' (Jn 10:3); and 'everyone who is of the truth,' Jesus says, 'listens to my voice' (Jn 18:37). In *John*, the 'Word' is also light: 'I am the light of the world; whoever follows me will not walk in darkness' (Jn 8:12; cf. 9:5). Elizabeth wants to bask in this light, fascinated and drawn irresistibly by it: 'I want to gaze on You always,' she prays, 'and remain in Your great light.'

> My Rule tells me: 'In silence will your strength be.' It
> seems to me, therefore, that to keep one's strength for
> the Lord is to unify one's whole being by means of
> interior silence, to collect all one's powers in order to
> 'employ' them in 'the one work of love,' to have this
> 'single eye' which allows the light of God to enlighten
> us. (LR 3)

Nor is she any stranger to the marked contrast between light and
darkness found in *John*. For her, too, the light shines in the darkness,
in what she calls her 'nights', her 'voids', her 'helplessness'. She
desires to be taught by the Word – 'to become,' she says, 'wholly
teachable'.

Taught by God

For any mind steeped in the fourth gospel, the transition to the role
of the Spirit which follows next in her prayer is both easy and
smooth: it is the Paraclete who will teach her everything. In *John*,
Jesus recalls the words of the prophets: 'They shall all be taught by
God' (Jn 6:45; cf. Is 54:13; Jer 31:33-34; Ez 36:27). Elizabeth
describes the Spirit as a 'consuming Fire, Spirit of Love' whose
action is *creative*: 'create in my soul a kind of incarnation of the
Word,' she prays. Earlier, Elizabeth had asked the Trinity that she
might be 'wholly surrendered to Your creative Action'. She will pray
a few lines later: 'I surrender myself to You'. She wishes to remain
always docile to this transforming action of the Spirit. At the outset
of his gospel, John introduces the Spirit who descends on Jesus as
the inaugurator of a new creation (cf. Jn 1:32; Gn 1:2) and who will
overflow from him onto the disciples by baptising them into a new
birth 'of water and the Spirit' (Jn 3:5).

The gospel of John draws to an end as the risen Jesus 'breathes'
the same Spirit into his first disciples (Jn 20:22), recreating them

and transforming them into his church, where Jesus himself will always be present in mystery until the end of time. So, Elizabeth surrenders herself to this same creative action of the Spirit, that she may provide the Word with 'another humanity... in which He can renew His whole Mystery'. She sees herself as the church in miniature: at one with the Vine and all the branches, to borrow John's image (Jn 15:1-17), embracing in herself the whole Body – Head and members – and making it present again, here and now, in 'a kind of incarnation of the Word'.

An eternal cycle

This true worship 'in spirit and truth' moves inexorably towards the Father. So, too, does the prayer of Elizabeth. She recalls the words of the Father at the transfiguration, asking him to see in her 'only the "Beloved in whom You are well pleased"' (cf. Mt 17:5). The Tabor scene does not appear in *John*, but Elizabeth's request here reaches the point of deepest intimacy between the believer and the Father as found in the fourth gospel – a relationship of love in and through Jesus, so close as to exclude, apparently, even the need for Jesus to pray for his disciples: 'I do not say to you that I shall pray the Father for you' (Jn 16:26). Jesus will not need to pray to the Father on behalf of the believer, for the believer's prayer will *be* Jesus' prayer.[23] When Elizabeth asks the Father to 'bend lovingly over' her and to see in her 'only the "Beloved"', she is asking him to grant the priestly prayer of Jesus in *John*, renewing itself within her: 'that the love with which you have loved me may be in them, and I in them' (Jn 17:26).

At the end, Elizabeth's prayer merges once again into the timeless life of the Trinity where it began. It has come full circle, reflecting in time the cyclic movement of eternal life in God as it flows unceasingly between the three persons: from its origin in the Father to the Son, and back from him to its source in the Father – and all through the Spirit. Elizabeth plunges us into that endless exchange of life and love in her prayer. As she lays down her pen, she awaits her departure 'to contemplate in Your light,' she tells the Trinity, 'the abyss of Your greatness'. Her prayer is a spontaneous cry of the heart.[24]

Elizabeth's prayer is written with calm, steady and even strokes, reflecting the 'peace' and 'rest' of the 'unchanging' Trinity in whose life she invites us to share and into whose mystery she challenges us to penetrate more deeply at every moment. Her prayer bears the distinctive mark of her personality and her own special and original interpretation of the Carmelite charism. Her words also remain permanently as a prayerful expression of some of the deepest truths of John's gospel – another priceless testimony, if any is needed, to the richness and variety of the Carmelite way of prayer always so deeply steeped, as it is, in the scriptures.

Her 'magnificent' Paul[25]

Much as Elizabeth loved John, the 'magnificent epistles' of Paul, as she called them, were her great passion, especially towards the end of her life.[26] She speaks of 'Saint Paul, whose beautiful letters I am studying with much enjoyment' (L 230), and adds that he writes 'splendid things' (L 239). For her, he is the 'great Saint Paul' (L 249) who has 'words that are so simple and at the same time so profound' (L 250). He is a man with a 'generous heart' (L 264) whose letters are 'magnificent' (L 299). She calls him her 'dear saint' (L 306), 'the father of my soul' (L 240, note 4). Although her time for reading the scriptures was limited to only short periods each day,[27] hers was not a casual or perfunctory reading. She studied Paul's letters seriously, even making indexes of them a year before her death.

Paul's words adorn almost every page of Elizabeth's later writings. She does not hesitate to fuse several of his texts into one with a single stroke of her pen: 'He has predestined you to be conformed to the image of His Son Jesus, and by holy baptism He has clothed you with Himself, thus making you His children, and at the same time His living temple' (L 240; cf. Rm 8:29; Gal 3:27.26; 2Cor 6:16). Here, three leading themes of her Trinity prayer blend. She will express them in her own characteristic style but the deep and underlying lessons are the same: our *identification* with Christ – our becoming *one* with him – as children of the heavenly Father, through *baptism*, by which every believer becomes a *temple* of God. She prays that the Trinity may make her soul their 'dwelling' or, in Paul's language, their 'temple' (1Cor 3:16-17; 6:19; 2Cor 6:16). Then, she turns directly to Christ and expands the implications of her union with him through baptism: 'clothe me with Yourself'. Again, 'clothe' is a Pauline expression: 'Every one of you that has been baptised in Christ has been clothed in Christ' (Gal 3:27; cf. Rm 13:14; Eph 4:24; Col 3:10). In Paul, she also finds the secret of her special vocation:

> I am going to tell you a very personal secret: my dream is to be 'the praise of His glory'; I read that in Saint Paul and my Bridegroom made me understand that this was to be my vocation while in exile, waiting to go sing the eternal Sanctus in the City of the saints. (L 256)

A praise of glory

Elizabeth identifies herself with this phrase, 'the praise of glory'. The first time, it is in a letter written nearly three years before her death (L 191). Afterwards, she will sign her letters repeatedly with it. The phrase occurs three times in *Ephesians* (1:6.12.14), running like a refrain through the magnificent hymn of praise which serves as a kind of prologue or overture to Paul's letter (1:3-14).[28] The Trinitarian perspective of this hymn must have appealed to Elizabeth. Not unlike her own prayer to the Trinity, Paul's praise of God's plan is directed to the Father, 'Blessed be the God and Father'

(1:3), is centred on the Son 'in [whom] we have redemption through his blood' (1:7) and provides a pledge of future glory because in Christ we 'were sealed with the promised Holy Spirit, who is the guarantee of our inheritance until we acquire possession of it, to the praise of his glory' (1:13-14). Elizabeth recalls this letter constantly in her writings. She has listened to it deep within herself, allowing the Spirit to unfold to her, through it, the hidden and mysterious depths of God's plan.

Perhaps nowhere else in his letters does Paul highlight so emphatically and so repeatedly our one-ness and identification with Christ and the mystery of God's love for us in him: 'God... has blessed us *in Christ*... he chose us *in him*... his glorious grace which he freely bestowed on us *in the Beloved*... *In him* we have redemption... his purpose which he set forth *in Christ*... to unite all things *in him*... *In him*... we... have been destined and appointed to live for the praise of his glory... *In him* you... were sealed with the promised Holy Spirit'. *Ephesians* also opens up for Elizabeth the profound spiritual depths that we find in her Trinity prayer, centred as it is on the '*exceeding* love' (Eph 2:4; GV 11) – a favourite phrase of hers[29] – which the Father has 'lavished' on us (Eph 1:8; cf. 1Jn 3:1) in Christ through the Spirit. For Elizabeth, a 'praise of glory' is the perfect imitation of Christ's life, reaching its culmination on Calvary.

Christ crucified

Much of Elizabeth's Trinity prayer is a variation on Paul's theme, 'For me, to live is Christ' (Ph 1:21). This identification with Christ is inseparably linked for Elizabeth, as for Paul, with the Crucified. She frequently quotes from this passage: 'With Christ I hang upon the cross, and yet I am alive; or rather, not I; it is Christ that lives in me. True, I am living, here and now, this mortal life; but my real life is the faith I have in the Son of God, who loved me, and gave himself for me' (Gal 2:19-20).[30] Paul chides his first converts in no uncertain terms: 'O foolish Galatians! Who has bewitched you, before whose eyes Jesus Christ was publicly portrayed as crucified?' (Gal 3:1). Text after text of his letters reinforce the lesson: 'Walk in love, as Christ loved us and gave himself up for us, a fragrant offering and sacrifice to God' (Eph 5:2).

Elizabeth shares Paul's passion for the Crucified. She prays: 'O my beloved Christ, crucified by love, I wish to be a bride for Your Heart... I wish to love You... even unto death!' She surrenders in love to crucified Love with an entire gift of herself in sacrifice. Again, the words of Paul are there to encourage her: 'I implore you by God's mercy to offer your very selves to him: a living sacrifice, dedicated and fit for his acceptance, the worship offered by mind and heart' (Rm 12:1). For Elizabeth, to be a 'bride' is to be identified with Christ's passion: 'I see the Master is treating you like a "bride" and sharing His Cross with you,' she writes to Madame Angles (L 207). At one with the crucified Jesus, she finds her missionary vocation in Carmel – to save souls:

> A Carmelite... is a soul who has *gazed on the Crucified*, who has seen Him offering Himself to His Father as a Victim for souls and, recollecting herself in this great vision of the charity of Christ, has understood the passionate love of His soul, and has wanted to give herself as He did! (L 133)

What Elizabeth said of her desire to love Christ 'even unto death' extends to his whole Body spread out in the world. Faced with death and the excruciating agony of her final illness, she could say: 'O, Love, love!... Exhaust the whole of my substance for your glory. May it be distilled drop by drop for your Church!'[31] This is Elizabeth's way of identifying totally with Paul's words, 'Now I rejoice in my sufferings for your sake, and in my flesh I complete what is lacking in Christ's afflictions for the sake of his body, that is, the church' (Col 1:24).

Glory in the face of Christ

This same Christ Elizabeth longs to 'cover with glory' and so fulfil her calling as a praise of that glory revealed to her in him: 'It is the God who said, "Let light shine out of darkness," who has shone in our hearts to give the light of the knowledge of the glory of God in the face of Christ' (2Cor 4:6). Again, Paul writes: 'We all, with unveiled faces, reflecting his glory as in a mirror, are being changed into his likeness from one degree of glory to another' (2Cor 3:18). In the spirit of Paul, Elizabeth wishes her life to radiate that same glory: 'A praise of glory... is a reflector of all that He is... like a crystal through which He can radiate... His own splendor' (HF 43). So, she prays to Christ that she 'may not withdraw from [His] radiance'.

But she admits and experiences her powerlessness: 'I feel my weakness'. Again, Paul is there to reassure her with the Lord's words to him: 'My grace is sufficient for you, for my power is made perfect in weakness' (2Cor 12:9). Her identification with Christ must know no reservation, as she prays: 'identify my soul with all the movements of Your Soul... possess me'. Elizabeth longs to be possessed or captivated by Christ: 'Ah, don't you see that when a heart has been taken captive by Christ, it must then give itself wholly?' (L 130). That word, 'captive', has a distinctly Pauline ring: 'I am still running, trying to capture the prize for which Christ Jesus captured me' (Ph 3:12). Elizabeth and Paul are indeed captive flames, both of them entirely possessed by Christ.

A 'terrible character'[32]

Elizabeth, however, was not some kind of blithe spirit gliding nonchalantly through life, with scant attention to the pain of others. In her prayer, she feels the need to invoke the Trinity in this way: 'help me to forget myself entirely'. 'A praise of glory is a soul that lives in God,' Elizabeth says, 'that loves Him with a pure and disinterested love, without seeking itself in the sweetness of this love' (HF 43). Her own attainment of such selfless love was to be a long, slow and painful process. She had to grow like others and struggle against what she called her 'dominant fault' (D 1). It was anger. She sometimes raged and boiled with fury. As a young child, she fumed against her local priest who had removed her doll: 'You wicked priest!' she exploded. 'Give me back my Jeannette!'[33] She had to battle constantly with her 'terrible character', as she called it (D 81). 'Elizabeth Catez,' said the priest who prepared her for first communion, 'with her nature, will be either an angel or a devil'.[34] Her mother had to threaten her young daughter with banishment to a house of correction for unruly children, even packing her bag in readiness! But Elizabeth's strong character and fiery nature became her greatest asset when transformed by the spirit of love. It kept alive the inner flame throughout the long, painful years of waiting to enter Carmel – tested by agonising scruples, dryness in prayer and her mother's initial refusal.

Enveloped in darkness

As a young religious, Elizabeth was quickly purified of any romantic ideas she might have had of Carmelite life. In her teens, she had been bursting with energy and brimming with mischief, exuberant and spontaneous – a very ordinary and normal young girl who loved to play, dance, picnic, hike and revel in nature's beauty, not to mention her passion for music. Enclosed within the bare convent walls, the contrast took its toll. A thick cloud enveloped her. She was again plagued with scruples – a by-product of the then prevalent Jansenism; her health became impaired; her vocation and suitability for Carmel were called in question. Elizabeth was 'overwhelmed with anguish,' she confessed (L 152). God seemed to have abandoned her. It was her dark night. But finally she did pronounce her vows. Recalling the previous evening, her vigil in prayer before the solemn day, she wrote, 'I understood that my Heaven was beginning on earth; Heaven in faith, with suffering and immolation for Him whom I love!' (L 169).

With Christ on the cross
Elizabeth wrote her *Prayer to the Trinity* two years before her death. But
she had not yet lived out fully its request, 'help me to forget myself
entirely'.[35] God was to answer that longing in her final illness and
death from the then incurable Addison's disease.[36] In her Trinity
prayer, she had also asked for support 'through all nights, all voids,
all helplessness'. Her intrepid faith never wavered, even as her
physical strength weakened and the complications of her illness
multiplied. The severity of her sufferings grew ever more intense.
On one occasion, Elizabeth, now terminally ill, pointed to the
window and said to her superior, 'My Mother, are you at peace
leaving me all alone like this?' And she added, in response to the
surprised expression of the prioress: 'I'm suffering so much that I
now understand suicide. But be at peace: God is there, and He
protects me' (L 329, note 2).[37]

Elizabeth did not desire suffering like this any more than did
Jesus on the cross. She recoiled from it, like him. But she well knew
that fear and anguish, pain and every human suffering, even death
itself, can be transfigured by trust and love. She longed for what
Jesus desired: the unfolding of God's plan of love for his people and
her place with him, through suffering, in the redemption of the
world. Towards the end of her life, she wrote: 'He wants to associate
His Bride in His work of redemption' (LR 13); 'Before I die, I
dream of being transformed into Jesus Crucified, and that gives me
so much strength in suffering' (L 324). To a world where euthanasia
is often thought of as 'mercy killing', Elizabeth's message is clear and
relevant: we can do much more than just put up with suffering; we
can, in fact, transform it by love and allow ourselves to be
transformed by it. 'Take your Crucifix, look, listen' (L 93) – this
could be her final word to all in pain.

Everything in a spirit of joy
For all her suffering, Elizabeth remained always faithful to the
teachings of her beloved Paul: 'Rejoice in the Lord always,' he says,

'again I say rejoice' (Ph 4:4). She lived out her own counsel, given to a young friend: 'a soul united to Jesus is a living smile that radiates Him and gives Him!' (L 252). Innumerable witnesses attest to her unfailing spirit of joy. Even summarised briefly, their testimonies provide a fitting record of her ever-cheerful disposition: 'She would fill you with joy… delightful, completely simple… loveable and engaging even during the most acute sufferings of her last days… Her smile never left her… equally amiable to all… each one could think herself the most loved… she was always smiling and always ready to do whatever one asked of her… When she met anyone she gave them a gracious smile… She was not rigid, but large-minded, full of delicacy and thoughtful for others, very forgetful of her own sufferings.'[38] These are only a few of many accolades. But tributes like these suffice to show how faithfully Elizabeth lived the teaching of Paul: 'God loves a cheerful giver' (2Cor 9:7). In her, grace was the hidden smile of her soul, reflected in her whole demeanour and in the radiance of her joy.

A practical teaching on prayer

At the age of ten, Elizabeth discovered a deep significance in her name. It meant 'House of God', she was told.[39] This was like finding 'the pearl of great price' (Mt 13:46). It helped her to locate a place within herself where she might easily commune alone with God. All who knew her as a young girl could witness her fidelity to prayer. To some, her teaching might appear too exalted, sublime, mystical. In fact, she is the most practical and helpful of spiritual guides. She does not write just for nuns or priests. Much of her most helpful advice was directed towards young persons and people struggling with the challenges of life outside the cloister. Like most of us, she was subject at times to all kinds of distractions. She was even tempted to run away at prayer time. Nor was she spared the trials of darkness and dryness so necessary for spiritual growth: 'how hard and difficult prayer ordinarily seems,' she writes. 'You have to work hard to gather all your powers together – how much it costs and how difficult it seems!' (D 14). She admits that when she went to prayer, 'try as I might, I could not rise above my "rags".'[40] But for all her difficulties, she was not discouraged: 'if Jesus seems to be asleep, oh, let us rest near Him; let us be very calm and silent; let us not wake Him but wait in faith' (L 239).

'Continual prayer'

Even while still in her teens, the phrase 'continual prayer' appears in her notes and journal: 'May my life be a continual prayer, one long *act of love. May nothing* distract me from you' (IN 5). This wish will again take shape in her Trinity prayer: 'May nothing trouble my peace or make me leave You'. She explains in her own simple way how this 'uninterrupted prayer' is possible, even without the support and structure of religious community, in her own heart – 'the cell of [her] heart', the Lord's 'little Bethany' (IN 5). She writes: 'even in the midst of the world one can listen to him in the silence of a heart that wants to belong to Him alone' (L 38).

Teresa of Avila told her sisters that 'the Lord walks among the pots and pans' (F 5:8). Elizabeth seems to be even more down to earth: 'I didn't go into ecstasy while holding the handle of the frying pan like my holy Mother Teresa, but I believed in the divine presence of the Master who was in the midst of us, and my soul, at its center, adored Him' (L 235). She assures us with her practical advice that it is possible to learn, by degrees, 'always to pray' (Lk 18:1). Writing to a friend, she says: 'think about this God who dwells within you, whose temple you are; Saint Paul speaks like this and we can believe him. Little by little, the soul gets used to living in His sweet company, it understands that it is carrying within it a little Heaven where the God of love has fixed His home' (L 249). For Elizabeth, the secret is perseverance, with attention and surrender to the indwelling presence of God. It is a gradual process.

A unique occupation

Elizabeth identified fully with the central precept of the Carmelite *Rule*: 'to ponder the Lord's law day and night and watch in prayer' (#10). For her, prayer is a Carmelite's 'unique occupation' (L 108; cf. 142; 335). She writes:

> It seems to me that I have found my Heaven on earth, since Heaven is God, and God is [in] my soul. The day I understood that, everything became clear to me. I would like to whisper this secret to those I love so they too might always cling to God through everything, and so this prayer of Christ might be fulfilled: 'Father, may they be made perfectly one!' (L 122)

In her Trinity prayer, she makes this request: 'make [my soul] Your heaven, Your beloved dwelling and Your resting place.' 'It is so good, isn't it,' she exclaims, 'to think that, except for the fact that we do not see him, we already possess him here as the blessed possess him above; that it is in our power never to leave him, never to let ourselves be drawn away from Him!' (L 62; cf. L 122). The indwelling presence of God is central to all Elizabeth's teaching on prayer. It gives it her own special slant and emphasis. It also stamps it with an authentic Carmelite seal. She is at one with the teaching of Teresa herself:

> wherever God is, there is heaven... Do you think it matters little... to understand this truth and see that there is no need to go to heaven in order to speak with one's Eternal Father or find delight in Him? Nor is there any need to shout. However softly we speak, He is near enough to hear us. Neither is there any need for wings to go to find Him. All one need do is go into solitude and look at Him within oneself... Those who

by such a method can enclose themselves within this little heaven of our soul, where the Maker of heaven and earth is present...should believe they are following an excellent path...for they will journey far in a short time. (WP 28:2.5)[41]

Heart to heart

The three heavenly Guests are always sharing and communing with each other in the deep heart's core. This personal exchange of love is taking place at the centre of our being – an unceasing dialogue. It is an active presence, creative, always reaching out to give, to communicate itself, and always inviting us to accept the outpouring and the inflow of its love. Elizabeth professes her openness to this transforming, *creative*, love, asking the three persons that she might be 'wholly surrendered to Your creative Action'. She reminds us, echoing the first letter of John: 'There is a Being who is Love and who wishes us to live in communion with Him' (L 327; cf. IJn I:3). Her words are an invitation to commune with God 'heart to heart' – a phrase that best sums up for her the dynamics of this exchange, but 'heart' understood here as the deepest centre of our being.[42] 'I pour out my heart,' she says, 'I catch myself saying all sorts of foolish things [to Him], but He likes me to be uninhibited and to speak to Him heart to heart' (D I35). Once asked by a family friend what she could find to say to God during the long hours of prayer, she replied simply, 'Oh, Madame, we love each other.'[43]

To pray is Christ[44]

Elizabeth's advice on prayer is simple and practical. It is also deeply embedded in the teachings of her beloved Paul. She makes his personal prayer her own when she writes to Abbé Chevignard:

In his magnificent epistles, Saint Paul preaches nothing but this mystery of the charity of Christ, so I borrow his words to express my wishes for you: 'May the Father of O.L. Jesus Christ grant, according to the riches of His glory, that you might be strengthened inwardly through His Spirit, that Christ might dwell in your heart through faith, that you might be rooted and grounded in charity so you can comprehend, with all the saints, the breadth, the length, the height, and the depth of the charity of Christ that surpasses all knowledge, so you might be filled according to all the fullness of God'... and let us be, as Saint Paul says, 'the praise of His glory'. (L 191; cf. Eph 3:14.16-19; I:12)[45]

The heart of Elizabeth must have thrilled to the mention of 'glory' in the opening words of this prayer and in the hymn to the praise of glory at the end: 'Glory to him whose power, working in us, can do infinitely more than we can ask or imagine; glory be to him from generation to generation in the church and in Christ Jesus for ever and ever. Amen' (Eph 3:20-21).[46] Paul speaks of all prayer as the prayer of Christ living in us through the Spirit: 'Likewise the Spirit helps us in our weakness; for we do not know how to pray as we ought, but the Spirit himself intercedes for us with sighs too deep for words. And he who searches the hearts of men knows what is the mind of the Spirit, because the Spirit intercedes for the saints according to the will of God' (Rm 8:26-27). Elizabeth makes this teaching her own.

The aim of all communion with God must be: to pray, and to let Christ pray in us. 'Since Our Lord dwells in our souls, His prayer belongs to us, and I wish to live in communion with it unceasingly... so that later I can communicate it to souls by letting its floods of infinite charity overflow' (L 191). Once asked, while still a postulant, to name her favourite book, she replied, 'The soul of Christ, it gives me all the secrets of the Father who is in Heaven'

(IN 12). In her Trinity prayer, she wants to be 'another humanity for [the Word] in which He can renew His whole Mystery'. She wishes her oneness with Christ's prayer to be total, so she pleads with him: 'identify my soul with all the movements of Your Soul... substitute Yourself for me... Come into me as Adorer'. She repeats the lesson for others: 'the divine Adorer is within us, so we have His prayer; let us offer it, let us share in it, let us pray with His Soul!' (L 179). For Elizabeth, Christ's prayer gives value and meaning to everything – silence, listening, self-forgetfulness, recollection: 'I'm never alone: my Christ is always there praying in me, and I pray with Him' (L 123). In this mystery of Christ's prayer, Elizabeth lived and moved. It was her whole existence. At the end of her life, she wished to bequeath her own experience of prayer to others.

A few days before her death, Elizabeth spoke of her posthumous 'mission'.[47] It is her precious gift to all:

> I think that in Heaven my mission will be to draw souls by helping them go out of themselves to cling to God by a wholly simple and loving movement, and to keep them in this great silence within that will allow God to communicate Himself to them and transform them into Himself. (L 335)

Notes

1 For Elizabeth's *Prayer to the Trinity*, see *Complete Works of Elizabeth of the Trinity*, vol. I, Washington, DC: ICS Publications, 1984, pp. 183-4; for Thérèse's *Act of Oblation to Merciful Love*, see SS, pp. 276-7 and Pri 6. For a new translation of Elizabeth's prayer, see *Mount Carmel*, vol. 47/3, 1999, pp. 51-2. The importance of this prayer by Elizabeth is highlighted by the inclusion of a large excerpt from it in the *Catechism of the Catholic Church* (#260).

2 Quotations from Elizabeth in this chapter are from her *Prayer to the Trinity*, unless otherwise stated.

3 This is how the *Catechism of the Catholic Church* expresses the mystery in precise terms: 'The Church uses (I) the term 'substance' (rendered also at times by 'essence' or 'nature') to designate the divine being in its unity, (II) the term 'person' or 'hypostasis' to designate the Father, Son and Holy Spirit in the real distinction among them, and (III) the term 'relation' to designate the fact that their distinction lies in the relationship of each to the others' (#252).

4 Carmel McCarthy, RSM explains well the profound implications of the revelation of Israel's God as the One whose name is 'I am who I am' (Ex 3:14) – 'the glory of Yahweh', his holiness, the 'otherness' of this covenant-God, his transcendence (incomprehensible and incomparable) and his 'awe-full' majesty: see McCarthy, *op. cit.*

5 For an insightful exploration of adoration and praise in Elizabeth, see Hans Urs von Balthasar, *Two Sisters in the Spirit: Thérèse of Lisieux and Elizabeth of the Trinity*, San Francisco: Ignatius Press, 1992, pp. 438-78; Luigi Borriello, OCD, *Spiritual Doctrine of Blessed Elizabeth of the Trinity: Apostolic Contemplative*, New York: Alba House, 1986, pp. 108-16.

6 For an excellent and succinct introduction to the theology of the Trinity, see Bernard Piault, *What is the Trinity?*, London: Burns & Oates, 1959; Karl Rahner, SJ, *The Trinity*, London: Burns & Oates/Herder & Herder, 1970.

7 The meaning of the Greek preposition *pros* means here not only 'with' in the sense of the Son being in the company of the Father, but also 'towards' in the sense of the dynamic thrust of their relationship: see Ignace de La Potterie, SJ, 'L'emploi dynamique de *eis* dans saint Jean et ses incidences théologiques', *Biblica* 43, 1962, pp. 366-87. See also above, ch. I, note 19.

8 *de Patris utero*: see Council of Toledo XI (AD 675) #6, in Denzinger &

Schönmetzer, *Enchiridion Symbolorum* #526.

9   For a brief and perceptive description of Rublëv's icon, see Luis Alvarez, 'The Icon of the Holy Trinity by Andrei Rublëv – A Reflection', *Mount Carmel*, vol. 52/1, 2004, pp. 48-50. This issue of *Mount Carmel* is devoted entirely to Elizabeth of the Trinity.

10   See Edith Stein's explanation in technical terms of the inner circle of the life of the Trinity (*perichoresis* in Greek, *circumincessio* in Latin): 'The Savior's high priestly prayer unveils the mystery of the inner life: the circumincession of the Divine Persons and the indwelling of God in the soul' (HL, p. 12).

11   Cf. Edith Stein: 'In these mysterious depths [of the circumincession of the Divine Persons] the work of salvation was prepared and accomplished itself in concealment and silence. And so it will continue until the union of all is actually accomplished at the end of time. The decision for the Redemption was conceived in the eternal silence of the inner divine life' (HL, p. 12); cf. Eph 1:9-10.

12   See the monumental work of Hans Urs von Balthasar, *The Glory of the Lord: A Theological Aesthetics*, vol. 4, Edinburgh: T & T Clark, 1989, part 2A, 'The Theological Apriori of the Philosophy of Beauty', pp. 317-412. See also John O'Donohue, *The Divine Beauty: The Invisible Embrace*, London: Transworld Books, 2003.

13   From his speech at the consistory of cardinals, Rome, 2001, quoted in *The Tablet*, December 21st/28th, 2002, p. 15.

14   This theme has been superbly expanded and developed with special reference to the writings of Thérèse, Teresa and John of the Cross and the symbolism of Mount Carmel as 'garden': see Teresa Clements, DMJ, 'What Carmel Means to Me: Beauty in all its Forms', *Mount Carmel*, vol. 51/4, 2003, pp. 8-13; see also Mary McCormack, OCD, 'What Carmel Means to Me: Garden-Land', *Mount Carmel*, vol. 52/4, 2004, pp. 9-15.

15   See the 'Annotations' to the prayer by Conrad De Meester, in *Complete Works*, vol. I, *op. cit.*, pp. 184-91. For an illustration of scriptural quotations in the Carmelite *Rule*, see the author's *The Carmelite Charism*, *op. cit.*, ch. 3, pp. 60-81 and 'The Carmelite Rule', *op. cit.*

16   As John Paul II said at Elizabeth's beatification: 'Elizabeth gives witness to a perfect openness to the Word of God. She had assimilated this Word of God to the point that it truly nourished her thought and her prayer and to such an extent that she found in it all her reasons for living...', in Conrad De Meester, OCD, *Your Presence is my Joy!: Life and*

Message of Blessed Elizabeth of the Trinity, Darlington Carmel, [no date], p. 50.

17 For a general survey of Elizabeth's use of scripture, see Patrick-Marie Févotte, *Aimer la Bible avec Élisabeth de la Trinité*, Paris: Cerf, 1991; also, the discussion by Conrad De Meester, in *Complete Works*, vol. I, *op. cit.*, pp. 137-8.

18 For John's influence on Elizabeth, see Févotte, *op. cit.*, *passim*.

19 See the author's 'Focus', *Mount Carmel*, vol. 52/1, 2004, pp. 5-8.

20 For a popular and insightful treatment of the prologue, see M-E Boismard, *St. John's Prologue*, Westminster: Newman, 1957.

21 See de La Potterie, 'L'emploi dynamique', *op. cit.*

22 See the classic work on truth in John's gospel: Ignace de La Potterie, SJ, *La Vérité dans saint Jean*, Rome: Editrice Pontificio Istituto Biblico (*Analecta Biblica* 73-74), 1977.

23 Raymond Brown expresses this point well: 'Jesus will not have to ask the Father on behalf of the Christian, for the Christian's prayer will be Jesus' prayer' and comments, quoting Loisy, 'In his glorified state Christ will not pray for his own; he will pray with them and through them in his Church. Here one comes to the deepest point of Christian mysticism. The Father sees in the Christians Christ himself, who is at the same time the object of their faith and love.': see Raymond E Brown, SS, *The Gospel according to John (xiii-xxi)*, London, Dublin & Melbourne: Geoffrey Chapman, 1971, p. 735.

24 Elizabeth later made only one small correction to the whole prayer: see *Complete Works*, vol. I, *op. cit.*, p. 191, note 36.

25 For a general treatment of prayer in Paul, see Jean Lévêque, OCD, 'Pastoral Prayer of St. Paul', in James McCaffrey, OCD, *A Biblical Prayer Journey in the Holy Land* [co-authored], Burgos: Editorial Monte Carmelo, 1998, pp. 539-70. On Paul in relation to Elizabeth, see Févotte, *op. cit.*, *passim*.

26 Elizabeth's great discovery of Paul can be dated to January 1904 (see L 191); her love of Paul continued to deepen and mature until her death in November 1906. She especially loved *Ephesians*, and although biblical scholars question the authorship of this book, Paul is retained as the author here, in line with Elizabeth's understanding.

27 Fifteen minutes were set aside in the morning for personal reading of a little from the gospels, epistles, psalms and the *Imitation of Christ*. There was also a period of spiritual reading for half an hour later in the day, or for one hour during Lent: see *Complete Works*, vol. 2,

Washington, DC: ICS Publications, 1995, pp. 371-2.

28 On Eph 1:3-14, see Lévêque, *op. cit.*, pp. 548-52.

29 See Févotte, *op. cit.*, pp. 51-7.

30 See *ibid.*, pp. 57-60.110-4.

31 De Meester, *Your Presence, op. cit.*, p. 80.

32 This human aspect of Elizabeth's character has been well treated in Joanne Mosley, 'The Splendour of the Ordinary Path: Exploring the Human Elizabeth', *Mount Carmel*, vol. 52/1, 2004, pp. 13-20.

33 De Meester, *Your Presence, op. cit.*, p. 2.

34 *Ibid.*, pp. 5-6.

35 Thérèse, too, wrote her own important prayer, the *Act of Oblation to Merciful Love*, two years before her death and had yet to live it out to the full.

36 For a description of Addison's disease, see Jennifer Moorcroft, *He is My Heaven: The Life of Elizabeth of the Trinity*, Washington, DC: ICS Publications, 2001, pp. 110-1.

37 This is strikingly similar to the sufferings and reaction of Thérèse: see ch. 5, section 'The final testing'.

38 See Discalced Carmelite Order, *To be a Carmelite with the Blessed Elizabeth of the Trinity*, Rome: Curia Generalis OCD, [no date], pp. 36-41; this document provides an extensive list of witnesses to Elizabeth's spirit of joy, her smiling countenance and her ever-cheerful disposition. See also the testimonies to Elizabeth's relationships in community given in the first biography of her, written by her former prioress, Mother Germaine: *The Praise of Glory: Reminiscences of Sister Elizabeth of the Trinity, a Carmelite Nun of Dijon, 1901-1906*, London: Burns Oates & Washbourne, 1912, pp. 100-7.

39 Elizabeth received this information on a prayer card given to her on the evening of her first communion during a visit to the Carmel of Dijon; see L 107, note 2. The card can be seen in Conrad De Meester & the Carmel of Dijon, *Elizabeth of the Trinity: Light, Love, Life — A Look at a Face and a Heart*, Washington, DC: ICS Publications, 1987, p. 35, photograph 110. It has also been suggested that the name designates 'My God is plenitude': see Discalced Carmelite Order, *To be a Carmelite, op. cit.*, p. 3. The true meaning of 'Elizabeth' comes from the Hebrew words *Eli sheir*, which signify 'God has sworn [made a promise/an oath]': my thanks to Rabbi Lionel Blue for this information.

40 Jean Lafrance, *Elizabeth of the Trinity: The Charism of her Prayer*, Darlington Carmel, c.1983, p. 38.

41   This passage is central to Teresa's whole teaching on prayer: see ch. I, section 'This little heaven of our soul'.

42   See the author's *The Carmelite Charism, op. cit.*, pp. 20-2.

43   Office for the Promotion of Causes, *Elizabeth Still Speaks...: In the Processes of Beatification and Canonization*, Eugene, Oregon: Carmel of Maria Regina, 1982, p. 7. Elizabeth's words echo those of Thérèse on her deathbed when she, too, was asked what she was saying in prayer: 'I say nothing to Him, I love Him!' (LC, p. 228).

44   On aspects of prayer in Elizabeth's writings, see Eugene McCaffrey, OCD, '"Within that Secret Place": Entering into Prayer with Elizabeth', *Mount Carmel*, vol. 52/1, 2004, pp. 51-60.

45   On the maturing of Elizabeth's vocation as 'praise of glory', of which this letter is the first mention, see L 191, notes I.11; another key letter is L 250. For a treatment of the theme of 'praise of glory' in Elizabeth, see M M Philipon, OP, *The Spiritual Doctrine of Elizabeth of the Trinity*, Washington, DC: Teresian Charism Press, 1947 (1985 reprint), pp. 81-100; Bouyer, *op. cit.*, pp. 159-68; Borriello, *op. cit.*, pp. 103-17.

46   On Paul's doxologies, see Lévêque, *op. cit.*, pp. 546-52. For a splendid treatment of doxology from a biblical and Trinitarian standpoint and with reference to the meaning of 'praise of glory', so central to Elizabeth's doctrine, see Arthur Michael Ramsey, *The Glory of God and the Transfiguration of Christ*, London, New York & Toronto: Longmans, Green & Co, 1949, ch. ix, 'The Praise of his Glory', pp. 91-100.

47   See the discussion by Conrad De Meester of Elizabeth's thoughts on her posthumous mission and of the influence of Thérèse of Lisieux in this regard, in *Complete Works*, vol. I, *op. cit.*, pp. 28-32.

CHAPTER FOUR

EDITH STEIN: INTO THE TRUTH OF THE CROSS

God's plan for his people

'Are they Hebrews? So am I. Are they Israelites? So am I. Are they descendants of Abraham? So am I' (2Cor 11:22). Edith Stein could have applied these same words to herself. Paul could then add, in view of his Damascus experience: '[All this] I have come to regard as loss because of Christ' (Ph 3:7). Again, Edith after her conversion could say the same. However, both Edith and Paul are visibly permeated by Jewish ideas; her writings, like his, are brimful of Old Testament references and rich with the traditions of Israel. Paul spoke of his people as 'my kindred according to the flesh' (Rm 9:3). Edith Stein spoke of her Jewish people with the same affection and sense of belonging. In fact, when an official offered her a chance of escape from Westerbork transit camp, he says that she replied to him: 'Wasn't it fair that baptism not be allowed to become an advantage? If somebody intervened at this point and took away her chance to share in the fate of her brothers and sisters, *that* would be utter annihilation.'[1]

Edith, like Paul, was convinced that the gospel of Christ 'is the power of God for the salvation of everyone who has faith, to the Jew first and also to the Greek' (Rm 1:16). Resistance to the 'good news' filled Paul's heart with 'great sorrow and unceasing anguish' (Rm 9:2). With Edith it could be no different. Paul was willing to be

129

branded 'accursed' (Rm 9:3) for the sake of his people. Edith was willing to face the risk of expulsion from her own home because of her conversion, as well as exile from her family through her entrance into Carmel — like a new Esther removed from her people all the better to plead on their behalf (SP, p. 291).[2] Both Paul and Edith preserved their belief in the ultimate redemption of Israel. Paul says: 'And so all Israel will be saved' (Rm 11:26); Edith writes: '[at the end of time] the twelve tribes will have found their Lord' (HL, p. 133).

In his *Letter to the Romans* (chs. 9-11), Paul wrestles with the problem of Israel's place in God's plan of salvation. He uses the image of an olive tree and explains the mystery by speaking of branches being cut off or grafted on (Rm 11:17-24). The 'cut-off' branches are those Israelites who have refused to believe in Christ — although this is by no means a definitive situation, as God has the power to graft them on again (Rm 11:23). The Gentile Christians have been grafted onto the same root. Paul preaches humility, reminding the Christians that they owe their grace of salvation to God's covenant with the Jewish people: 'it is not you that support the root, but the root that supports you' (Rm 11:18). Moreover, he adds that the salvation of the Jews actually takes precedence in a sense, since they themselves belong to the original 'olive tree' (Rm 11:24). Jesus assures us that 'salvation is from the Jews' (Jn 4:22).[3] So, too, the final unfolding of God's plan is full of hope for the chosen people. Paul explains: 'as regards election, they are beloved for the sake of their ancestors' (Rm 11:28). Elsewhere, he expands: 'They are Israelites, and to them belong the sonship, the glory, the covenants, the giving of the law, the worship, and the promises; to them belong the patriarchs, and of their race, according to the flesh, is the Christ' (Rm 9:4-5). In the ultimate analysis, the Jews are assured of God's saving mercy and the fulfilment of his covenant with them (Rm 11:27.31; cf. Jer 31:33).

A heritage rediscovered

Paul also speaks of the Jewish people in the Christian era, and to explain their situation takes up an idea that pervades the Old Testament: the 'remnant' of Jews that remained ever faithful to Yahweh.[4] He says: 'So too at the present time there is a remnant, chosen by grace' (Rm 11:5), referring now to those who, like Paul himself, believe in Christ. Edith Stein, as a convert, is also part of this 'remnant'. However, like Paul, she retained immense respect for her Jewish heritage and for those who remained faithful to it. 'As children,' she said, 'we read right conduct in our mother's example as if in a mirror of the virtues.'[5] Edith spoke, too, of the 'high human and moral heritage' that is received in the Jewish home.[6] Even after her conversion, she continued to attend the synagogue with her mother and was highly sensitive to the views of Jewish people. When at home, she practised her Catholic faith as discreetly as possible, slipping out secretly to the early Mass each morning. She may also have supported the decision of her sister Rosa to delay her own reception into the Catholic Church until after their mother's death, so as not to cause unnecessary hurt to Frau Stein.

Edith had complete confidence, possibly unlike many of her Christian contemporaries, that the prayers of a Jew were effective. The same official at Westerbork recalled his conversation with Edith Stein: 'When I asked her if she thought God was listening to her prayers, she answered, [pointing to her fellow Jews,] "He is listening to their pleading. I have no doubt of that."'[7] In fact, Edith sincerely believed that her mother was interceding for her in heaven. No doubt it was part of God's providence, in support of her conviction, that she received an almost tangible sense of her mother's presence at her side, the very moment that Frau Stein died, many miles away.

As Edith's new-found faith developed, she never felt that she had to renounce her Jewish heritage. Rather, she found that she was steeping herself more and more in the Jewish roots of the Christian faith. She had a special love for *Genesis* and the Hebrew scriptures in general. Her former novice mistress remarks: 'Whenever she was discussing the Old Testament this joy used to radiate like a peaceful light from her beautiful eyes'.[8] In particular, Edith identified with the figures of Elijah and Esther. Her niece has these surprising words: 'Edith Stein tells us that by becoming a Catholic she felt truly Jewish for the first time in her life' (SEL, p. 117).

A special vocation

Edith's special grace of belief in Christ did not mark her out, in her own eyes, as superior in any way to her Jewish brothers and sisters. It consisted in a personal calling within God's saving plan, centred on the redeeming cross of Christ. Speaking in retrospect of her first awakening to the power of the cross – which could be called her first or 'Christian' conversion – she says that at that very moment her 'unbelief was shattered'.[9] By 'unbelief' she does not mean 'tepid faith' but 'lack of belief [in Christ]'. 'Unbelief' is the exact term that Paul uses in Romans (11:20.23) to refer to the Jews who do not believe in Christ. Later, when Edith wrote her will, she prayed that she might atone for 'the unbelief of the Jewish people'.[10] But, like Paul, she believed that 'God has not rejected his people' (Rm 11:2). Rather, she prayed for their eventual conversion – not as a judgment on her contemporaries but as part of God's final plan – because only in this way would his kingdom finally come. She therefore added these words immediately after her prayer for the Jewish people: 'so that the Lord may be received by his own and that his kingdom may come in glory'.[11] As Paul explains: 'I want you to understand this mystery, brethren: a hardening has come upon part of Israel, until the full number of the Gentiles come in, and so all Israel will be saved' (Rm 11:25-26).

For Edith, a special vocation or mission entailed a full acceptance of what she was conscious of being called to do. It did not imply any guilt on the part of those who had not received a similar call. When her distressed mother asked Edith if she thought that Jews, who do not believe in Christ, could be devout, she answered: 'Certainly, if one has not come to know anything else' (SEL, p. 28). In terms of accepting her own special vocation – a call to carry the cross – Edith describes her response to Jesus in just such terms of *awareness* of one's personal call: 'I knew that it was His cross that was now being placed upon the Jewish people; that most of them did not understand this, but that those who did, would have to take it up willingly in the name of all. I would do that' (SEL, p. 17).

As we shall see, Edith's whole life would be a search for the truth, a profound penetration of the truth of the cross. But while her conversion and entrance into Carmel appeared to distance her from her Jewish people, her path was nothing other than a deepening and rediscovering of her Jewish roots. How thrilled Edith must have been to find the core of Carmel's *Rule* expressed with echoes of her beloved Old Testament: 'pondering the Lord's law day and night' (#10; cf. Ps 1:2; Jos 1:8). We can only surmise what her joy would have been to discover that the two greatest figures of the reformed Carmel, Teresa of Avila and John of the Cross, shared her Jewish blood.[12]

An unknown God

In her search for truth, Edith lived discipleship to the full as we find it described in the gospels. Like the first disciples in *John*, she was already searching for Jesus without knowing it,[13] even before she, like them, ever encountered him personally. When the Baptist 'looked at Jesus as he walked past, he exclaimed, "Behold, the Lamb of God!" The two disciples heard him say this and they *followed* Jesus' (Jn 1:36-37). They were already following Jesus before he 'turned and saw them *following* him, and said to them, "What do you seek?"' (Jn 1:38). The original verb 'to follow' (*akolouthein*), twice repeated here, is highly significant. It designates a following of Jesus precisely as his disciple (cf. Jn 13:36-37). These followers are already his disciples in some deep mysterious way and already searching, unwittingly, for an unknown God. Theirs is the *cor inquietum* of the Christian experience, the human heart that is always restless until it rests in God. For the psalmist, it is a painful 'thirsting for God... Like the deer that yearns for running streams' (Ps 41:3.2). In the gospels, Jesus offers to slake that thirst: 'Let anyone who is thirsty come to me and drink' (Jn 7:37). 'What do you seek?' Jesus had asked (Jn 1:38). There is as yet no indication that these first disciples are in search of a *person* and that he is the one who alone can still their beating minds and hearts or give them rest (cf. Mt 11:28). In fact, God is searching for them much more than they are searching for him. Jesus is explicit: 'No one can come to me unless drawn by the Father' (Jn 6:44; cf. 6:37).[14]

This facet of discipleship in *John* is like a gospel commentary of the workings of God in the life of Edith Stein. Determined and headstrong by nature, she volunteered at the outset of the First World War for service with the Red Cross, and was sent to a hospital for contagious diseases in Austria: 'my mother declared with all the energy she could muster: "You will not go with my permission." My reply was every bit as determined. "Then I must go without your permission."' Edith observed: 'granite was striking granite' (LJF, p. 319). This was the virtue Teresa loved to encourage in her Carmelite daughters: '*determinada determinación*' – 'determined determination' or 'resolute determination' (WP 21:2). It was to serve Edith well in her constant search for the truth.

Passion for the truth
Edith Stein was a brilliant philosopher. By definition, then, a 'lover of wisdom' (from *philo*, 'I love' and *sophia*, 'wisdom'). Her life was a search for truth at all costs, a shining example and witness to the gospel promise, 'the truth will make you free' (Jn 8:32). At fifteen, Edith became an atheist. It was her own conscious and deliberate choice. At the same time, she also decided to give up praying. Later,

she would say: 'My longing for truth was a prayer in itself.'[15] Those who at times find it hard even to believe can take comfort from her. The search for truth itself is a search for God. It is prayer. Edith was a woman of great moral integrity who hated hypocrisy. She knew, as if by instinct, that 'whoever lives by the truth comes to the light' (Jn 3:21). She could not abide any opportunistic attitude or compromising of principles. Adamant as ever in her search for truth, to her own self she remained always true.

Examples abound of her exploring and probing mind and her nobility of character. On her return from the Red Cross hospital, letters which Edith was carrying back on behalf of some of the patients were confiscated at the border. Her mother urged her to feign ignorance of the law. 'No matter what the cost might be,' Edith said, 'I refused to say I was ignorant of the prohibition; I would rather face a prison term than lie about it' (LJF, p. 364). Edith was resonating with the word of God, walking in the light: 'God is light and in him there is no darkness at all... while we walk in darkness, we lie and do not live according to the truth' (IJn 1:5-6).

Edith walked at ease with the great original thinkers of her day. She would even become a friend and assistant of her revered 'Master', Edmund Husserl, a Protestant and the pioneer of phenomenology. As he lay dying, she wrote of him: 'I am not at all worried about my dear Master. It has always been far from me to think that God's mercy allows itself to be circumscribed by the visible church's boundaries. God is truth. All who seek truth seek God, whether this is clear to them or not' (SP, p. 272). The Lord, in his own mysterious way, was preparing Edith for her future entrance into Carmel. 'God is supreme Truth,' writes Teresa of Avila, 'and to be humble is to walk in truth' (IC VI:10:7). Edith was already walking in the tradition of Carmel by her humble submission to the truth. One Carmelite sister sums up this aspect of her own call to Carmel: 'I think the essence of what Carmel means to me lies in this: that its whole spiritual teaching affirms and supports the pursuit of truth as the central quest of life.'[16] Little wonder that Thérèse of Lisieux, on her deathbed, could sum up her whole life in this way: 'Yes, it seems to me I never sought anything but the truth; yes, I have understood humility of heart' (LC, p. 205).

Conversion through encounter

Jesus invites his disciples to a personal encounter with himself: 'Come and see' (Jn 1:39; cf. 4:29). It is a faith-challenge. They accept: 'They came and saw... and stayed with him that day' (Jn 1:39). In Jesus, they find the Messiah of Jewish expectations. 'We have found the Messiah,' Andrew says to his brother Simon Peter, and the evangelist adds by way of explanation, 'which means the Christ' (Jn 1:41). In dialogue with the Samaritan woman, Jesus explicitly owns the title: 'I know the Messiah is coming,' she remarks; and Jesus replies, 'I who speak to you am he' (Jn 4:25-26). Together with *Kyrios* ('Lord'), the title most frequently used in the gospels to identify Jesus is 'Christ' or 'Messiah'. It sums up the mystery of the disciples' discovery.

This expression of Andrew's faith is followed by another one, even more explicit, on the lips of Philip: 'We have found him of whom Moses in the law and also the prophets wrote, Jesus of Nazareth, the son of Joseph' (Jn 1:45). Much later, after the resurrection, Jesus himself will assure his disciples 'that everything written about [him] in the law of Moses and the prophets and the psalms *must* be fulfilled' (Lk 24:44). The 'must' (in Greek: *dei*) is significant. It refers, throughout the gospels, to a divine necessity for the fulfilment of God's plan (cf. Mt 16:21; Mk 8:31; Lk 9:22; 17:25). The Torah, or the law, was God's special *gift* to his people: 'the law was *given* through Moses; grace and truth came through Jesus Christ' (Jn 1:17). It served as a 'pedagogue' leading to Christ (Gal 3:24); or, as Paul explains elsewhere: 'Christ is the fulfilment of the law' (Rm 10:4). Matthew's expression of the same truth is more nuanced, explaining that Jesus did not come 'to abolish the law and the prophets... but to complete them', and in order that the purpose of the law might be 'achieved' (Mt 5:17-18). In a unique gesture, Paul 'called together the local leaders of the Jews' (Acts 28:17), we are told, 'to convince them about Jesus both from the law of Moses and from the prophets' (Acts 28:23).

'I am the way, the truth and the life'

Edith Stein's search for truth led her inexorably, like the first disciples, to the person of Jesus as the promised Messiah of her rich Jewish heritage. In the end, it was not arguments of philosophy, theology or even scripture that convinced her. The moment of discovery came for Edith when she chanced on the autobiography of Teresa of Avila, the reformer of Carmel.[17] She read all night until she finished the book. Then, with the first streaks of daybreak, the inner light also dawned. 'That,' she exclaimed, 'is the truth.'[18] Through Teresa, Edith had found a *Person* who claimed to be, and was, *the* truth (cf. *Life* 40:1-4). At the very outset of his gospel, John reveals this great secret of the Christian faith: 'The Word was made flesh... full of grace and truth' (Jn 1:14). Again, during the last supper, Jesus claims to be himself the truth in person: 'I am the way, the truth and the life; no one can come to the Father except through me' (Jn 14:6). Edith had always been, in gospel terms, 'of the truth' (Jn 18:37). Now, having discovered *the* truth, she would henceforth, like every true disciple of Jesus, 'listen to [his] voice' (Jn 18:37).

In Jesus, Edith would rediscover the law, now fulfilled, of her own people. For them, the Torah was the highest source of wisdom.[19] She well knew, like the first disciples, that it occupied a central place in the Jewish scriptures: it was God's word to his people, the revelation of his will, a lesson not just for Israel but for all the nations of the world (Dt 4:6). In his vision of salvation history, Isaiah sees all peoples as pilgrims on a universal exodus at the end of time, on the march towards God's temple: 'For out of Zion shall go forth the law, and the word of the Lord from

Jerusalem' (Is 2:3; Mic 4:2). A devout Jew is one 'whose delight is the law of the Lord and who ponders his law day and night' (Ps 1:2). This is the challenge for all Carmelites summoned by their *Rule* (#10) to a life of prayer. Edith Stein's continuing love of that law – fulfilled, completed and its purpose achieved (cf. Mt 5:17-18) in the person of Jesus – was to colour her whole understanding of prayer and stamp it with her own original touch.

Later, writing as a Carmelite about prayer in the light of her Jewish tradition, Edith asks the question: 'What is meant by "the Law of the Lord"?' She refers to psalm 118 as being 'entirely filled with the command to know the Law and to be led by it through life' and explains: 'The Psalmist was certainly thinking of the Law of the Old Covenant.' 'But,' she says, 'the Lord has freed us from the yoke of this Law.' Edith then adds, 'We can consider the Savior's great commandment of love, which he says includes the whole Law and the Prophets, as the Law of the New Covenant... But we understand the Law of the New Covenant, even better, to be the Lord himself' (HL, p. 4). Here, we are already close to the heart of Teresian prayer, with Edith's emphasis on the priority of love and her focus on the person of Jesus – announced in the Old Testament and revealed in the New.[20]

Prayer in the spirit of Carmel

Edith has also recaptured a central message of the Old Testament prophets who promised 'an inner law' (cf. Jer 31:33) and 'a new heart... a new spirit' (Ez 36:26; cf. 11:19) which Paul later describes as 'the law of the life-giving Spirit in Christ Jesus' (Rm 8:2). This law of love is 'poured into our hearts by the Holy Spirit who has been given to us' (Rm 5:5); it is the fruit of Christ's prayer, 'that the love with which you [Father] have loved me may be in them, and I in them' (Jn 17:26); and it is 'written not with ink but with the Spirit of the living God, not on tablets of stone but on tablets of human hearts' (2Cor 3:3). Edith reminds us of the depths to which this eternal love of God can penetrate the human heart when she comments on the teaching of John of the Cross in her final work, *The Science of the Cross*:

> The flame of divine life *touches* the soul with the tenderness of God's life and *wounds* her so mightily in her innermost depth that she dissolves wholly in love... This happens in the *inmost region* of the soul where neither the devil nor sensuality can penetrate, therefore what occurs is the more secure, substantial, and delightful. (Sci Cr, p. 188)

We, too, must enter into these depths in the spirit of the same mystical doctor. As Edith writes, echoing John of the Cross: 'To erect the structure of holiness... one must dig deep and build high, must descend into the depths of the dark night of one's own nothingness in order to be raised up high into the sunlight of divine love and compassion' (HL, p. 6; cf. DN; P 6).

One apparently insignificant event in Edith's life, some five years before her conversion, throws light on her approach to prayer. She was captivated, as is well known, by phenomenology. It answered a personal need, for she was never concerned with mere theory, and this new philosophical movement enabled her to explore life: all human experience was her field of research, and her studies had even led her to an openness to questions of faith. She later records her awe and wonder when witnessing at that time a certain experience of Catholic devotion. She entered the cathedral in Frankfurt as a tourist, where she observed a simple woman come in with her shopping basket and soon become deeply immersed in prayer. Edith reflected on the contrast with Jewish synagogues and Protestant churches, which she had seen visited during religious services only. Catholic churches, by contrast, were obviously meant for what she called 'an intimate conversation' with God (LJF, p. 401). This was a new experience for Edith, and one which she felt compelled to explore.

Love responding to Love

'God is love,' Edith would later write in Carmel, 'and love is goodness giving itself away' (HL, p. 38; cf. IJn 4:8; Mt 20:28). For her, 'Prayer is the communication of the soul with God' (HL, p. 38). The call of the first disciples reaches its climax with the words of Jesus: 'You shall see greater things... you will see heaven opened, and the angels of God ascending and descending upon the Son of man' (Jn 1:50-51). Here, the Old Testament scene of Jacob's ladder, pitched between heaven and earth with the angels of God ascending and descending on it, opens up by way of background (Gn 28:10-17). Edith sees this unceasing communication between heaven and earth as a significant image of prayer within her Jewish tradition. 'Prayer is a Jacob's ladder,' she writes, 'on which the human spirit ascends to God and God's grace descends to people' (HL, p. 38).

The human spirit, like those angels, is in an unbroken link between heaven and earth. It is able, Edith explains, 'to receive God's love with understanding and to return it freely' (HL, p. 38). She then says, significantly, 'Prayer is the highest achievement of which the human spirit is capable. But it is not merely a human achievement' (HL, p. 38). Ever true to the spirit of Teresian silent prayer, Edith reminds us of 'the one thing necessary' (Lk 10:42) for this prayer: 'The only essential,' she says, 'is that one finds, first of all, a quiet corner in which one can communicate with God as though there were nothing else' (SP, p. 54). And she also says, pointing to the effects of this quiet prayer: 'No human eye can see what God does in the soul during hours of inner prayer. It is grace upon grace' (HL, p. 6).

In the prophet Elijah, 'Father of all Carmelites', Edith finds the great model of this kind of prayer within the Jewish tradition.[21] He is her shining exemplar of someone in a personal relationship and loving communion with God. She writes: 'Prayer is looking up into the face of the Eternal' (HL, p. 3), and she explains this in terms of the great prophet: 'Elijah stands before God's face because all of his love belongs to the Lord... He stands before God's face like the angels before the eternal throne' (HL, p. 2). She further relates this to life in Carmel – her own life and that of her Carmelite sisters: 'To stand before the face of God continues to be the real content of our lives' (HL, p. 4).

But Elijah is merely a reflection of the figure of Jesus at prayer who, Edith says, 'stands, always and everywhere, before the face of God' (HL, p. 12). It is to Jesus as supreme model that Edith turns for her last word on the Carmelite vocation of 'meditating on the Law of the Lord day and night and watching in prayer' (HL, p. 3; cf. *Rule* 10): 'We thus fulfill our Rule when we hold the image of the Lord continually before our eyes in order to make ourselves like him' (HL, p. 4). For that reason, she concludes, 'We can never finish studying the Gospels' (HL, p. 4).

'From failure up'[22]

Another apparently insignificant incident in the life of Edith Stein was to mark an important breakthrough in her understanding of Jesus as the promised Messiah. In 1917, a good friend of hers, the philosopher Adolf Reinach, died in combat. He and his wife Anne were Christians, converts from Judaism. Edith wondered how she might comfort the bereaved widow. But she observed, in amazement, how Anne had accepted the pain of her husband's death: the young widow was at one with Christ's suffering. Anne's strength seemed to console Edith. 'It was then that I first encountered the Cross,' said Edith later, 'and the divine strength which it inspires in those who bear it. For the first time I saw before my very eyes the Church, born of Christ's redemptive suffering, victorious over the sting of death. It was the moment in which my unbelief was shattered, Judaism paled, and Christ streamed out upon me: Christ in the mystery of the Cross.'[23] Edith was now facing the challenge of what Paul describes: 'Christ crucified... the power of God and the wisdom of

God… For the foolishness of God is wiser than human wisdom, and the weakness of God is stronger than human strength' (1Cor 1:23-25). Here was a God unknown to Edith, a stumbling block for her as it was for her own people – a suffering Messiah. Later, she was to reveal her conformity with him in one of her prayers, describing the conversion journey of her sister Rosa:

> You have led me by a long, dark path,
> Rocky and hard.
> Often my strength threatened to fail me.
> I almost lost all hope of seeing the light.
> But when my heart grew numb with deepest grief,
> A clear star rose for me.
> Steadfast it guided me – I followed,
> At first reluctant, but more confidently later.
> (SEL, p. 59)

A Suffering Servant

But how was Edith to reconcile a suffering Messiah with Jewish expectations? There was nothing in the tradition of her people linking the Messiah with suffering, pain, abasement and humiliation. However, there is a line of prophetic tradition which attests the necessity of personal suffering and its fruitfulness in God's design. It has its foundation in the story of several outstanding Old Testament characters. Abraham, destined to be the 'father of all believers', leads Isaac to the slaughter at God's command: 'Take your son, your only son Isaac, whom you love, and go to the land of Moriah, and offer him there as a burnt offering upon one of the mountains of which I shall tell you' (Gn 22:2). Joseph, sold by his envious brothers to some passing merchants, becomes their eventual saviour in exile. They receive the assurance through him: 'God will be with you, and will bring you again to the land of your fathers' (Gn 48:21). Moses is rejected by the people whom he has led to freedom: 'Israel murmured against Moses…

"you have brought us out into this wilderness to kill this whole assembly with hunger'" (Ex 16:2-3). The rejected prophets proclaim the word of God and, with it, challenge the conscience of the rebellious Israelites: 'my people... have forsaken me, the fountain of living waters' (Jer 2:13). The plaintive tones of the just in their suffering fills the psalms with their sobbing music: 'How long, O Lord? Will you hide yourself for ever?' (Ps 88:47); 'This is what causes my grief; that the way of the Most High has changed' (Ps 76:11). But perhaps nobody has grappled more intensely with this problem of innocent suffering than Job, only to conclude with a change of heart: 'I was the man who misrepresented [God's] intentions... I retract what I have said and repent in dust and ashes' (Jb 42:3.6).

This imposing array of biblical figures reaches its summit in Isaiah's prophecy of the Servant of Yahweh who is '[without] form or comeliness... despised and rejected... a man of sorrows... Surely he has borne our griefs and carried our sorrows... stricken, smitten by God, and afflicted... with his stripes we are healed... no deceit in his mouth... it was the will of the Lord to bruise him' (Is 53:2-5.9-10). He gave his life in sacrifice as 'an offering for sin... bore the sin of many, and made intercession for the transgressors' (Is 53:10.12). His humiliation and suffering are the paradoxical means chosen by God to bring about the glorification of his Servant: 'he shall be exalted and lifted up' (Is 52:13). As we have seen, the tradition of the Messiah and that of the Suffering Servant were never united in the Old Testament Jewish tradition. This shattering revelation had to await the coming of Christ.

'The folly of the cross'
The union of these two traditions in the good news of the gospel is the dazzling light that blinded the minds of Jesus' listeners, his disciples no less than the crowds. It is the central revelation of Mark's gospel: Jesus *is* the suffering Messiah. This was something

entirely new, unexpected, astounding. Jesus had to try and stun people into accepting it. Mark describes a miracle in slow motion which may be taken to illustrate the gradual dawning of this baffling light of faith. 'Do you see anything?' Jesus asked a blind man (Mk 8:23). 'I see people,' he replied, 'but they look like trees, walking' (Mk 8:24). Then Jesus touched the man's eyes a second time and the blind man 'looked intently and was restored, and saw everything clearly' (Mk 8:25). The scales had finally dropped from his eyes.

Immediately afterwards, the evangelist records the scene at Caesarea Philippi. 'Who do people say that I am?' Jesus asks his disciples (Mk 8:27). Peter answers in the name of all: 'You are the Christ' (Mk 8:29). Right answer! He is the Messiah. But not a victorious wonder-worker expected to restore the political power of Israel. So, Jesus now foretells his passion: 'The Son of man must suffer... be rejected... and killed, and after three days rise again' (Mk 8:31). Peter is appalled. He remonstrates with Jesus. But Jesus in turn rebukes Peter harshly: 'Get behind me, Satan!' (Mk 8:33). There must be no mistaking his message. This is a hard saying, a profound mystery: the *suffering* Messiah. He goes on to endorse the lesson with a challenge to all his disciples: 'Let them take up their cross and follow me' (Mk 8:34). Edith Stein was to discover that in order to follow Jesus as her suffering Messiah, she too, like every faithful disciple, would have to shoulder that cross. In fact, her whole life was to unfold under the sign of the cross. This was the core of Edith's own vocation: to carry the cross at one with Jesus.[24]

The path to Carmel

Like her newly discovered Messiah, Edith would be battered by the winds of adversity, misunderstanding and rejection, and in time eventually by the destructive powers of evil unleashed by the Nazis. She was no stranger to pain, even from her earliest years. A sensitive and loving child, she lost her father before she was two. Her hard-working mother successfully carried on the family lumber business and Edith had to endure the daily absence of a caring mother from the family home. She may have been a born philosopher and lecturer, but she was not a born saint. Later, at Breslau University, she did not hesitate to call some of her fellow students, who did not share her own high ideals, 'The Idiots' (LJF, p. 191)! This kind of sharpness needed to be tempered; she had still to grow and mature under the shadow of the cross.

Edith was baptised on New Year's Day, 1922. When she broke the news of her conversion, it was the first time Edith had ever seen her mother weep. Edith wept too. She was experiencing the gospel truth: 'I have come to set... a daughter against her mother... Whoever loves... mother more than me, is not worthy of me' (Mt 10:35.37). The recent convert was determined to become a Carmelite immediately after her conversion. But her wise spiritual director, Canon Joseph Schwind, advised against it in deference to her mother and because her conversion was so recent. A disappointed Edith obeyed – as she did with her second director, Raphael Walzer, who considered her role as a public lecturer too important to be abandoned.

Destined for a university post by her great intellectual talents and consummate skill as a communicator, Edith never obtained one – not just because she was a woman but also because she was a Jewess. Finally, as a lecturer at a Catholic institute, she was barred from her profession, like all her fellow Jews, by the Third Reich. It was a cruel blow, but 'we know that in everything, God works for good with those who love him, who are called according to his purpose' (Rm 8:28). In fact, it proved a blessing in disguise. Her spiritual director waived his objections to her embracing the religious life, now that Edith was no longer permitted to lecture. The door to Carmel was open to her at last.

Carmel at last

In October 1933, Edith entered the Carmelite convent of Cologne: 'it always seemed to me that the Lord was saving something for me in

Carmel,' she said, 'which I could find there and nowhere else' (SEL, p. 21). She took the religious name 'Teresa Benedicta of the Cross'. It epitomised her life before she entered – 'Teresa', recalling her conversion experience; 'Benedicta', because 'Benedict... adopted me,' she said (SP, p. 182), referring to her close links with Beuron Abbey in the Black Forest; 'of the Cross', a reminder of her inner vocation to share in the passion.[25] In Carmel she did not escape the cross. She described religious life as 'a silent, life-long martyrdom', with 'all the little sacrifices... a regimen structured day after day in all its details... the self-control...achieved with a loving smile... serving others in love' (HL, p. 6). Neither was she spared the pain of ingrained anti-Semitic prejudice. Recalling her first meeting with Edith, her future prioress at Echt commented with a sigh of relief: 'not a Jewish type at all'.[26] For Edith, the cross represented the religious vows: 'The Crucified One looks down on us,' she wrote for her religious sisters. '...Will you remain faithful to the Crucified?... If you decide for Christ, it could cost you your life' (HL, p. 94). It did cost Edith no less.

But Edith did not enter the contemplative life to escape the cross of the menacing powers of evil running riot outside the cloister. Rather, she withdrew from the world to listen more intently in prayer to the painful voices she had left behind. 'You can be at all fronts, wherever there is grief, in the power of the cross,' she said. 'Your compassionate love takes you everywhere, this love from the divine heart' (HL, p. 96). Such was her constant refrain. She once wrote to a friend: 'even in the contemplative life, one may not sever the connection with the world. I even believe that the deeper one is drawn into God, the more one must "go out of oneself"; that is, one must go to the world in order to carry the divine life into it' (SP, p. 54). This was Edith's comment on *fuga mundi* – religious life as a so-called 'escape from the world'! 'Whoever enters Carmel is not lost to his own,' she reassured a Jewish friend distressed at the thought of her disappearance out of his life, 'but is theirs fully for the first time; it is our vocation to stand before God for all' (SP, pp. 177-8).

'They will persecute you'

In January 1933, Adolf Hitler came to power and Edith soon saw that there was no place for her in the darkening shadows of Nazi Germany. 'I talked with the Savior,' she wrote, 'and told Him that I knew that it was His cross that was now being placed upon the Jewish people... I would [help carry it]. He should only show me how... I was certain that I had been heard. But what this carrying of the cross was to consist in, that I did not yet know' (SEL, p. 17). Edith had no illusions about the future. She wrote personally to Pius XI, urging him to write an encyclical condemning Nazi ideology. Outside the convent, anti-Jewish feeling was mounting. By the end of 1938, especially after the pogrom of *Kristallnacht*, open persecution was rife. Edith was not looking for death but she was ready to face her Gethsemane 'as a sacrifice... for true peace' (SP, p. 305). She would later keep pinned under her scapular a slip of paper with the words, 'When they persecute you in one town, flee to the next' (Mt 10:23). Edith followed this gospel advice. The Carmel of Echt in the Netherlands offered her asylum, and she joined their community on New Year's Eve. However, in 1940 the Germans occupied the country. Two years later, when the Dutch Catholic bishops made a public protest against the treatment of the Jews, the Nazi authorities retaliated and ordered the arrest of all Catholics of Jewish origin in the Netherlands. Edith was among the victims. As she walked calmly to her death, she turned to her sister and said, 'Come, Rosa. We're going for our people.'[27]

Jesus had foretold the persecution of his followers: 'When they deliver you up, do not be anxious how you are to speak or what you are to say; for what you are to say will be given to you in that hour; for it is not you who speak, but the Spirit of your Father speaking through you' (Mt 10:19-20). Edith was to experience the truth of these words during the last days before her death on 9th August, 1942 in the gas chambers of Auschwitz. 'If the world hates you,'

Jesus warned, 'know that it has hated me before it hated you... A servant is not greater than his master. If they persecuted me, they will persecute you... They hated me without a cause' (Jn 15:18.20.25). Edith was entirely one in mind and heart with her suffering Messiah. Her final days among her own anguished people in a squalid transit camp, where she comforted the children and combed their hair, were a shining witness to the power of the Holy Spirit at work in her: 'the Spirit of truth,' Jesus had said, '...will bear witness to me' (Jn 15:26).

One eyewitness, a woman who was later released from Westerbork, described Edith praying in the camp as 'a Pietà without the Christ'.[28] But the Christ was there in Edith, living his passion at one with her and deep within her, invisible to the naked eye. In fact, not quite invisible. Others have borne witness to the radiant presence all around her. One man, working as an official in the camp, described Edith with these remarkable words:

> The one sister who impressed me immediately, whose warm, glowing smile has never been erased from my memory, despite the disgusting 'incidents' I was forced to witness, is the one whom I think the Vatican may one day canonize. From the moment I met her in the camp at Westerbork... I knew: here is someone truly great. For a couple of days she lived in that hellhole, walking, talking, and praying... like a saint. And she really was one... When she spoke, it was impossible not to be moved by her humility and conviction. Talking with her was like... journeying into another world, where for the moment, Westerbork ceased to exist.[29]

Yet Edith herself, in one of her earlier prayers, speaks not of her own testimony, but of the love and power of the Spirit bearing witness within her:

Who are You, sweet light that fills me
And illumines the darkness of my heart?
You guide me like a mother's hand,
And if You let me go, I could not take
Another step.
You are the space
That surrounds and contains my being.
Without You it would sink into the abyss
Of nothingness from which You raised it into being.
You, closer to me than I to myself,
More inward than my innermost being –
And yet unreachable, untouchable,
And bursting the confines of any name:

> Holy Spirit –
> Eternal love![30]

Her life – a priestly prayer

Edith was born into an observant Jewish family. Her birth, on October 12th, 1891, fell on the Jewish feast of *Yom Kippur*, the Day of Atonement. This holy day, described in *Leviticus* (ch. 16) and evoked again in *Hebrews* (9:11-12),[31] was destined to take on profound significance in Edith's life. She recalls the prayer of Jesus at the last supper, when 'he lifted his eyes to heaven and spoke to the Father' (HL, p. 11; cf. Jn 17:1). She then comments: 'We call these words Jesus' great high priestly prayer, for this talking alone with God also had its antecedent in the Old Covenant' (HL, pp. 11-12). She goes on to explain the link:

> Once a year on the greatest and most holy day of the year, on the Day of Atonement, the high priest stepped into the Holy of Holies before the face of the

Lord 'to pray for himself and his household and the whole congregation of Israel'... This solitary dialogue took place in deepest mystery... And the high priest descended from Aaron foreshadows the eternal high priest... [Jesus] stands, always and everywhere, before the face of God... He gazes upon the uncovered face of the Eternal One... The Savior's high priestly prayer unveils the mystery of the inner life: the circumincession of the Divine Persons and the indwelling of God in the soul. (HL, p. 12)[32]

Edith also speaks of 'attentive souls in whom Jesus' high priestly prayer comes to life again and again... steeped in the life and suffering of Christ, [they] were the Lord's preferred choice as instruments to accomplish great things in the church' (HL, p. 13). Edith refers explicitly to Teresa of Avila as one such person of prayer, together with Bridget of Sweden and Catherine of Siena (HL, p. 13). But Edith herself would also surely qualify to take her place among them and indeed has already done so: she has been named co-patroness of Europe together with Bridget and Catherine.[33] Her whole life is an eloquent commentary on this priestly prayer of Jesus and a profound insight into its deepest meaning.

Carmel and the priestly prayer

As such a person of prayer, Edith forms part of a long Carmelite tradition nourished and inspired by the priestly prayer of Jesus. Teresa of Avila returns to it when she describes the highest form of the mystical life in the seventh or innermost mansions. She calls this prayer of Jesus a mirror in which the soul on the peaks can see its own reflection, while she complains that through our own fault 'we do not see ourselves in this mirror that we contemplate, where our image is engraved' (IC VII:2:8). We know that on his journeys John of the Cross constantly repeated, quietly and with great devotion, this same priestly prayer of Jesus.[34] John was at a loss for words to explain the mystery of final transforming union, even allowing for the lines of his incomparable lyric poetry: 'the breathing of the air…/in the serene night, with a flame that is consuming and painless' (SC, stanza 39). For him, only the words of the priestly prayer could express the deepest action of God in prayer. 'No knowledge or power can describe how this happens' (SC 39:5), he says; and, by way of explanation, he simply quotes from the priestly prayer (Jn 17:20-24) and concludes: *The glory which you have given me I have given them that they may be one as we are one, I in them and you in me*' (SC 39:5; cf. Jn 17:22-23).

The abiding fascination of this same prayer of Jesus is also evident in two more recent Carmelites. Elizabeth of the Trinity, with her profound insights into the mystery of the indwelling presence of God, highlights her own slant on Carmelite spirituality by recalling practically every verse of the priestly prayer, throughout her writings, even some verses again and again (Jn 17:4.13.21). It is her inspiration for a life of prayer, as she explains in the spiritual treatise bequeathed to her sister. Recalling 'Christ's last wish, His supreme prayer before returning to His Father', she opens with the words: '"Father, I will that where I am they also whom You have given Me may be with Me"… He wills that where He is we should be also, not only for eternity, but already in time' (HF 1; cf. Jn 17:24). In the final pages of *Story of a Soul*, Thérèse of Lisieux, just before her death, speaks of the all-embracing intercessory power of this priestly prayer: 'I dare to borrow the words You addressed to the heavenly Father, the last night which saw You on our earth,' she writes. '…I do not know when my exile will be ended… but for me will finally come *the last night*' (SS, pp. 254-5). At that moment, she chooses to speak to God in the words of the priestly prayer, which she repeats at great length, verse by verse. It is like her dying gasp, a prelude to her prayer of intercession for others throughout eternity.

A sacrifice of atonement

Edith saw her own life as a 'sacrifice of atonement' (SP, p. 305).[35] But the phrase takes on a significance for her far beyond the sacrificial action of the Jewish high priest on the Day of Atonement (cf. Lv 16). The term 'atonement' means 'reconciliation' – that is, 'at-one-ment'.[36] It does not refer only to *prayer* of intercession: it also involves *sacrifice*. The priestly prayer of Jesus is a great prayer of intercession, but right at the heart of it – or, we might say, at the crucial turning point in the prayer – Jesus speaks in equivalent terms of his own sacrificial self-offering: 'For their sake do I sanctify myself' (Jn 17:19). Here, 'to sanctify' (*hagiazein*), which designates in the Greek 'to take something out of profane usage and to hand it over to God', also takes on a *sacrificial import* (cf. Dt 15:19-21).[37] Jesus is here interceding, handing himself over to his Father as a sacrificial victim. As the Old Testament high priest interceded for himself, his household and the whole community of Israel, so too Jesus prays for these three concerns: for himself – 'Father... glorify your Son...' (cf. Jn 17:1-5); for his disciples – 'those whom you [Father] have given me...' (cf. Jn 17:6-19); and for the wider community of the Church – 'those who believe in me through [the disciples'] word...' (cf. Jn 17:20-26). The gradual expanding movement of Jesus' prayer ultimately extends to embrace the whole world.[38]

But the parallel with the high priest in the Old Testament ritual of atonement goes even further. Once a year, he entered the Holy of Holies, the inner sanctuary behind the veil, to stand before the presence of God; there, he offered sacrifice, interceding for the sins of the people. In his priestly prayer, Jesus is striding across the threshold of eternity in anticipation of his return to the Father through his passion-resurrection. It is the sacrificial movement of redemption for sin enacted in prayer. The priestly prayer of Jesus lays bare the spontaneous and free surrender of Jesus to his Father in his passion, as he had previously explained it to his disciples: 'For this reason the Father loves me, because I lay down my life in order that I may take it up again... I lay it down of my own accord... This command I have received from my Father' (Jn 10:17-18). The return of Jesus to his Father makes possible an 'at-one-ment' of Jesus with all believers: 'that they may be one, even as we are one, I in them' (Jn 17:22-23).

Jesus now stands before the face of God as the great mediator or priest, that is, 'pontifex' or 'bridge-builder' (from *pons*, 'bridge' and *facere*, 'to make'). He builds a bridge of reconciliation between God and his people, interceding for all believers, carrying them in his heart and presenting them before the throne of God.

Standing before God for others
The life of Edith Stein is like a modern re-enactment of this priestly prayer in our own times. Long before she entered Carmel, she already felt called to make of her own life a 'holocaust': 'After every encounter in which I am made aware how powerless we are to exercise direct influence, I have a deeper sense of the urgency of my own *holocaustum*' (SP, p. 60). The 'holocaust' or 'burnt offering' was the specific type of sacrifice described in *Leviticus* (1:1-17; 6:8-13), by which the victim was wholly consumed by fire; it is the offering associated with the Day of Atonement (Lv 16), so special to Edith who was born on that feast. Now, on Passion Sunday, March 26th, 1939, having recently moved to the Carmel of Echt, she made her formal self-offering: 'Dear Mother: please, will [Your Reverence] allow me to offer myself to the heart of Jesus as a sacrifice of atonement' (SP, p. 305).[39] Later in the same year, on June 9th, she wrote her will in which she repeated her offering: 'I joyfully accept the death which God has destined for me in complete submission to his most holy will... in atonement...'[40] There is no doubt who Edith's model was: Jesus, she writes, went to his death out of obedience to his Father (cf. HL, pp. 94-5). It is this free and spontaneous offering of herself that gave value to Edith's sacrifice as it did to the sacrifice of Jesus' life right from its beginning: 'Lo, I

have come to do your will' (Hb 10:9) – and to the very end: 'Not my will but yours be done' (Mk 14:36). As Edith expresses it: 'Thus the road from Bethlehem leads irresistibly to Golgotha, from the manger to the cross' (MC, p. 22).

But Edith's sacrifice of atonement was of necessity an act of intercession – like the entreaties of Jesus in his priestly prayer, or the pleading of Esther called by God to represent her people before the king. Edith identifies herself with this Old Testament queen: 'I keep having to think of Queen Esther,' she says, 'who was taken from among her people precisely that she might represent them before the king' (SP, p. 291).[41] Edith, like Esther, would step into the presence of her king; and, like Esther, she would stand before him for her people. But we might also say that she represented her people like Moses who 'carried them in his bosom' (cf. Nb 11:12). Just as Jesus in his priestly prayer carries all believers in his heart, interceding for them in the presence of the Father, so Edith would hold her people with her in her self-offering, carrying them in her heart. Like Jesus, Edith would 'die for the nation, yet not for the nation only, but to gather into one the scattered children of God' (Jn 11:51) – that is, the whole world.

Edith is explicit that her offering is not only 'in atonement for the unbelief of the Jewish people' – which, as we have seen, does not imply condemnation but is a prayer to hasten the coming of the kingdom.[42] She was, in fact, tormented by the pressing need to 'atone for what is happening to the Jewish people in the name of the people of Germany'. Moreover, she felt that the victims were precisely those who could atone for the sins of the Nazis.[43] But Edith's love was all-embracing. As she wrote in her will, she offered herself also for the concerns of Jesus and Mary; for the Church and the Carmelite Order; 'for the salvation of Germany and world peace'; and 'for my family members, living and dead'. Finally, the concluding words of her self-offering have a distinct ring of the priestly prayer of Jesus, his own last will and testament: she prays 'for all whom God has given me: that not one of them may be lost' (cf. Jn 17:6.12; 18:9).[44]

A spirituality of truth

From her whole background, Edith Stein would seem at first sight to be a most unlikely candidate for sainthood and martyrdom. She was for much of her early life an atheist, later a leading feminist, then a distinguished scholar, prolific writer and accomplished educationalist; she was also a brilliant philosopher, a woman at home in the world of thought, but with an eye ever-open to the signs of the times. However, her lasting legacy lies elsewhere: in her life 'hidden with Christ in God' (Col 3:3). Her special Carmelite contribution may rightly be called a spirituality of truth. We do not need to be philosophers to understand her message, though that may help. A priest once expressed his surprise to Edith that she had not lost her faith through her study of philosophy. 'On the contrary,' she replied, 'I found it.'[45] But the truth that transformed Edith's life was 'God's word and not some human thinking' (1Th 2:13), or more precisely what Paul calls 'the word of the cross' (1Cor 1:18).

Edith discovered truth in the person of a suffering Messiah who said, 'I am the way, the truth and the life' (Jn 14:6). Her great message is the gospel lesson: 'The truth will make you free... So if the Son makes you free, you will be free indeed' (Jn 8:32.36). She knew the truth of her own vulnerability and loved to compare herself to Esther in her weakness: 'I am a very poor and powerless little Esther, but the King who chose me is infinitely great and merciful. That is such a great comfort' (SP, p. 291). This knowledge of her own littleness led Edith to an ever-greater trust in God. Even when writing as a philosopher, she sums up the confidence that sustained her at all times:

> In the knowledge that being holds me, I rest securely.
> This security, however, is not the self-assurance of one

who under her own power stands on firm ground, but rather the sweet and blissful security of a child that is lifted up and carried by a strong arm. And, objectively speaking, this kind of security is not less rational. For if a child were living in the constant fear that its mother might let it fall, we should hardly call this a 'rational' attitude. In my own being, then, I encounter another kind of being that is not mine but that is the support and ground of my own unsupported and groundless being. (FEB, p. 58)

In her search for truth, the Spirit guided Edith inexorably towards the solitude and silence of Carmel, an ideal setting for 'meditating on the Law of the Lord day and night and watching in prayer' (HL, p. 3; cf. *Rule* 10). There she could continue to deepen her spiritual life. There, too, she found the space to keep her eyes of faith open to the light of truth, and to have her sight constantly cleansed by the dark beams of contemplation. Amid all the hectic vicissitudes of the turbulence of life around her, Edith's heart remained always an oasis of silence and prayer where the Spirit could continue to guide her ever more deeply into the truth of the cross. In this, she extends Carmel's message beyond the confines of the cloister, to embrace all who are in search of a life of prayer in our hectic modern world.

A candle still burning

Edith's prophetic mission as a teacher of prayer also derives from a mind and heart steeped in her rich Jewish tradition and its scriptures. Her writings continue to remind us that 'the New Testament cannot be fully understood except in the light of the Old Testament'[46] and to reaffirm the vigorous spiritual ties that unite the church of Christ to the Jewish people. 'You don't know what it means to me when I come into the chapel in the morning,' Edith said one day to a priest, 'and, looking at the tabernacle and the picture of

Mary, say to myself: they were of our blood.'[47]

Edith was noble in the face of death – proud, to the end, to be Jewish, German and Catholic. Obliged to wear the yellow star of David as a badge of ignominy, she carried it with dignity. A woman of prayer, she never felt the need to abandon her Jewish heritage but rediscovered it in greater depth: 'All authentic prayer is prayer of the church,' she said. And: 'The prayer of the church is the prayer of the ever-living Christ. Its prototype is Christ's prayer during his human life... The Gospels tell us that Christ prayed the way a devout Jew faithful to the law prayed' (HL, pp. 15.7). Edith – through her example and her writings – may have done much to silence what has been called 'the teaching of contempt'[48] for the Jewish people. In our day, the notion of 'deicide' or 'killers of Jesus' has – hopefully – been finally laid to rest and irrevocably consigned to history. Witness, for example, the recent Roman document, *We Remember: A Reflection on the Shoah*, which the writings of Edith so eloquently anticipated, in its acknowledging that 'the Jews are our dearly beloved brothers' (cf. HL, pp. 132-3).[49]

Edith Stein acknowledged the transforming power of her early Jewish faith. How ironic it would be if her search for truth and her gift to the Church as a canonised saint should fuel misunderstanding and controversy today.[50] Her official declaration as a saint and martyr[51] is the Church's celebration of a life, wonderful and humbling in a quest which plunged her ever more deeply into truth and which reached its high point with her sharing as a martyr in the mystery of Christ's cross. Her voice still echoes, '*Ave Crux, spes unica!*' – 'Hail, Cross, our only hope!'[52]

Notes

1   Waltraud Herbstrith, OCD, *Edith Stein: A Biography*, San Francisco: Ignatius Press, 1992, p. 187.

2   The *Book of Esther*, in particular the pleading of Esther for the lives of her people, is the first reading for the liturgy of the Mass on Edith's feastday, August 9th, in the Carmelite missal.

3   This passage from *John* is contained in the gospel reading for the liturgy of the Mass on Edith's feastday.

4   Examples in the Old Testament abound: 2Kgs 19:30-31; Is 10:20-22; 37:4.31-32; Mic 2:12; cf. 1Kgs 19:18; 2Kgs 25:12; Is 4:2-3; Zeph 3:12-13.

5   Sister Teresia de Spiritu Sancto [Posselt], OCD, *Edith Stein*, London & New York: Sheed & Ward, 1952, p. 9.

6   Waltraud Herbstrith, OCD, 'Edith Stein and Christian-Jewish Dialogue', in Waltraud Herbstrith, OCD (ed.), *Never Forget: Christian and Jewish Perspectives on Edith Stein*, Washington, DC: ICS Publications, 1998, p. 82.

7   Herbstrith, *Edith Stein, op. cit.*, p. 187.

8   Posselt, *op. cit.*, p. 188.

9   *Ibid.*, p. 59.

10   Romaeus Leuven, OCD, *Heil im Unheil: Das Leben Edith Steins – Reife und Vollendung*, Druten: De Maas & Waler/Freiburg, Basle & Vienna: Herder, 1983, p. 148.

11   *Ibid.*, pp. 148-9.

12   On Teresa's lineage, see Teófanes Egido, OCD, 'The Historical Setting of St Teresa's Life', *Carmelite Studies*, vol. I, Washington, DC: ICS Publications, 1980, pp. 122-82 (see especially pp. 132-49); on John, see Hardy, *op. cit.*, p. 3.

13   See SP, p. 272: 'All who seek truth seek God, whether this is clear to them or not.'

14   See John of the Cross: 'if anyone is seeking God, the Beloved is seeking that person much more' (LF 3:28); and Elizabeth of the Trinity: 'when I look back I see a divine pursuit of my soul' (L 151).

15   Posselt, *op. cit.*, p. 64.

16   McCormack, *op. cit.*, p. 14.

17   Edith insisted that Teresa was the reformer rather than the founder of Carmel: see ch. I, note 4.

18   Posselt, *op. cit.*, p. 64.

19   See Kurt Hruby, 'The Torah', in Edward Malatesta, SJ (ed.), *The Spirituality of Judaism*, Wheathampstead: Anthony Clarke, 1977, pp. 59-67.

20   Edith's writings are permeated by both the Old and New Testament: see Francisco Javier Sancho Fermín, OCD, *La Biblia con ojos de mujer: Edith Stein y la Sagrada Escritura*, Burgos: Editorial Monte Carmelo, 2001.

21   On Elijah in the Carmelite tradition, see the author's *The Carmelite Charism*, *op. cit.*, pp. 38-59; Jane Ackerman, *Elijah: Prophet of Carmel*, Washington, DC: ICS Publications, 2003; *Mount Carmel*, vol. 51/3, 2003, an issue devoted entirely to the many aspects of Elijah's story in relation to the Carmelite charism. For a treatment of Elijah in the writings of Edith Stein, see Joanne Mosley, *Edith Stein — Woman of Prayer: Her Life and Ideals*, Leominster: Gracewing, 2004, pp. 113-20.

22   The title of a poem by Patrick Kavanagh.

23   Posselt, *op. cit.*, p. 59.

24   Edith's specific vocation to carry the cross can be dated in a special way to April 6th, 1933 when, in prayerful communion with Jesus, she offered to carry the cross (SEL, p. 17). See also four essays which she wrote in Cologne and Echt, relating the Carmelite vocation to the cross: HL, pp. 91-104.

25   During Edith's interview in Cologne, when it was suggested that she could still accomplish so much in the world, she replied, 'It is not human activity that can help us, but the sufferings of Christ. To have a share in them is what I long for.': see Maria-Baptista a Spiritu Sancto [Pohl], OCD, *Edith Stein, Schwester Teresia Benedicta a Cruce: Kleines Lebensbild der grossen Philosophin und Karmelitin*, Cologne Carmel, 1962, p. 66.

26   Leuven, *op. cit.*, p. 128.

27   Herbstrith, *Edith Stein*, *op. cit.*, p. 180.

28   Elisabeth Prégardier & Anne Mohr, *Passion im August (2.-9. August 1942): Edith Stein und Gefährtinnen — Weg in Tod und Auferstehung*, Annweiler: Plöger, 1995, p. 52.

29   Account from the Dutch official, Wielek, quoted in Herbstrith, *Edith Stein*, *op. cit.*, p. 186. For two other eyewitness accounts, those of P O van Kempen and Pierre Cuypers who visited Edith in the camp, see Herbstrith (ed.), *Never Forget*, *op. cit.*, pp. 272-8.

30   Translation by Edith's niece, Susanne Batzdorff, in SEL, p. 93.

31   For the significance of the ritual of the Day of Atonement by way of background for a better understanding of the journey of Jesus to his Father through his passion-resurrection in John's gospel, see the

author's *The House with Many Rooms: The Temple Theme of Jn. 14,2-3*, Rome: Editrice Pontificio Istituto Biblico (*Analecta Biblica* 114), 1988, pp. 81.88.208. See also, in relation to *Hebrews*, Albert Vanhoye, SJ, *Our Priest is Christ: The Doctrine of the Epistle to the Hebrews*, Rome: Editrice Pontificio Istituto Biblico, 1977 and his 'Par la tente plus grande et plus parfaite...He 9,11', *Biblica*, vol. 46, 1965, pp. 1-27.

32   See ch. 3, note 10, with reference to the circumincession of the three Persons in Rublëv's icon of the Trinity.

33   This title was given on October 1st, 1999; see the Apostolic Letter of John Paul II, *Spes aedificandi*, of the same date (especially #8-11).

34   See Ruiz Salvador, *op. cit.*, p. 82.

35   See note 39.

36   For a discussion of the meaning of atonement in relation to Edith Stein, see Mosley, *Edith Stein, op. cit.*, pp. 50-2. For Edith's description of the sacrifices of the Day of Atonement as an act of reconciliation, see HL, pp. 97-8.

37   See the author's *The House with Many Rooms, op. cit.*, pp. 233-4, also note 45. 'The work of the Lord [in sanctifying or consecrating himself] is here presented under the aspect of absolute self-sacrifice.': see Westcott, *op. cit.*, p. 245.

38   See the author's *Prayer – The Heart of the Gospels*, Oxford: Teresian Press, 1985, pp. 83-107.

39   The standard translation is 'sacrifice of propitiation' but the German means, equally, 'sacrifice of atonement'.

40   Leuven, *op. cit.*, p. 148.

41 · For a discussion of Esther's intercession in relation to Edith Stein, see Mosley, *Edith Stein, op. cit.*, pp. 96-111.

42   See above, section 'A special vocation'.

43   See Herbstrith, *Edith Stein, op. cit.*, p. 194.

44   For the text of the self-offering in Edith's will, see Leuven, *op. cit.*, pp. 148-9; an English translation can be found in Mosley, *Edith Stein, op. cit.*, p. 46.

45   See Joachim Feldes, *Edith Stein und Schifferstadt*, Schifferstadt: Geier-Druck-Verlag, 1998, p. 46.

46   Pontifical Biblical Commission, *The Jewish People, op. cit.* #21, p. 49.

47   Johannes Hirschmann, SJ, 'Schwester Teresia Benedicta vom heiligen Kreuz', in Waltraud Herbstrith, OCD (ed.), *Edith Stein: Ein Lebensbild in Zeugnissen und Selbstzeugnissen*, Mainz: Matthias-Grünewald-Verlag (Topos Taschenbücher), 1998, p. 134.

48 A term coined by the French Jewish historian, Jules Isaac, to describe the overall effect of Patristic polemics against Jews and Judaism: see Eugene J Fisher, 'Introduction', in Eugene J Fisher (ed.), *Catholic Jewish Relations: Documents from the Holy See*, London: Catholic Truth Society, 1999, p. 5, also note 3.

49 For the full text of this document, see Vatican Commission for Religious Relations with the Jews, *We Remember: A Reflection on the Shoah*, March 16th, 1998, in Fisher (ed.), *op. cit.*, pp. 58-72; the text quoted is on p. 70.

50 There have been several recent contributions on the issues surrounding the beatification and canonisation of Edith Stein, in the light of Catholic and Jewish perspectives. See Harry James Cargas (ed.), *The Unnecessary Problem of Edith Stein*, Lanham, New York & London: University Press of America (Studies in the Shoah, vol. IV), 1994; Herbstrith (ed.), *Never Forget, op. cit.*, pp. 3-196; Susanne M Batzdorff, *Aunt Edith: The Jewish Heritage of a Catholic Saint*, Springfield, IL: Templegate, 1998, pp. 196-211 and her 'Catholics and Jews: Can We Bridge the Abyss?', in SEL, pp. 115-8; Freda Mary Oben, *The Life and Thought of St. Edith Stein*, New York: Alba House, 2001, pp. 121-52; Sarah Borden, *Edith Stein*, London & New York: Continuum, 2003, pp. 135-43; María Ruiz Scaperlanda, *Edith Stein: St. Teresa Benedicta of the Cross*, Huntington, IN: Our Sunday Visitor, 2001, pp. 163-76.

51 Remarkably, Edith was beatified because of both heroic virtue and martyrdom. 'On January 25, 1987, in the presence of the Holy Father, the Decree confirming the *heroic degree of the virtues*, as well as the *martyrdom* of Sr Teresa Benedicta, was read – an event without precedent in the centuries-old history of the Congregation.': see Ambrose Eszer, OP, 'Edith Stein, Jewish Catholic Martyr', in *Carmelite Studies*, vol. 4, *op. cit.*, p. 314.

52 The subtitle of her 'Elevation of the Cross' (September 14th, 1939), in HL, pp. 94-6. She wrote these words again, a few months before her death, in a letter to her prioress: 'A *scientia crucis*...can be gained only when one comes to feel the Cross radically. I have been convinced of that from the first moment and have said, from my heart: *Ave, Crux, spes unica!*' (SP, p. 341).

CHAPTER FIVE

THÉRÈSE OF LISIEUX: JOURNEYING INTO WEAKNESS

Vatican II anticipated

Thérèse of Lisieux died at the age of twenty-four. One might readily be forgiven for expecting to find little in her writings to better our understanding of the scriptures. Moreover, she was brought up in a narrow and rigid family environment and was not particularly well-educated. She was hidden for nine years in an enclosed Carmelite convent, practically unrecognised – even within her own community. She died unknown to the world at large. The milieu in which she lived would appear to be one of intellectual poverty. There had not yet been a Vatican II to restore the word of God to its rightful place at the heart of the Christian life. In her day, the people of God were ill-prepared for the new and challenging insights of our modern approaches to the scriptures.[1] Biblical renewal had hardly begun in earnest. So, we may well ask: has Thérèse anything significant to tell us about the word of God? In fact, her teaching in many ways anticipates some of the richest insights of Vatican II – it explains, deepens, expands and develops them. Both her life and her writings can help us understand better the Council's teaching on the scriptures.

On her deathbed, Thérèse could say, 'Yes, it seems to me I never sought anything but the truth' (LC, p. 205). It is hardly surprising, then, that the Holy Spirit drew Thérèse, in this quest, to the truth of the gospels. Long before Vatican II, she was to discover for herself this lesson of the Council: 'It is common knowledge that among all the Scriptures, even those of the New Testament, the Gospels have a special pre-eminence'.[2] For her, too, the gospels were, in the words of the Council, 'the principal witness of the life and teaching of the incarnate Word, our Saviour'.[3] She once wrote: 'as yet I had not discovered the treasures hidden in the Gospels' (SS, p. 102); but later she could say: 'I have only to cast a glance in the Gospels and immediately I breathe in the perfumes of Jesus' life' (SS, p. 258). Only the gospels could satisfy her fully. She was always discovering in them 'new lights, hidden and mysterious meanings' (SS, p. 179). One sentence says it all: 'with the exception of the Gospels, I no longer find anything in books. The Gospels are enough' (LC, p. 44). It is little wonder that she cries out: 'Show me the secrets hidden in the Gospel./Ah! that golden book/Is my dearest treasure' (PN 24, stanza 12).

Thérèse was also to discover for herself, as the Council expresses it, 'the true word of God in the books of the Old Testament'.[4] She wrote deeply and movingly of God's mercy and justice. She would not have needed the Council's reminder that the Old Testament reveals 'the ways in which God, just and merciful, deals with people'.[5] It was in the Old Testament that she found reassurance for the truth of her 'little doctrine' (SS, p. 189): 'Whoever is a little one, let him come to me [Pr 9:4]... For to him that is little, mercy will be shown [Wis 6:7]... God shall feed his flock like a shepherd; he shall gather together the lambs with his arm, and shall take them up in his bosom [Is 40:11]... As one whom a mother caresses, so will I comfort you; you shall be carried at the breasts and upon the knees they will caress you [Is 66:13.12]' (SS, p. 188; cf. p. 208). Vatican II stresses the perennial value of the Old Testament, reminding us that 'these books, therefore, written under divine inspiration, remain permanently valuable' and that 'Christians should receive them with reverence'.[6] Thérèse did revere them: 'So speaks the Holy Spirit,' she says, 'through the mouth of Solomon'

(SS, p. 188); and she writes a few lines later: 'this same prophet [Isaiah] whose gaze was already plunged into the eternal depths cried out in the Lord's name' (SS, p. 188).

Thérèse the reader

When Thérèse read scripture, she had an eye to detail. She mentions Jesus' '*look of love*' which pierces into the heart of the rich young man (LT 247; cf. Mk 10:21). She draws attention to the '*pillow*' on which Jesus rests his head during the storm at sea, this time observing explicitly: 'The Gospel gives us this detail' (LT 144; cf. Mk 4:38). She reminds us that Jesus, at prayer, gave thanks 'in a transport of joy' to the Father (SS, p. 209; cf. Lk 10:21). Even the presence of Tobias' dog will not escape her observant eye (LT 18a; cf. Tb 11:4). Such minute attention to detail is indeed striking.

We might readily conclude that Thérèse had lots of time for study of the Bible. Nothing could be farther from the truth. For reading, she had at her disposal half an hour each day, a little longer perhaps on special days.[7] But pressure of work, and her duties with the novices, rarely left her free. Still, she copied and compared, repeated and memorised, meditated and lived the word of God. So close was her intimacy with it that she *became* a 'Word of God'.[8] Many of us today lead busy, tense and often chaotic lives. Thérèse challenges us to plunge ourselves into scripture, however little time we have, however great the pressure. She is an example and inspiration for all of us.

But Thérèse did not just *read* the Bible. She also anticipates the lesson of Vatican II: 'prayer should accompany the reading of sacred Scripture'.[9] And so she writes, 'it is especially the *Gospels* that sustain me during my hours of prayer' (SS, p. 179). The discovery of truth in the word of God, however, did not always come easily to Thérèse. Speaking of the scriptures, she explains: 'this *vast field* seems to us to be a desert, arid and without water... We *know no longer* where *we are*; instead of peace and light, we find only turmoil or at least darkness'

(LT 165). Still, she persevered. Even the arid word was a word of life.

Open to new insights

At first sight, it might appear that Thérèse was anti-intellectual in her approach to reading. A casual remark to her sister Céline is often quoted. When they were one day standing in front of a library, Thérèse exclaimed gaily: 'Oh! I would have been sorry to have read all those books!' Céline asked why. She could understand regretting having to read them, but not already having read them. Thérèse explained: 'If I had read them, I would have broken my head, and I would have wasted precious time that I could have employed very simply in loving God' (LC, p. 261). However light-hearted the tone, the point is a serious one. For, as Thérèse wrote to a missionary priest shortly before her death: 'At times, when I am reading certain spiritual treatises in which perfection is shown through a thousand obstacles, surrounded by a crowd of illusions, my poor little mind quickly tires; I close the learned book that is breaking my head and drying up my heart, and I take up Holy Scripture' (LT 226). But her priority of loving God does not mean abdicating the intellect.

Vatican II has reaffirmed the importance of the study of biblical languages: 'the Church with maternal concern sees to it that suitable and correct translations are made into different languages, especially from the original texts of the sacred books.'[10] The mature Thérèse would have embraced this teaching: 'Had I been a priest, I would have learned Hebrew and Greek,' she said wistfully, 'and wouldn't have been satisfied with Latin. In this way, I would have known the real text dictated by the Holy Spirit' (LC, p. 132). She chose carefully between this or that translation and confessed that she was 'sad to see so many different translations' (LC, p. 132). She felt a need to know the exact meaning of the original biblical terms. We know that Thérèse tried to harmonise the resurrection texts of all four gospels.[11] We have to admire the seriousness of her work. It was a minute, careful and painstaking task. In her day, making a gospel harmony – which today we know to be quite impossible – was common practice among biblical experts; even her own novice would later put together a harmony of the gospels.[12] Thérèse's attempt shows that she was open to the scholarly approach and prepared to try it herself.

To the heart of the gospels[13]

Thérèse seems to have discovered for herself that each evangelist has his own particular slant in his portrait of Jesus. Mark's Jesus is the Suffering Messiah – weak, rejected and misunderstood even by his own disciples. Generally speaking, we are closer in *Mark* to the historical Jesus than in any of the other gospels. Thérèse focuses repeatedly on his scene of Jesus with the disciples in the storm-tossed boat (Mk 4:35-41).[14] Here, she finds a Jesus after her own heart who fully accepts the human condition. He is weak, tired and eminently human. But Thérèse will also interpret the scene with her own original touch: 'Living on Love, when Jesus is sleeping,/Is rest on stormy seas./Oh! Lord, don't fear that I'll wake you./I'm waiting in peace for Heaven's shore' (PN 17, stanza 9). She will not disturb him. He can sleep on and take his rest until eternity dawns. She decides he will get weary of waiting for her before she grows tired of waiting for him.

One small incident helps us to see how Thérèse penetrates to the core of Jesus' message in *Matthew* also. A few weeks before she died, she asked her sister to read the Sunday gospel for her. 'I didn't have the missal,' comments Pauline, 'and told her simply: "It's the Gospel where Our Lord warns us against serving two masters." Then, imitating the voice of a little child reciting her lesson by heart, she said it from memory from beginning to end' (LC, pp. 188-9). A significant warning runs through the passage like a refrain: 'Do not be anxious about your life... do not be anxious about tomorrow, let tomorrow take care of itself' (Mt 6:25.34). It contains the kernel of her 'Little Way' of surrender and confidence.

Luke, in turn, is the gospel of God's mercy. His Jesus is the compassionate and merciful Saviour, with the message that 'repentance and forgiveness of sins should be preached in his name to all nations' (Lk 24:47). Thérèse echoes the central message of his gospel: 'I don't hasten to the first place but to the last; rather than advance like the Pharisee, I repeat, filled with confidence, the publican's humble prayer. Most of all I imitate the conduct of Madgalene; her astonishing or rather her loving audacity which charms the Heart of Jesus also attracts my own... I know how much He loves the prodigal child who returns to Him' (SS, pp. 258-9). All these gospel characters are found in *Luke*. The first words of Thérèse's life story express admirably the purpose of his gospel: 'I shall begin to sing what I must sing eternally: "*The Mercies of the Lord*"' (SS, p. 13; cf. p. 205).

So, too, Thérèse pierces straight to the heart of John's gospel: 'It seems to me that the *word* of Jesus is *Himself*... He, *Jesus*, the *Word*, the *Word* of *God!*' Then she reminds us how 'Jesus teaches us that He is the way, the *truth*, the life' (LT 165). This is John's special slant on the mystery of Jesus. He is the Word: the revelation in person of the Father, 'full of grace and truth' (Jn 1:14) – that is, full of God's enduring and merciful love. This is the love to which Thérèse offers herself as a victim of holocaust, 'until the shadows having disappeared I may be able to tell You of my *Love* in an *Eternal Face to Face!*' (SS, p. 277).

A free and easy approach

In her approach to the Bible, Thérèse is uninhibited. She will not hesitate to fuse texts, even from different gospels. She asks a question in the words of *John*, 'Master, where do you live?', and replies with a variation of *Luke*: 'I [Jesus] have no place to rest my head' (LT 137; cf. Jn 1:38; Lk 9:58). She recalls the words of the fourth gospel, 'Lift up your eyes and see how the fields are already white enough to be harvested', but then continues in the words of

Matthew: 'the harvest is abundant but the number of laborers is small' (LT 135; cf. Jn 4:35; Mt 9:37).

Thérèse does not hesitate to interpret the silences of the gospels. When Jesus speaks of 'things' that 'are hidden from the wise and prudent and revealed to little ones' (Mt 11:25), he does not tell us what they are. Thérèse tells us: they are 'the *things* of His *love*' (SS, p. 105). She will even change the words of Jesus himself. 'You will find rest for your souls' (Mt 11:28), he says; and Thérèse interprets: 'you will find rest for your *little* souls' (LC, p. 44). Again, Jesus gives no indication of who will 'sit at my right or at my left' in the kingdom (Mt 20:23). For Thérèse, these places are 'reserved to little children' (LC, p. 215). She recalls the priestly prayer of *John* 17 at length, skips over some verses and inverts the order of others (cf. SS, pp. 255-7). Most of all, she makes this prayer of Jesus her own: 'I dare to borrow the words You addressed to the heavenly Father' (SS, p. 254). We could also take her great discovery in reading *1 Corinthians* 13: that 'the Church *had a Heart*' (SS, p. 194). In fact, Paul does not here use the word 'heart'. It is Thérèse who infers it from his context. She adds to the text without betraying it.

Her superior spoke of Thérèse as of one 'whose head is filled with tricks... a *comedienne*... She can... make you split your sides with laughter' (LC, p. 16). This sense of humour saved Thérèse from taking herself too seriously, even in her approach to the scriptures. 'It is a curious thing,' she said, 'when I open the Gospels, I nearly always come across the phrase "little children".' Then she added, tongue in cheek: 'Unless it's..."brood of vipers"!'[15] Even on her deathbed, she read the story of the Good Samaritan with a touch of humour: 'I'm like this "half-dead" traveller,' she said: 'half-dead, half-alive' (LC, p. 174). At times, she was conscious of even shocking those around her with her daring, with her free and easy approach.

In and with the Church
Thérèse felt that she was fully in tune with the voice of the Church. She also, in the spirit of Teresa of Avila, read the scriptures as a true

daughter of the Church. Likewise, Thérèse willingly submitted her insights to the scrutiny of Church representatives, as she wanted to be one in mind and heart with the community of believers in everything. When she wrote her *Act of Oblation to Merciful Love*, she asked her prioress to have it checked by a theologian. He approved everything except for one word. She had written of her 'infinite' desires; he changed it to 'immense'. Thérèse accepted. Her offering had been approved – officially. She was at peace. She was living the word of God in communion with the praying Church, in the heart of the Church and at the service of the Church – the whole Church.

The 'Little Way' itself, like the scriptures, was born in response to particular needs and problems. It sprang from Thérèse's lived experience in the day-to-day struggle of faith. Like the early Christian community, Thérèse read the scriptures in the light of her own experience. Before taking up her pen to write *Story of a Soul*, she knelt in prayer at the foot of Mary's statue and 'opening the Holy Gospels,' she said, 'my eyes fell on these words: "And going up a mountain, he called to him men of his *own choosing*, and they came to him" [Mk 3:3]. This is the mystery of my vocation, my whole life' (SS, p. 13). It is scripture that would give her the key to this unfolding mystery.

Thérèse's vocation to pray for sinners developed gradually. It was confirmed at the age of fourteen and a half at the time of the Pranzini affair – a notorious criminal for whom she prayed earnestly and who repented on the scaffold. She writes: 'The cry of Jesus on the Cross sounded continually in my heart: "*I thirst!*".' (cf. Jn 19:28). Thérèse then comments: 'These words ignited within me an unknown and very living fire' (SS, p. 99). She pleaded in vain with Pope Leo XIII for permission to enter Carmel at fifteen. She later recorded her feelings: 'filled with confidence, for the Gospel of the day contained these beautiful words: "Fear not, little flock, for it is your Father's good pleasure to give you the kingdom"' (SS, p. 133; cf. Lk 12:32). Half a year later, she was a Carmelite.

Later, in Carmel, the word of God would continue to answer to her deepest needs. Totally unaware of Thérèse's troubled state of mind, the saintly Mother Geneviève reminded her of the words of Paul, *'Our God is a God of peace'* (1Cor 14:33; SS, p. 169), which diminished her anguish. Thérèse was deeply affected by her father's mental illness and in this Gethsemane experience found special meaning in the song of Isaiah's Suffering Servant, 'We esteemed him stricken, smitten by God, and afflicted' (Is 53:4).

Thérèse's greatest spiritual discovery – her legacy to the Church – began in painful questioning that only scripture could resolve. She was tormented by the problem of how a 'little' person like herself could reach the heights of sanctity. She found the solution in the words of Isaiah, *'you shall be carried at the breasts'* (Is 66:12; SS, pp. 188.208). Later, in her overriding desire to share every vocation, she read Paul's hymn to love (1Cor 13). With it, she found her true place in the Church, having discovered in that moment that this vocation would embrace all the others: 'MY VOCATION IS LOVE!' (SS, p. 194), she exclaimed.

Words of love

As Christians privileged to live in the wake of Vatican II, we are blessed with the incomparable fruits of recent biblical research. Not so Thérèse. She was not aware of the textual composition of the biblical books, the so-called literary forms, the 'synoptic question', the theories of inspiration.[16] Rarely, if ever, did she have direct access to a complete copy of the Bible.[17] Many of her favourite scripture texts were only discovered at second hand, mostly from spiritual books such as *The Imitation of Christ*, the writings of John of the Cross, or the little black leather notebook in which Céline had copied out scriptural passages before entering Carmel.[18] Today, works on the Bible can help us enormously to discover, read and assimilate the scriptures better. We should accept these admirable helps in the spirit of Thérèse: with openness, enthusiasm and gratitude. But they are of little value unless we are resolved to listen to the word of God like Thérèse: with the heart of a child, surrendered to the movements of the Spirit. The charism of Thérèse may be expressed in these words of Vatican II: 'the nourishment of the Scriptures for the people of God, thereby enlightening their minds, strengthening their wills, and setting hearts on fire with the love of God'.[19] At the top of one of her poems, Thérèse jotted down some words which our Lord addressed to St Gertrude. They speak reams about Thérèse's approach to the scriptures:

> My daughter, seek those words of mine which most exude love. Write them down, and then, keeping them preciously like relics, take care to reread them often. When a friend wishes to reawaken the original vigour of his affection in the heart of his friend, he tells him: 'Remember what you felt in your heart when I said such and such a word,' or 'Do you remember your feelings at such a time, on such a day, in such a place?'... Be assured then that the most precious relics of mine on earth are my words of love, the words which have come from my most sweet Heart.[20]

In this passage, we can hear again the voice of God through the prophet Hosea: 'I will speak tenderly to her heart... she will answer as in the days of her youth' (Hos 2:14-15). For Thérèse, the word of God comes straight from the heart of God. It is a word of love, calling for a response of love. She was to learn this lesson early on in life. She was only fourteen when she developed what she calls 'an extreme desire for learning' (SS, p. 101). Her mind expanded and her thirst for knowledge grew, she tells us. But already she had discovered that the deeper knowledge of God's word could come only through love. It was a crucial moment in her spiritual growth. God spoke to her through the prophet Ezekiel: 'Behold, you were at the age for love' (Ez 16:8; cf. SS, p. 101).

Love must take priority. The scriptures are not just an intellectual exercise. Thérèse echoes the important lesson of the Council: 'in the sacred books, the Father who is in heaven meets His children with great love and speaks with them'.[21] She reaffirms with her life that 'the force and power in the word of God is so great that it remains the support and energy of the Church, the strength of faith for her children, the food of the soul, the pure and perennial source of spiritual life'.[22] It is the scriptures that have been canonised in the life of Thérèse.[23]

Jesus, 'my only love'[24]

The experience of her weakness drove Thérèse to the gospels. She had a tremendous need for love. 'The Spirit of Love sets me aflame with his fire,' she says in one of her poems; 'I want to be set on fire with his Love' (PN 17, stanzas 2.15). She must find someone to love who is weak, frail and vulnerable like herself; and, like herself, passionately in need of love. She does. It is Jesus. He is the human face of God. 'The Word became flesh' (Jn 1:14), with all the weakness to which flesh is heir, except sin (Hb 4:15). Jesus sleeps through a storm — which, as we have seen, is one of Thérèse's favourite gospel scenes (Mk 4:35-41); and he stops to rest by Jacob's Well, tired and thirsty (Jn 4:4-42). She needs a God like this: weak, little, needy — quite simply, human. She can walk with this Jesus at her side, even run, for he is a companion and a friend. Jesus is her 'only Friend whom I love' (PN 23, stanza 5).

The Word truly became weakness for Thérèse. She repeats his cry, '*I thirst!*' (SS, p. 99; Jn 19:28). His 'thirst' was a thirst for love, reaching out for love when he said to the Samaritan woman, 'Give me to drink' (Jn 4:7). Thérèse says, 'it was the *love* of His poor creature the Creator of the universe was seeking. He was thirsty for love' (SS, p. 189). At the heart of the fourth gospel, Jesus cries out again for that love: 'If anyone thirsts, let that person come to me and drink' (Jn 7:37). In her poem to the Sacred Heart, the thirst of

Thérèse becomes one with the thirst of the Magdalen. She does not dwell on the symbol of the pierced heart so popular in her day but lingers with the Magdalen, weeping, looking for the one she loves. Thérèse cries out:

'I need a heart burning with tenderness,
Who will be my support forever,
Who loves everything in me, even my weakness...
And who never leaves me day or night.'...
I must have a God who takes on my nature
And becomes my brother and is able to suffer!
(PN 23, stanza 4)

Mercy and justice meet
On the feast of the Trinity, 1895, Thérèse made her celebrated *Act of Oblation to Merciful Love* (Pri 6).[25] But right at the heart of this prayer to God's *mercy*, she also speaks of his *justice*: 'I wish... to be clothed in Your own *Justice*'. She writes that before making her offering, 'I was thinking about the souls who offer themselves as victims of God's Justice in order to turn away the punishments reserved to sinners, drawing them upon themselves' (SS, p. 180). The Baptist speaks of this God of justice with his words, 'Who taught you to flee from the wrath to come?' (Mt 3:7). Here we have a God of vengeance, threatening 'fire and brimstone' – a kind of heavenly Shylock exacting his pound of flesh, even the last drop of blood.

This was not the God Thérèse found reflected in the heart of Jesus. Her God proclaimed himself 'gentle and humble of heart' (Mt 11:29) – another of Thérèse's favourite gospel texts. She knew, as if by intuition, that mercy and justice, in a true biblical sense, do not necessarily exclude or contradict each other but can sit easily side by side. As we read in the *Book of Wisdom*: 'Ever should justice and mercy go hand in hand' (Wis 12:19). They are significant parallels, the one explaining the other. As the psalmist writes:

I have not hidden your *justice* in my heart but declared
your *faithful help*...
  Your *merciful love* and your *truth* will always guard me.
    (Ps 39:11-12)

Here, we might add the words of Isaiah: 'The Lord... exalts himself
to show mercy to you. For the Lord is a God of justice' (Is 30:18).
No wonder Thérèse could cry out: 'To be just is not only to exercise
severity in order to punish the guilty; it is also to recognize right
intentions and to reward virtue. I expect as much from God's justice
as from His mercy. It is because He is just that "He is
compassionate and filled with gentleness, slow to punish, and
abundant in mercy, for He knows our frailty, He remembers we are
only dust. As a father has tenderness for his children, so the Lord
has compassion on us!"' (LT 226; cf. Ps 102:8.14.13).

Thérèse is drawn especially by the unrequited love of God in
which justice and mercy fuse. 'On every side this love is unknown,
rejected,' she writes sadly. 'Is Your disdained Love going to remain
closed up within Your Heart?' (SS, pp. 180-1). Her prayer of
oblation ends with her own painful cry of love to God, asking him
to allow 'the waves of *infinite tenderness* shut up within [him] to
overflow into [her] soul' (SS, p. 277). Mercy and justice fuse for
Thérèse in the 'real tenderness of His infinite Love' (SS, p. 189) –
this is the heart of our God who thirsts, so often in vain, to share
his love with his people.

The weakness of God[26]
Thérèse longed to be ever more identified with the weakness of
Jesus. She expressed it all in one simple aspiration: 'Make me
Resemble you, Jesus!...' (Pri 11). And her prayer was certainly
answered. This deep longing led her inexorably to the passion.[27]
There, she was to plunge ever more deeply into the mystery of love
revealed in human weakness. She recalled that as a young girl, 'The

first [sermon] I *did understand* and which *touched me deeply* was a sermon on the Passion' (SS, p. 42). But she was to discover the passion again later, in a strange and entirely new way – in the face of Jesus.

At first, devotion to the Holy Face had no special appeal for Thérèse. But the discovery of it was to coincide with the mysterious mental illness of her father, who had always radiated for her the beauty of God's love. That experience now gave way to the image of her father as a man of sorrows: 'Until my coming to Carmel, I had never fathomed the depths of the treasures hidden in the Holy Face,' she said (SS, p. 152). It was, however, through the Servant Songs of Isaiah that Thérèse really entered deeply into the mystery of love hidden and revealed in human weakness: 'There was no beauty in him… no comeliness…' (Is 53:2). She confided to Pauline: 'These words of Isaiah…have made the whole foundation of my devotion to the Holy Face, or, to express it better, the foundation of all my piety' (LC, p. 135). Thérèse would continue to contemplate the love of God in her 'gentle and lowly' Saviour, his radiant face now distorted by pain, like a beautiful object reflected on rippling water. In the infirmary where Thérèse lived out her final agony, there was a fresco on the wall representing Jesus in Gethsemane. He surrenders to the pain and suffering; he accepts the sorrow and confusion, the fear and loneliness: 'Abba, Father!…not what I will but what you will' (Mk 14:36). It is all part of the mystery of God's infinite love revealed in human weakness.

Thérèse would not in any way soften the lesson of Isaiah's words and their impact on her life. 'Let us not believe we can love without suffering, without suffering much,' she said (LT 89). Even on her deathbed, she recited phrases from the Servant Songs, making them her own: 'I desired that, like the Face of Jesus, "my face be truly hidden, that no one on earth would know me"' (SS, p. 152; cf. Is 53:3); 'I, too, have desired to be without beauty, alone in treading the winepress, unknown to everyone' (LC, p. 135; cf. Is 53:2; 63:3). In Carmel, Thérèse had chosen a life of prayer and sacrifice 'hidden with Christ in God' (Col 3:3). She had embarked on a way of total self-giving in love and had found her model in the Suffering Servant – forgotten, hidden and unknown. For her, a life of sacrifice meant taking up her cross daily to follow this Jesus. It was love in action.

Thérèse expresses beautifully her desire to remove all the layers of selfishness and to be stripped of everything for love of Jesus in her simple image of 'an unpetalled rose' (PN 51). Naïve, childish, sentimental it may seem to some, even mawkish. But the reality it speaks of for Thérèse is the total and absolute self-giving of her response to love, revealed in what she calls 'the HIDDEN BEAUTIES of Jesus', the Suffering Servant (LT 108). She is never deterred by weakness in her resolve to give everything. She assures us that we do not have to suffer heroically, nor even courageously. Here again, we glimpse something of the originality of Thérèse. The worst kind of suffering, she tells us, is not being able to suffer *well* (cf. LC, p. 152) – though 'well' does not mean 'grandly'. 'What an unspeakable joy to carry our Crosses FEEBLY,' she said (LT 82). 'Let us suffer…without courage!… (Jesus suffered in *sadness!* Without sadness would the soul suffer!…) And still we would like to suffer generously, grandly!… Céline! what an illusion!… We'd never want to fall?… What does it matter, my Jesus, if I fall at each moment; *I see* my weakness through this and this is a great gain for me' (LT 89). Her Jesus cried out in Gethsemane; he 'sweated blood' (Lk 22:44) and 'offered up prayers and supplications, with loud cries and tears' (Hb 5:7). On his way to Calvary, he stumbled and fell – again and again and again.

Grace and truth

Thérèse was also to discover that the Word made weakness was 'full of grace and truth' (Jn 1:14). We know that she regretted not knowing the original biblical languages of Hebrew and Greek (LC, p. 132). So we can only surmise her delight, had she known that the Hebrew word for 'grace' is *hesed*[28] and that it refers to God's saving love, his *merciful* love: 'It is for love of you,' God tells his people, 'and to keep the oath he swore to your fathers that Yahweh brought you out with a mighty hand and redeemed you from the house of slavery' (Dt 7:8). It is God's covenant love, his mercy through and through. In the Old Testament, 'grace' and 'truth' are linked: 'Your merciful love and your truth will always guard me' (Ps 39:12). The Hebrew for 'truth' is *emeth*: it refers to 'truth' as God's 'fidelity' to his covenant love, enduring in spite of the weakness of his people – their sins, their failures, their infidelities. The psalmist expresses it well: 'Indeed, how good is the Lord, eternal his merciful love. He is faithful from age to age' (Ps 99:5). *Hesed* and *emeth* express God's enduring love for his people. Paul's words capture the meaning exactly: 'We may be unfaithful, but he is always faithful for he cannot disown his own self' (2Tm 2:13; cf. Ps 116.135).

But *hesed* is also closely linked to another Hebrew term, *rahamim*, which denotes a mother's love for the child of her womb. The psalmist cries out at the marvels of this love: 'For it was you who created my being, knit me together in my mother's womb' (Ps 138:13). This love has all the feminine qualities of a caring mother's tender love – patience, understanding, always the readiness to forgive. In Jesus, Thérèse discovered the maternal heart of God, eternal and merciful love shining through human weakness, thirsting for her love. She says: 'I felt at the bottom of my heart that... God is more tender than a mother' (SS, p. 174). She expresses it beautifully in one of her poems, 'Jesus Alone':

> O you who knew how to create the mother's heart,
> I find in you the tenderest of Fathers!
> My only Love, Jesus, Eternal Word,
> For me your heart is more than maternal.
> (PN 36, stanza 2)

A celebration of littleness

Thérèse explains how her way to God grew out of the experience of her own weakness. She calls it a 'Little Way' – 'very straight, very short, and totally new' (SS, p. 207). When asked about it, she replied, 'It is to recognize our nothingness, to expect everything from God as a little child expects everything from its father' (LC, p. 138). In the words of the psalmist, it is to remain before God like a 'child on its mother's breast' (Ps 130:2). In *Story of a Soul* she explains it in almost identical terms: 'this road is the *surrender* of the little child who sleeps without fear in its Father's arms' (SS, p. 188).

It would be easy to heap up quotations from the gospels in support of what Thérèse calls '*my little* doctrine' (SS, p. 189). The reply of Jesus to the question of the disciples, 'Who is the greatest in the kingdom of Heaven?' (Mt 18:1), readily comes to mind: 'In truth I tell you, unless you change and become like little children you will never enter the kingdom of Heaven. And so, those who make themselves as little as this little child are the greatest in the kingdom of Heaven' (Mt 18:3-4).[29] In *Story of a Soul*, Thérèse develops at length the further implications of her gospel teaching on spiritual childhood. We find it in the record of her last retreat (SS, pp. 187-200) – just a few brief pages of incredible spiritual depth.[30] These are not simply a collection of beautiful thoughts, nor are they mere speculation or theory. They are a faith-filled interpretation, illumined by scripture, of her personal experience of living out her 'Little Way'. Love, trust, surrender, confidence and her vast desires are here linked, and have to be linked, with littleness. For Thérèse, greatness in the gospel sense is inseparable from the weakness of a child.

Part of the 'Little Way' – an integral aspect, though still only a part – is about doing little things for God and doing them well. Again and again, Thérèse insists on this. 'Jesus does not demand great actions from us,' she writes, 'but simply *surrender* and *gratitude*... He has no need of our works but only of our *love*... love is proved by works... Jesus, I am too little to perform great actions... I am a *very little soul* and... I can offer God only *very little things*' (SS, pp. 188.189.196.200.250). Echoing John of the Cross, she says: '*the smallest act of* PURE LOVE *is of more value to [the Church] than all other works together'* (SS, p. 197; cf. SC 29:2). Thérèse's 'nothings' will please Jesus (SS, p. 197). She will prove her love to him, she says, by 'not allowing one little sacrifice to escape, not one look, one word, profiting by all the smallest things and doing them through love' (SS, p. 196). It is God's love that makes these tiniest actions 'infinitely valuable' (SS, p. 197) and pleasing to God.

But doing little things for God is all part of acknowledging and accepting our own littleness and weakness. This, she confesses repeatedly, is essential for all who wish to follow her 'Little Way': 'Is there a soul more *little*, more powerless than mine?' she asks (SS, p. 193); 'I am the smallest of creatures; I know my misery and my feebleness' (SS, p. 195). All these facets of Thérèse's teaching are summed up briefly in one sentence: 'I feel that if You found a soul weaker and littler than mine...You would be pleased to grant it still greater favors, provided it abandoned itself with total confidence to Your Infinite Mercy' (SS, p. 200). Yet, for all her 'extreme littleness' (SS, p. 198), Thérèse experiences 'great aspirations' (SS, p. 197), 'measureless desires' (SS, p. 197), *'infinite desires'* (LT 107) – 'desires and longings which reach even unto infinity' (SS, p. 193). She was confused by this and asked the question: 'O Jesus, my Love, my Life, how can I combine these contrasts? How can I realize the desires of my poor *little soul?*' (SS, p. 192). Her 'Little Way' is not a contradiction of the greatness of her desires: it is precisely the 'Little Way' that can provide the explanation.

A 'Little Way' of vast desires

The remarkable thing about the 'Little Way' is that these vast desires of Thérèse spring from the experience of her own powerlessness and weakness. In fact, the deeper she plunged into the abyss of her own littleness, the greater and more intense her desires became. At an early age, Thérèse already felt that she was destined for *'glory'* – the glory of 'becoming a great *saint'* (SS, p. 72). One incident speaks volumes. 'Father,' she once said to a visiting priest, 'I want to become a saint, I want to love the Good God as much as St Teresa.' 'What pride and what presumption!' he replied. 'Moderate your rash desires.' Undaunted, she insisted, 'But, Father, I do not regard these as rash desires, I can truly aspire to sanctity, even to a more exalted sanctity, if I wish, than that of St Teresa, for Our Lord said, "Be perfect as your heavenly Father is perfect." You can see, Father, how vast the field is; and it seems to me that I have the right to run in it.'[31] But by the time she came to describe her 'Little Way', her desires were virtually limitless, infinite. Technically, we might call this an experience of self-transcendence. She found that there was a longing in her that went beyond every boundary, breaking open every goal. It was a need, a hunger, a thirst to embrace every vocation in the Church, including that of the priest, apostle, doctor, martyr – in short, to be 'everything' (SS, pp. 192.194).

Again, it was the scriptures that provided an answer to the 'veritable martyrdom' (SS, p. 193) which her unsatisfied desires were causing her. 'I opened the Epistles of St. Paul,' she tells us, 'to find some kind of answer' (SS, p. 193). In vain, she sought for her place among the different members of the Church listed by Paul (1Cor 12). Then he goes on to speak of the 'way' of love (1Cor 13). We can only marvel at Thérèse's astounding and original development of the apostle's teaching on love. Paul never mentions the 'heart' among the members of the Church. But Thérèse does: 'I understood that the Church *had a Heart*,' she exclaims, *'and that this Heart was BURNING WITH LOVE*... I understood that LOVE COMPRISED ALL VOCATIONS... THAT IT WAS ETERNAL!... MY VOCATION IS LOVE!... in the heart of the Church, my Mother, I shall be *Love*. Thus I shall be everything' (SS, p. 194). Yes, love is eternal, infinite – like her own infinite desires. But Thérèse reminds us explicitly that it was through entering deeply into her own weakness and littleness that she attained all her desires: 'I, abasing myself to the very depths of my nothingness, raised myself so high that I was able to attain my end' (SS, p. 194).[32] And she repeats this lesson in no uncertain terms: 'because of my weakness,' she cries out, 'it has pleased You, O Lord, to grant my *little childish desires* and You desire, today, to grant other desires that are *greater* than the universe' (SS, p. 193).

Capacity for the infinite

The human heart can go to the lengths of God; it is 'capable of God'.[33] The theologian who changed Thérèse's expression in her *Act of Oblation* from 'infinite desires' to 'immense desires' missed the full import of her experience.[34] She wrote 'infinite', she repeated it elsewhere (LT 107; cf. SS, p. 192), and she meant it. In fact, the nature of desire is determined not by the person who desires, but by the object of longing. John of the Cross speaks of the 'deep caverns' of the human spirit – its faculties of memory, intellect and will: 'They are as deep as the boundless goods of which they are capable,' he explains, 'since anything less than the infinite fails to fill them' (LF 3:18). He continues: 'capable of infinite goods... they cannot receive these infinite goods until they are completely empty' (LF 3:18). Augustine repeats the same lesson: 'This is our life, to be exercised by desire. But we are exercised by holy desire only in so far as we have cut off our longings from the love of the world... empty that which is to be filled.'[35]

It was precisely this emptying out of herself, entering into the profound depths of her own weakness or nothingness, that put Thérèse in touch with her vast desires, her sheer emptiness and capacity for God, for the infinite. She draws on her own original interpretation of a rather strange gospel text in support of her experience. It is the conclusion to the parable of the unjust steward (Lk 16:1-9): 'Make use of the riches which render one unjust in order to make friends who will receive you into everlasting dwellings' (Lk 16:9). For Thérèse, these 'riches' are *my desires of being everything* (SS, p. 195). It is these that will open to her the kingdom of heaven. But they need not necessarily do so. The wealth of her desires can be misdirected to something other than God. The psalmist laments these disordered appetites that restrict the human spirit: 'how long will your hearts be closed, will you love what is futile and seek what is false?' (Ps 4:3). Thérèse saw clearly that misguided desires 'were the riches that would be able to render me unjust' (SS, p. 195). Any such inordinate and self-centred desire would savour of yielding to the primeval temptation, 'You will be like God' (Gn 3:5), stifling our deepest need of God by gratifying our selfish desires with something less than him.

In describing her own desire for littleness, Thérèse may give the impression, at times, that she is proud of her own weakness: 'I am simply resigned to see myself always imperfect and in this I find my joy... It seems to me I'm humble...' (SS, p. 158; LC, p. 205). But even if she appears to be boasting, she is in fact speaking the language of Paul who 'glories in [his] weakness' (2Cor 12:9) so as to experience the strength of Christ: 'it is in my weakness that I glory,' writes Thérèse, 'and I expect each day to discover new imperfections in myself' (SS, p. 224). And she does not hesitate to link the greatest grace of her life to the discovery of her own weakness: 'I prefer to agree very simply that the Almighty has done great things in [me]... and the greatest thing is to have shown [me my] *littleness*, [my] impotence' (SS, p. 210). 'I feel that if You found a soul weaker and littler than mine,' she says to Jesus, and then adds, 'which is impossible' (SS, p. 200). Is this false modesty or lack of humility, her claiming to be littler than anyone else could ever be? Quite the contrary: it confirms that Thérèse is in touch with her own infinite emptiness for God. Nobody can be smaller than one who is immeasurably small. In this sense, nobody can be more little than anyone else. Thérèse has recognised that she is limitlessly small, immeasurably empty for God. How much littler can anyone possibly be than Thérèse in the immensity of her sheer desire for God?

Infinite emptiness

In his discussion of the human faculties, or 'caverns', John of the Cross explains: 'when these caverns are empty and pure, the thirst, hunger, and yearning of the spiritual feeling is intolerable' (LF 3:18). Thérèse, likewise, speaks of her desires as 'a veritable martyrdom' (SS, p. 193).[36] In her language, this emptiness is her littleness and weakness and neediness – the radical poverty of her total capacity for God. Her heart, in John's words, is 'emptied, purged and cleansed of every affection for creatures' (LF 3:18) – infinitely little and totally empty for God. Limitlessly little, Thérèse experiences the *vast emptiness* of her boundless capacity for the infinite. John of the Cross explains: 'The capacity of these caverns is deep because the object of this capacity, namely God, is profound and infinite. Thus in a certain fashion their capacity is infinite, and their languishing and suffering are infinite death' (LF 3:22).

Entering into the abyss of her own littleness, weakness and powerlessness, Thérèse experienced her total capacity for God released in the vast hunger and yearning of her painful desires which only an infinite God of love could activate and fully satisfy. Her limitless capacity was at full stretch, her restless heart in the pain of separation but not yet completely at rest in God. Thérèse experienced herself as an immense and limitless capacity for God, and it was precisely her unsatisfied desires that impelled her forward in absolute confidence and trust towards the promised gift of God himself: 'Not that I have secured it already,' she could have said with Paul, 'nor reached my goal, but I am still running trying to capture the prize for which Christ Jesus captured me... I do not reckon myself as having taken hold of it; I can only say that forgetting all that lies behind me, and straining forward to what lies in front, I am racing towards the finishing-point to win the prize of God's heavenly call in Christ Jesus' (Ph 3:12-14).

At first, Thérèse seemed troubled by her vast desires. But all that changed as they became highly important for her in defining her 'Little Way'. They gave meaning to her experience of endless need, the transcendent aspect of what it means to be made for God – fully human in her endless desire, and in her openness to be touched by

God's love in her sheer nothingness. These desires are not
unreasonable, even though they reach beyond reason: to a self-
transcendence that is sublime. Thérèse's 'Little Way' is, in fact, a
perfect way to be fully human. The challenge of it is to recognise
this and to live it fully in total confidence, relying unreservedly on
God's merciful love. To do this requires a trust as infinite as desire –
again, reasonable beyond reason: 'my own folly is this: to trust,'
writes Thérèse (SS, p. 200). This requires especially a radical self-
emptying, like the self-emptying of God himself in his Son – the
divine *kenosis* in the Word made flesh (Ph 2:7). 'I have found the
secret of possessing Your flame,' Thérèse says. 'Yes, in order that
Love be fully satisfied, it is necessary that It lower Itself... to
nothingness and transform this nothingness into *fire*' (SS, p. 195).
For love to be love in God, it needs to give itself away, empty itself;
for love to be love in Thérèse, it needed to do the same: empty itself,
give itself away.[37] So, in the 'Little Way' of self-emptying surrender
to God's merciful love, the heights and the depths are one.

Discovering love
For all her great desires, the spirituality of Thérèse is deeply
embedded in the daily demands of community living. Keenly aware
of her own weakness, she found in the new commandment[38] the key
to the mystery of that same human frailty in others. Near the end
of her life, Thérèse wrote of love: 'God has given me the grace to
understand what charity is; I understood it before, it is true, but in
an imperfect way... I applied myself especially to *loving God*, and it
is in loving Him that I understood my love was not to be expressed
only in words' (SS, p. 219). All her life, she had walked the way of
God's commandment of love, never refusing him anything since the
age of three (cf. SS, p. 279). But it was only in loving him that she
discovered the deeper mysteries of that love. This discovery was
God's gift to her – his gift in response to her love: 'those who love
me will be loved by my Father, and I will love them and reveal myself
to them' (Jn 14:21).

As always, Thérèse focuses on Jesus. He is the exemplar. He points to Calvary and says: 'Love one another as I have loved you' (Jn 15:12; 13:34). 'How,' Thérèse asks, 'did Jesus love His disciples and why did He love them?' (SS, p. 220). She replies: 'it was not their natural qualities that could have attracted Him... they were poor ignorant fishermen filled with earthly thoughts. And still Jesus called them *his friends, his brothers*' (SS, p. 220). In using the word 'friends', she is here borrowing from *John*: 'I have called you friends' (Jn 15:5). Jesus does not love his disciples *because* they are his 'friends'; rather, they are his friends because he *first loved them*: 'In this is love, not that we loved God but that he loved us... We love, because he first loved us' (1Jn 4:10.19). The thought-pattern of Thérèse is often the same as that of the fourth evangelist, and her words echo clearly the teaching of his gospel. She writes: 'He desires to see [His disciples] reign with Him in the kingdom of His Father, and to open that kingdom to them He wills to die on the cross, for He said: *"Greater love than this no man has than that he lay down his life for his friends"*' (SS, p. 220; Jn 15:13; cf. 13:34). There, on Calvary, Thérèse finds the full and complete revelation of Jesus' pure and selfless love – redemptive and sacrificial. And so, she can say, 'I am prepared to lay down my life for [my Sisters]' (SS, p. 239).

Love's stark realism
'*Illusions,*' said Thérèse, 'God gave me the grace *not to have* A SINGLE ONE when entering Carmel. I found the religious life to be *exactly* as I had imagined it, no sacrifice astonished me' (SS, p. 149). With a clear, keen eye sharpened by her own struggle to love others and by her observations of community living, Thérèse discovered 'that all souls have very much the same struggles to fight' (SS, p. 239) and lays bare for us, in the final part of *Story of a Soul*, the full demands of fraternal love.[39] Yet, for all her realism, she touches human weakness with deep sympathy, understanding and warmth. Like Jesus, she 'could tell what someone had within' (Jn 2:25): the challenges, the temptations and the difficulties.

For Thérèse, every sacrifice demanded by human relationships was a real death to self. The little grains of self-love, self-complacency, self-pity, self-assertiveness provided so many occasions of self-mastery: not to insist that an object borrowed be returned because this 'would satisfy self-love' (SS, p. 229); a smile for the ungracious 'when I was tempted to answer her back in a disagreeable manner' (SS, p. 223); resisting 'a great desire to turn my head and stare at the culprit' who was irritating her (SS, p. 249), or a temptation in the laundry 'to draw back and wipe [her] face to show the Sister who was sprinkling [her]' (SS, p. 250); a kindly service done to one with 'poor crippled hands... because I knew it was not easy to please [her]' (SS, pp. 248.247); seeking out at recreation 'the least agreeable to me in order to carry out with regard to these wounded souls the office of the good Samaritan', knowing that a 'word, an amiable smile, often suffice to make a sad soul bloom' (SS, p. 246); running away 'like a deserter whenever my struggles became too violent' (SS, p. 223); when disturbed, taking 'care to appear happy and especially *to be so*' (SS, p. 228); not insisting on her rights when 'my heart was beating' with indignation (SS, p. 224).

At first glance, her language might sometimes appear exaggerated. But Thérèse was keenly sensitive and so, too, the struggle was all the more intense. When, for example, an article for her work is removed, 'patience is very close to abandoning me and I must take my courage in both hands in order to reclaim the missing object without bitterness' (SS, p. 226); refusing in 'such a delightful way... what cannot be given that the refusal gives as much pleasure as the gift itself' (SS, p. 228). She exclaims, 'Ah! how contrary are the teachings of Jesus to the feelings of nature!' (SS, p. 229) and sums up everything so well: 'Ah! I understand now that charity consists in bearing with the faults of others, in not being surprised at their weakness, in being edified by the smallest acts of virtue we see them practice. But I understood above all that charity must not remain hidden in the bottom of the heart' (SS, p. 220).

The utter candour of her self-analysis and the frank confession of her struggle holds up the mirror to the stark reality and truth of the demands of community living and its essential core of sacrifice. But her humanity and sympathy for others never deserted her. She experienced the truth of John's words: 'We know that we have passed out of death into life, because we love the brethren. Whoever does not love remains in death' (1Jn 3:14-15). The fruits of victory in her conflicts, Thérèse tells us, were peace and joy as an abiding possession: 'Ah! what peace floods the soul when she rises above natural feelings' (SS, p. 226).

Love in action
'Bear one another's burdens and so you shall fulfil the law of Christ', writes Paul (Gal 6:2). And Thérèse: 'it isn't enough to love; we must prove it' (SS, p. 225). For her, the words of scripture were not a mere repertoire of beautiful thoughts and sentiments – a mirror to look into, only to forget later what manner of person one is (cf. Jas 1:23-24). Thérèse was 'a doer of the word' and not a hearer only, deceiving herself (cf. Jas 1:22). She reiterates the lesson of Teresa of Avila, 'good works, good works' (IC VII:4:6): 'The most beautiful thoughts are nothing,' Thérèse tells us, 'without good works' (SS, p. 234). She recalled this when she felt challenged to put it into practice – practical Christianity! 'Not wishing to give in to the natural antipathy I was experiencing,' she writes, 'I told myself that charity must not consist in feelings but in works... I understood my love was not to be expressed only in words' (SS, pp. 222.219). Again, her thinking is along the mind of John: 'Little children, let us not love in word or speech, but in deed and in truth' (1Jn 3:18).

Thérèse illustrates the dynamism of her love with a beautiful example which goes straight to the heart of community living. A sister in her community was displeasing to her in every way. But, as Thérèse had reminded herself that charity consists not in feelings but in works (SS, p. 222), 'I set myself to doing for this Sister,' she said, 'what I would do for the person I loved the most' (SS, p. 222). This was love in action. But even more important is the lesson of Thérèse on the true vision of faith that made this possible: 'what attracted me,' she confesses, 'was Jesus hidden in the depths of her soul' (SS, p. 223). Thérèse did not see just another sister – weak, frail, imperfect like herself. She responded to her with love and discovered Jesus in her. Or rather, it was Jesus 'hidden' in brokenness who revealed himself to Thérèse in response to her love. She experienced the truth of Matthew's gospel: 'I was hungry... thirsty... a stranger... You did it to me' (Mt 25:35-40). Beneath the surface in every human person lies the hidden beauty of God's presence waiting to be discovered.

Jesus says, in the gospel of John: 'I am the vine and you are the branches' (Jn 15:5). Every word is significant for community living. Jesus is the vine – the stock and the branches – that is, the whole community. He lives on in the whole community, just as every person lives in him (cf. Jn 15:4). He works his own masterpiece in each person differently, so that everyone reflects in a unique way the face of Jesus.[40] Thérèse resonates to this teaching on Jesus as the vine: 'when especially the devil tries to place before the eyes of [her] soul the faults of such and such a Sister' (SS, p. 221), she looks deeper to the truth beneath the surface and into the hidden beauty of that person. She looks with the eyes of faith and sees Christ working there. Thérèse does not linger on the faults, failings or limitations of another sister: 'I hasten,' she says, 'to search out her virtues, her good intentions' – that is, Jesus at work in her sister. With startling insight, Thérèse comments: 'what appears to me as a fault can very easily be an act of virtue because of her intention' (SS, p. 221). Again, her thoughts run on the lines of John, even without explicit reference: 'Do not judge by appearances... you judge according to the flesh' (Jn 7:24; 8:15) – by human, natural standards. 'In order that this judgment be favorable,' writes Thérèse, 'or rather that I be not judged at all, I want to be charitable in my thoughts toward others at all times, for Jesus has said: *"Judge not, and you shall not be judged"* (SS, p. 222).

An impossible commandment?[41]

Thérèse is aware of the exalted and radical demands of fraternal love: 'Love one another as I have loved you' (Jn 15:12; 13:34). So she asks the question: is this love possible? In one of the deepest and loveliest passages she ever penned, Thérèse discovers the truth of Jesus' teaching in *John*: 'Ah! Lord,' she exclaims, 'I know you don't command the impossible' (SS, p. 221). She is still aware of her weakness and imperfection. She is always conscious of that illusive 'beam' in her own eye. 'You know very well,' she writes, 'that never would I be able to love my Sisters as You love them'; then comes the solution: 'unless *You*, O my Jesus, *loved them in me*. It is because You wanted to give me this grace that You made Your *new* commandment... it gives me the assurance that Your Will is *to love in me* all those You command me to love!' (SS, p. 221). Ever practical, Thérèse goes on to draw out the implications of her teaching: 'it is Jesus alone who is acting in me, and the more united I am to Him, the more also do I love my Sisters' (SS, p. 221). That is how real community grows. We can so easily miss the reality beneath the surface, a truth open only to the eyes of faith: 'Abide in me... abide in my love' (Jn 15:4-7.9-10).

Few have ever lived the new commandment as fully as Thérèse. Her final word speaks of God's vast plan of salvation and of her – and our – place in it, as channels of his love. Again, it is scripture that helps her to express her thoughts: *'therefore have I raised you, that I may show* MY POWER *in you, and my name may be spoken of throughout all the earth'* (SS, p. 234; Ex 9:16). She goes on to explain: 'Century has followed on century since the Most High has spoken those words, and since then His conduct has undergone no change, for He is always using His creatures as instruments to carry on His work in souls' (SS, pp. 234-5). *All* believers have a mission – God's mission

— as channels of his love. Yes, we are Christ, who is present, spread out everywhere, until the end of time. Like Thérèse, we are Christ's love let loose in the world.

The prayer of a child

Thérèse admits to another form of weakness: the difficulties of prayer, which is an experience common to all who try to pray. This is what makes her teaching so engaging and compelling. She herself was no stranger to distractions, the inability to concentrate, unanswered requests, aridity, loss of fervour, emptiness, and the apparent absence of God. She often slept during prayer. At times, we have all suffered such disappointments and frustrations. We, too, know what it is to struggle as she did. But for Thérèse, weakness is not an obstacle to communion with God: it is a stepping-stone to closer intimacy with him. With characteristic originality, she writes, 'I learned very quickly… that the more one advances, the more one sees the goal is still far off. And now I am simply resigned to see myself always imperfect and in this I find my joy' (SS, p. 158).

Thérèse has lessons for all of us on how to deal with our difficulties and struggles in prayer: 'I do not have the courage to force myself to search out *beautiful* prayers in books… it really gives me a headache!' (SS, p. 242). So, what does she do? Powerless and weak like a little child, she relates to God exactly as a child: 'I do like children who do not know how to read, I say very simply to God what I wish to say, without composing beautiful sentences, and He always understands me' (SS, p. 242). In her weakness, Thérèse prays like a child who dares to say, 'Father'. This was how Jesus himself prayed at his moment of greatest desolation in Gethsemane: 'Abba, Father!' (Mk 14:36). It is also the way the early Christian community prayed: 'When we cry, "Abba, Father!" it is the Spirit himself bearing witness with our spirit that we are children of God' (Rm 8:15-16). This prayer is possible, Paul explains, because 'God has sent the Spirit of his Son into our hearts, crying, "Abba,

Father!"' (Gal 4:6). Thérèse echoes his teaching: 'we cannot, without the Spirit of Love, give the name of *"Father"* to our Father in heaven' (SS, p. 234). She teaches us to pray like Jesus: a child communing in love with its Father. Whenever we, like Thérèse, 'do not know how to pray as we ought, it is the same Spirit who helps us,' says Paul, 'in our weakness' (Rm 8:26).

When Thérèse speaks of her powerlessness to pray, she confesses to sometimes finding it 'impossible to draw forth [from prayer] one single thought to unite me with God' (SS, p. 243). In the spirit of Teresa, she teaches us by her own example to resort to vocal prayer: 'I *very slowly* recite an "Our Father",' she says, 'and then the angelic salutation... they nourish my soul much more than if I had recited them precipitately a hundred times' (SS, p. 243).[42] As Teresa herself had discovered (cf. WP 30:7), so Thérèse, too, found that the Our Father could lead into deep prayer and contemplation. One day, her sister found Thérèse alone in her room, 'lost in profound contemplation'. Céline asked what she was thinking about, and Thérèse replied with tears in her eyes what a wonderful thing it was 'to call God our Father'; she was, Thérèse explained, 'meditating on the *Our Father*'.[43] Her heart had gone out to him – in an endless, aching hunger. There is a pain beyond all telling, hidden in the heart of love. It is there also in the heart of prayer – a thirst, and a longing unsatisfied. It is an aspiration of the heart, a reaching out in love.

'An aspiration of the heart'

Thérèse's teaching on prayer is embedded not just in the experience of her own weakness. It is also inseparably linked with her great desires. She describes prayer briefly, in these striking terms:

> For me, *prayer* is an aspiration of the heart, it is a simple glance directed to heaven, it is a cry of gratitude and love in the midst of trial as well as joy; finally, it is something great, supernatural, which expands my soul and unites me to Jesus. (SS, p. 242)[44]

An aspiration of the heart! 'To aspire' means, literally, 'to breathe' (*spirare*) 'towards' (*ad*) – to long, or to sigh, for *something* or *someone*. In a word, it is a desire. When the object is God, it is an outburst of love – a fling of the heart to the heart of God.

Thérèse recalls fishing expeditions with her father in the countryside. She would sit there on a river bank bedecked with flowers: 'my thoughts became very profound,' she said. 'Without knowing what it was to meditate, my soul was absorbed in real prayer. I listened to distant sounds, the murmuring of the wind… Earth then seemed to be a place of exile and I could dream only of heaven' (SS, p. 37). That was her prayer – her aspiration: her pilgrim soul in exile, longing for heaven. But Thérèse never longed for heaven alone. Her deepest longing was for Jesus. As she later wrote, again speaking of her desire for heaven:

> I think that the Heart of my Spouse is mine alone, just as mine is His alone, and I speak to Him then in the solitude of this delightful heart to heart, while waiting to contemplate Him one day face to face… (LT 122)

In these few words, we find an emphasis on the heart of God, which is integral to Carmelite prayer. When Thérèse expresses her need for solitude, she says: 'I want to hide myself for you, O Jesus!/Lovers must have solitude,/A heart-to-heart lasting night and day' (PN 17, stanza 3). Her need for withdrawal to pray means, in the words of Teresa, 'taking time frequently to be alone with [God]' (*Life* 8:5). For both Teresa and Thérèse, the essence of prayer lies in a communion or exchange of love: for Teresa, an 'intimate sharing between friends' (*Life* 8:5); for Thérèse, a 'heart-to-heart'. In her *Act of Oblation to Merciful Love*, Thérèse expands on her understanding of prayer as love. She implores God: 'look upon me only in the Face of Jesus and in His heart burning with *Love*' (SS, p. 276). This prayer of oblation is like an extended litany of love's passionate longings. Her pleadings, 'I desire... I want... I long... I wish...', ring out the variations on her ardent need to love.

It is desire that accepts every pain: 'let us love Him enough to suffer for Him all that He wills, even spiritual pains, aridities, anxieties,' she exhorted her sister Céline and added, 'That is love pushed to the point of heroism' (LT 94). Years later, her deathbed conversation with this same sister illustrates how well Thérèse practised what she preached. 'What are you doing?' Céline asked her, finding her awake in the middle of the night. 'You should try to sleep.' 'I can't sleep,' replied Thérèse, 'I'm suffering too much, so I am praying.' 'And what are you saying to Jesus?' 'I say nothing to Him, I love Him!' (LC, p. 228). Such was her prayer: one long, ceaseless aspiration of love in her weakness and in her pain – while, in her own phrase, 'waiting to contemplate Him one day face to face' (LT 122). She was, in the spirit of the Carmelite *Rule*, 'watching in prayer' (#10) – a woman of prayer, right to the end.

Pondering the word

Thérèse also prayed – again in the spirit of her *Rule* – by 'pondering the Lord's law day and night' (#10). Her prayer time seems to have been mainly a prolonged meditation on the gospel, listening to it prayerfully in response to the action of the Holy Spirit – even if Thérèse rarely mentions the Spirit explicitly. 'This is... what Jesus has done in my soul during my retreat,' she says: he told her to 'descend' like Zacchaeus. She then comments at length on the way of *descending*: into a place of poverty where we may 'serve as an abode for Jesus' (LT 137; cf. HF 7; LR 42). On another occasion, she retired in silence to her room and reflected on what Jesus thought of her many failings: 'I recalled these words He addressed one day to the adulterous woman: "Has no one condemned you?" And I, tears in my eyes, answered Him: "No one, Lord"' (LT 230; cf. Jn 8:10-11).

The life of Thérèse, like that of Mary, was one of treasuring God's word in her heart (cf. Lk 2:51; cf. 2:19), open to the Spirit.

'The Holy Spirit…will bring back to your memory everything I have said to you,' Jesus remarked (Jn 14:26). The Spirit will often 'recall' a word of scripture for Thérèse.[45] She repeats it and lets it seep into her mind and heart: 'I repeated constantly to myself these words of St. Paul: "It is no longer I that live, it is Jesus who lives in me!"' (SS, p. 79; cf. Gal 2:20). Her method of 'repetition' is as old as the *lectio divina* of the Desert Fathers and the monastic tradition. 'I repeated over and over the words of love burning in my heart,' she writes (SS, p. 103). As sacristan, she often *recalls* these words: 'You are to be holy, you who carry the vessels of the Lord' (SS, p. 172: cf. Is 52:11).

The words of scripture just came to her memory as she tried to explain God's mercy to one of the sisters. This nun later said of Thérèse: 'I was amazed that this sister, who was so young, knew so well how to show me the mercy of God, quoting passages of the psalms for me as easily as if she had read them in a book'.[46] It *was* a book: the book of Jesus' own words communicated to her directly. As Thérèse once wrote:

> Jesus has no need of books or teachers to instruct souls; He teaches without the noise of words. Never have I heard Him speak, but I feel that He is within me at each moment; He is guiding and inspiring me with what I must say and do… I have frequently noticed that Jesus doesn't want me to lay up *provisions*; He nourishes me at each moment with a totally new food; I find it within me without my knowing how it is there. I believe it is Jesus Himself hidden in the depths of my poor little heart: He is giving me the grace of acting within me, making me think of all He desires me to do at the present moment. (SS, pp. 179.165)

But the Spirit does not just 'recall' the word of God in a general way. He makes it actual and relevant to the individual person. He shows Thérèse how it is realised in herself and in others: 'I... see the words of Psalm 22 realized in me,' she said: '"The Lord is my Shepherd, I shall not want..."' (SS, p. 15; cf. Ps 22:1). She says of herself and of her companion: 'in us was realized this passage from Scripture: "*A brother who is helped by a brother is like a strong city*"' (SS, p. 236; cf. Pr 18:19). Through the Spirit, Thérèse discovered, too, the significance of the word of God for the here and now, the concrete circumstances of her daily living. In keeping with a custom in the Carmel at that time, she often opened the Bible at random,[47] receiving the word that God chose to give her at that precise moment. It was a word of life for herself personally, and also for others.

Soon after entering Carmel, she wrote to her sister Céline: 'I read this morning a passage of the Gospel where it says: "I have not come to bring peace but the sword"' (LT 57; cf. Mt 10:34); this strengthened her for the trials that lay ahead. Céline also once wrote to her with a problem and Thérèse replied, 'After having read your letter, I went to prayer, and taking the gospel, I asked Jesus to find a passage for you, and this is what I found: "Behold the fig tree..." I closed the book, I had read enough' (LT 143; cf. Lk 21:29). A year before her death, Thérèse was still meditating, pondering, praying the word of God: 'This evening, during my prayer, I meditated on some passages from Isaias which appeared to me so appropriate for you' (LT 193). As Thérèse ponders the scriptures, she comes to the point where she can say: 'a single word uncovers for my soul infinite horizons' (LT 226).

Surrender and trust
'Jesus deigned to show me the road that leads to this Divine Furnace,' Thérèse writes, speaking of the fire of love, 'and this road is the *surrender* of the little child who sleeps without fear in its

Father's arms' (SS, p. 188). It took her years to achieve this total surrender, to walk in the way of absolute confidence and trust. The Lord seems to have kept her waiting and waiting, patiently. Then comes the breakthrough – 'in one instant' (SS, p. 98). This succinct phrase runs almost like a refrain throughout her writings (cf. SS, pp. 58.97.277; PN 17, stanza 6).

Thérèse's temperament did not take kindly to surrender. Her mother described the young Thérèse as a 'little imp', commenting: 'one doesn't know how things will go, she...has a stubborn streak in her that is almost invincible' (SS, p. 22). These words were later echoed by her confessor: 'had [God] abandoned you, instead of being a little angel, you would have become a little demon' (SS, p. 149). After her sister Pauline entered Carmel, the young Thérèse, once so happy and carefree, became timid, scrupulous and more sensitive than ever, easily dissolving in tears, retiring and introspective. Eventually, she emerged from the struggle. She called this her 'complete conversion' (SS, p. 98). It was Christmas Eve: 'that luminous *night*,' she says, when 'Jesus... changed the night of my soul into rays of light' (SS, p. 97). Thérèse comments significantly: 'The work I had been unable to do in ten years was done by Jesus in one instant' (SS, p. 98).

After Thérèse had spent three years in Carmel, she still agonised over her 'faults' and worried constantly about offending God. Then, during a retreat, the visiting priest who had spoken no more than a few words to her 'launched me full sail upon the waves of *confidence and love* which so strongly attracted me, but upon which I dared not advance' (SS, p. 174). Her surrender to God's action had now reached another significant turning-point in her life. Again, it happened in an instant. Her experience would take away the fear of death, for she well knew that God had transformed her in one moment and could do so again. Her *Act of Oblation* sums this up well, echoing and adapting the words of scripture: 'a single day is like a thousand years. You can, then, in one instant prepare me to appear before You' (SS, p. 277; cf. 2Pt 3:8). In one of her poems, Thérèse writes: 'Living on Love is banishing every fear,/Every memory of past faults./I see no imprint of my sins./In a moment love has burned everything…' (PN 17, stanza 6).

We are fortunate to have many telling photographs of Thérèse. Conrad De Meester, a distinguished commentator on her life and works, uses the image of her hand to great effect. It describes well, he says, how her surrender gradually deepened:

> To use an analogy, we could say that, at first, her hand was held with palm downward and fingers clenched, seeking to grasp as best they could. Then, with the passage of time and a change of attitude and perspective, her fingers relaxed gradually and eventually released their hold, while her hand turned until her palm was outstretched, ready to offer and to receive much in return. It took Thérèse almost her entire lifetime to reach this point.[48]

The final testing

We discover the real cost of total surrender for Thérèse in the great and final testing of her faith. Shortly before her death, she wrote to a priest friend: 'my way is all confidence and love' (LT 226). But soon afterwards, she is writing about the 'thickest darkness' (SS, p. 211) which had invaded her soul fourteen months earlier. It was Easter. Thérèse had coughed up blood just a few days before. This was the first summons – a *distant murmur*', she called it, '*that announced the Bridegroom's arrival*' (SS, p. 211).

It is risky to assume that we can understand what Thérèse was experiencing at this time. She herself found it almost impossible to explain: 'One would have to travel through this dark tunnel to understand its darkness' (SS, p. 212), she wrote starkly. Or, as she expressed it again: she was covered in 'thick fog', which suddenly became 'more dense' (SS, pp. 213-4). Her torment redoubled. The psalmist, at his bleakest, expresses Thérèse's experience only too well: 'my one companion is darkness' (Ps 87:19). This darkness borrowed the voice of sinners and said to her, mockingly, that death would not give her what she hoped for, but only 'the night of nothingness' (SS, p. 213). She confided to one of her community: 'I don't believe in eternal life, it seems to me that after this mortal life there is nothing left... Everything has disappeared for me, love is all I have.'[49] She could not discern any trace of heaven. Everything, it seemed, had vanished. Even her own 'Little Way' seemed lost, swallowed up in its own littleness.

A month before Thérèse died, her sister Pauline was sitting by her bed. Thérèse pointed to the chestnut trees near the cemetery and said, 'Look! Do you see the black hole where we can see nothing; it's in a similar hole that I am as far as body and soul are concerned. Ah! what darkness! But I am in peace' (LC, p. 173). Near the end, she confided that the pain was enough 'to make her lose her reason'. She asked her sister not to leave any poisonous medicines around her and said, 'If I had not had any faith, I would have committed suicide without an instant's hesitation' (LC, p. 196; cf. pp. 162-3). Earlier that summer, Thérèse had said, quoting Job: 'Although he should kill me, I will trust in him' (LC, p. 77; cf. Jb 13:15). That trust was tested in so many ways, not least by the uncertainty concerning her illness. Her doctors had given conflicting views. Thérèse was perplexed. Was death imminent? Or would this excruciating pain last for years? However, she refused to submit to anxiety. Her phrase 'everything is a grace' (LC, p. 57) sums up her response at all times. When she felt she could take no more, she said to the prioress who was at her bedside, 'I assure you, the chalice is filled to the brim!... But God is not going to abandon me, I'm sure... He has never abandoned me' (LC, p. 205). These words were uttered the day of her death: the ultimate trust.

Speaking the truth in love

Thérèse, we have seen, had no illusions about religious life. Nor did she have any illusions about the Church. She was of one mind with another future Doctor of the Church, Catherine of Siena, who felt that those are truly blessed who suffer at not seeing the Church as fair as they would like and are all the more faithful because of it. It is often assumed that criticism in the Church is a voice of the angry and disgruntled. It may be, but it is not necessarily so. Honest criticism is a function of love and was part of Thérèse's vision of church as communion, in which each member belongs fully, as family. 'I am the *Child of the Church*,' she said. 'I love the Church, my Mother!' (SS, pp. 196-7).

To avoid the challenge of speaking out is the easy option. But it was precisely her love for the Church that enabled Thérèse to discern things clearly, and unmask deception and pretence. She was to discover that criticism of this kind was 'a painful operation' but added: 'truth always wins out' (SS, p. 240). As a young religious, she became uneasy with the attachment which one of her companions had to the superior. Thérèse felt that she must act, in true love, to open the eyes of the young nun, even though it could be at some cost to herself.[50] One commentator has referred to this episode as 'a fight for truth'.[51] Thérèse writes: 'the moment had come and I must no longer fear to speak out... [I told this sister] *everything I was thinking about her*' (SS, p. 236). She followed the words of *Ephesians* (4:15) and told her companion the truth – with love. The young nun recognised that Thérèse's motives were genuine and took the lesson to heart. Thérèse would say later: 'If I'm not loved, that's just too bad! I tell the whole truth, and if anyone doesn't wish to know the truth, let her not come looking for me' (LC, p. 38).

It was the same sense of conviction that led Thérèse to voice constructive criticism wherever she found it necessary. She asked the unwilling superior that there be more frequent communion – a custom not yet accepted by the Carmel of Lisieux.[52] Thérèse also expresses the hurt which many women feel today with regard to the Church. She is not a strident voice, but is no less a challenge to the Church she loved so deeply. She recalls how she travelled in Italy as a young girl, and 'every minute someone was saying [to the women]: "Don't enter here! Don't enter there, you will be excommunicated!"' (SS, p. 140). In desperation, she releases her indignation:

> Ah! poor women, how they are misunderstood! And yet they love God in much larger numbers than men do and during the Passion of Our Lord, women had more courage than the apostles since they braved the insults of the soldiers and dared to dry the adorable Face of Jesus. It is undoubtedly because of this that He allows misunderstanding to be their lot on earth, since He chose it for Himself. In heaven, He will show that His thoughts are not men's thoughts, for then the *last will be first*. (SS, p. 140)

A fragile Church

There is considerable disappointment today at the discovery of clerical failings. Thérèse had a special love for priests but, observing them on the train to Rome, she records her shock upon seeing that they were 'weak and fragile men' who '[showed] in their conduct their extreme need for prayers' (SS, p. 122). To be human is an essential part of what it means to be a priest.[53] The priest is weak and fragile like Jesus, because like Jesus he is human. To exalt the priest above this shared humanity is to deny the incarnation: 'He can deal gently with the ignorant and wayward, since he himself is beset with weakness' (Hb 5:2). This is not to minimise in any way the clerical sins and glaring abuse of trust highlighted recently by the press and media. These failings have rightly outraged, pained and angered many – not least the vast majority of priests themselves who are good, committed and often heroic in their service of the Church.

However, much support and sympathy is still needed for the scarred victims and their families, as well as soul-searching by the Church, together with healing and reconciliation. The clerical voice must join the cry of the repentant Church to ask forgiveness for the wounds inflicted and suffered.

Peter was one of Thérèse's favourite gospel characters. She said that she could understand perfectly why he fell: 'he was relying upon himself instead of relying only upon God's strength... Before Peter fell,' she reminds us, 'Our Lord had said to him: "And once you are converted, strengthen your brethren"' (LC, pp. 140-1). Then she proceeds to comment on what Jesus had said: 'This means: Convince them of the weakness of human strength through your own experience' (LC, p. 141). In the gospel, Jesus spoke these words to Peter: 'I have prayed for you that your faith may not fail' (Lk 22:32). Jesus did not pray that Peter himself would not fail. He is bound to fail, almost by definition, because he is human. Jesus prayed that Peter's *faith* might not fail, and so guaranteed the only permanent foundation of a community of believers: a Church supported in its weakness by the prayer of Jesus. Little wonder that the story of the Pharisee and the publican was a special favourite with Thérèse: 'He told this story to some who trusted in themselves that they were virtuous...' (Lk 18:9-14). She comments: 'I repeat, filled with confidence, the publican's humble prayer... Like the publican, I felt I was a great sinner. I found God to be so merciful!... My confidence is not lessened' (SS, p. 258; LC, p. 147). These words may surprise us. For as sinners go, Thérèse was not in the top league! She was not even in the ranks of the 'sinner' saints, Augustine and the Magdalen. But she did not miss the point of the parable: the opposite of sin is not virtue, it is God's grace, his merciful love. So, she can identify with the prayer of the publican: 'God, be merciful to me a sinner!' (Lk 18:13; cf. SS, p. 212).

Thérèse is now a 'Doctor of the Church'.[54] This confirms that her message is universal – that is, for the whole people of God. Her teaching provides all believers with a deeply scriptural way of living their faith in the full acceptance of human frailty. Thérèse also encourages a fragile and repentant Church to face the future with renewed trust in God's limitless mercy: 'Yes, I feel it; even though I had on my conscience all the sins that can be committed, I would go, my heart broken with sorrow, and throw myself into Jesus' arms... I go to Him with confidence and love...' (SS, p. 259). These are the last words she ever wrote.[55]

Notes

1   See ch. 2, note 4.

2   *Dei Verbum* (*Dogmatic Constitution on Divine Revelation*) 18.

3   *Ibid.* 18.

4   *Ibid.* 14.

5   *Ibid.* 15.

6   *Ibid.* 14-15.

7   At the Carmel of Lisieux, half an hour a day was assigned to 'spiritual reading' (2.30-3.00pm), a time which was, however, also designated for the meeting of the novices. Otherwise, there was one hour's 'free time' during the silence before Matins (8.00-9.00pm) and, during the summer when the night's sleep was curtailed, an additional hour in the middle of the day for 'free time' or 'siesta' (12.00-1.00pm). See Sainte Thérèse de l'Enfant-Jésus et de la Sainte-Face, *Œuvres complètes*, Paris: Cerf & Desclée De Brouwer, 1992, pp. 1523-4.

8   An expression used by Pius XI in his Italian discourse of February 11th, 1923, quoted in *La Bible avec Thérèse de Lisieux*, compiled by Sr Cécile, OCD & Sr Geneviève, OP, Paris: Cerf & Desclée De Brouwer, 1979, p. 40. Edith Stein speaks of Thérèse in the same way: '[her] entire life in the Order was a translation of Sacred Scripture into life': see SP, pp. 218-9 (also p. 219, note 3, which shows that these words almost certainly refer to Thérèse).

9   *Dei Verbum* (*Dogmatic Constitution on Divine Revelation*) 25.

10   *Ibid.* 22.

11   For the full text of this harmony, see *La Bible, op. cit.*, pp. 183-5.

12   See Pierre Descouvemont, *Thérèse of Lisieux and Marie of the Trinity: The Transformative Relationship of Saint Thérèse of Lisieux and her Novice Sister Marie of the Trinity*, New York: Alba House, 1997, p. 44.

13   See the author's *Prayer, op. cit.* and, for a brief synthesis of prayer in the gospels, his *A Biblical Prayer Journey, op. cit.*, pp. 310-22.

14   For a complete list of texts, see *La Bible, op. cit.*, pp. 187-90.

15   See *ibid.*, p. 32.

16   An observation well made in T E Bird, 'The Use of Sacred Scripture in the "Autobiography"', *Sicut Parvuli*, vol. lxviii, no. 1, 2004, p. 29.

17   See Christopher O'Donnell, O Carm, *Prayer: Insights from St Thérèse of Lisieux*, Dublin: Veritas, 2001, p. 76.

18   *Ibid.*, pp. 72-3.

19   *Dei Verbum* (*Dogmatic Constitution on Divine Revelation*) 23.

20 See *The Life and Revelations of Saint Gertrude*, Westminster: Christian Classics, 1983, p. 460.

21 *Dei Verbum (Dogmatic Constitution on Divine Revelation)* 21.

22 *Ibid.* 21.

23 'I love the story told by Canon Taylor, one of the first translators of her autobiography into English, about two parish priests who met on the steps of St Peter's on May 17th, 1925, the day Thérèse was canonised. "Do you know what has happened today?" one said to the other. "Of course I do," came the reply, "a saint was canonised." "No," his friend replied, "it was the gospel itself that was canonised."': see Eugene McCaffrey, OCD, 'Thérèse of Lisieux: A Pilgrim Saint', *Mount Carmel*, vol. 50/4, 2002, p. 25.

24 Thérèse engraved the words, 'Jesus is my only love!' on the lintel of her door: see Pierre Descouvemont & Helmuth Nils Loose, *Thérèse and Lisieux*, Toronto: Novalis/Grand Rapids, MI: Eerdmans, 1996, p. 261, which also contains a photograph of it.

25 The *Act of Oblation* can also be found in SS, pp. 276-7.

26 See the author's *St Thérèse: The Gospels Rediscovered*, Darlington Carmel, [1983], section 'The Weakness of God', pp. 53-61.

27 For an in-depth treatment of the theme of suffering in Thérèse, see André Combes, *St. Thérèse and Suffering: The Spirituality of St. Thérèse in its Essence*, Dublin: M H Gill & Son, 1951; Christopher O'Donnell, O Carm, *Love in the Heart of the Church: The Mission of Thérèse of Lisieux*, Dublin: Veritas, 1997, pp. 71-98. See also the popular and practical approaches of: Vincent O'Hara, OCD, '"His face was as though hidden": St Thérèse's Understanding of Suffering', *Mount Carmel*, vol. 48/4, 2001, pp. 25-33; Frances Hogan, *Suffering and Prayer in the Life of St Thérèse*, Darlington Carmel, 1988; Murchadh Ó Madagáin, *Thérèse of Lisieux: Through Love and Suffering*, London: St Pauls, 2003.

28 See section 'God's Enduring Love', in the author's *Fire of Love: Praying with Thérèse of Lisieux*, Boston, MA: Pauline Books & Media, 2004, pp. 61-3.

29 Although there are several gospel passages on spiritual childhood which Thérèse does not quote in her writings, we know from the testimony of others how familiar she was with these texts: see *La Bible, op. cit.*, pp. 192-3; LC, p. 213.

30 This central section of *Story of a Soul* is also known as 'Manuscript B'. See below, section 'A "Little Way" of vast desires', for a treatment of Thérèse's discovery of 'love in the heart of the Church'. Conrad De

Meester examines this turning-point in Thérèse's life: see his *The Power of Confidence: Genesis and Structure of the 'Way of Spiritual Childhood' of Saint Thérèse of Lisieux*, New York: Alba House, 1998, pp. 183-208.

31 See *La Bible, op. cit.*, p. 158; also, Guy Gaucher, OCD, *The Spiritual Journey of St Thérèse of Lisieux*, London: Darton, Longman & Todd, 1987, p. 107. The visiting priest was Fr Blino, SJ.

32 These words are an allusion to the poem of John of the Cross, '*I went out seeking love...*' (P 6).

33 Thomas Aquinas, commenting on the writings of Augustine, describes the human person as *capax Dei* ('capable of God' or 'fit to receive God'): see *Summa Theologica* I-II q. 113 a. 10; cf. Augustine, *De Trinitate* 1.14 c. 8. See, too, *Catechism of the Catholic Church*, section 'Man's Capacity for God', 27-43. Augustine also writes: 'by delaying the fulfilment of desire God stretches it, by making us desire he expands the soul, and by this expansion he increases its capacity': from his treatise on the *First Letter of St John*, in *Divine Office*, vol. I, p. 538.

34 Although 'immense' literally means 'measureless' or 'without measure or limit' and so may rightly be used as a synonym for 'infinite' – as John of the Cross himself uses it: *inmensos...infinitos bienes* (LF 3:18) – the effect of the theologian's change was to lessen the impact of Thérèse's 'infinite' desires.

35 From the treatise of St Augustine on the *First Letter of St John*, in *Divine Office*, vol. I, p. 538. See also, on desire as exercised in prayer, his letter to Proba, in *Divine Office*, vol. III, pp. 661-2.

36 See also Teresa's treatment of anxious and painful desires: IC VI:11:2.5.

37 Cf. the definition of God's love by Edith Stein: 'God is love, and love is goodness giving itself away' (HL, p. 38).

38 See note 41.

39 This is the third section of *Story of a Soul*, often referred to as 'Manuscript C', and written right at the end of her life.

40 Thérèse remembered well what a priest had once taught her: '*There are really more differences among souls than there are among faces*' (SS, pp. 239-40).

41 See the author's *St Thérèse, op. cit.*, section 'An Impossible Commandment', pp. 43-52; also his 'Saint Thérèse and the New Commandment', in Thomas M Curran, OCD (ed.), *The Mind of Saint Thérèse of Lisieux*, Dublin: Carmelite Centre of Spirituality/Bury, Greater Manchester: Koinonia, 1977, ch. 3, pp. 26-36.

42 See ch. I, section 'Praying with words'.

43   See Sister Geneviève of the Holy Face (Céline Martin), *My Sister St. Thérèse*, Rockford, IL: Tan Books, 1997, p. 109.

44   The first half of this passage of Thérèse has been used in the *Catechism of the Catholic Church* as the opening definition of prayer (#2558).

45   On the 'recalling' action of the Holy Spirit who brings the word of God back to our memory, see the author's *The Carmelite Charism, op. cit.*, pp. 18-20.

46   Testimony of Sr Marie of Jesus, quoted in *La Bible, op. cit.*, p. 14.

47   See O'Donnell, *Prayer, op. cit.*, p. 81.

48   Conrad De Meester, OCD, *With Empty Hands: The Message of St Thérèse of Lisieux*, London & New York: Burns & Oates, 2002, p. 119.

49   A confidence made to Sr Teresa of Saint Augustine: quoted in PN, p. 184.

50   Her sister Pauline had warned Thérèse that she might even be sent away, if the superior heard of it: see Gaucher, *op. cit.*, p. 123. For Thérèse's own description of the episode, see SS, pp. 235-7.

51   Gaucher, *op. cit.*, p. 122.

52   *Ibid.*, p. 190.

53   See *Mount Carmel*, vol. 52/3, 2004 – an issue devoted to the priesthood.

54   See Steven Payne, OCD, *Saint Thérèse of Lisieux: Doctor of the Universal Church*, New York: Alba House, 2002; Eugene McCaffrey, OCD, *Heart of Love: Saint Thérèse of Lisieux*, Dublin: Veritas, 1998, pp. 74-9.

55   I am referring here to the last words of *Story of a Soul*, abandoned at the beginning of July 1897 because of her illness (see LC, p. 70); she did, however, write a few letters and prayers after this date.

EPILOGUE

For Carmelites, Mary is *the* woman of prayer, the Virgin who 'treasured' and 'pondered' God's word in her heart (Lk 2:19; cf. 2:51). A little chapel, now in ruins and once dedicated to our Lady, still bears witness to Mary's presence in the first Carmelite community. Those early hermits who became known as 'Brothers of the Blessed Virgin Mary of Mount Carmel' were, in time, to shape their own special devotion to the mother of God. She was honoured as *Domina* – that is, Lady or Mistress; as *Mother*, Mother of Carmel; as *Sister*, sister in the faith; as *Most Pure Virgin*; and sometimes quite simply as *Carmelite*. The scapular, a brown cloth worn over the shoulders, is a traditional Carmelite expression of devotion to Mary. It is not a talisman or magical charm but a sign approved by the Church for over seven centuries, and it speaks of the resolve to follow Jesus like Mary. As intimacy with Jesus grows in prayer, so too does friendship with his mother. The two are inseparable and have always remained so in the prayer tradition of Carmel and its saints.

Mary – Mother of Carmel

Teresa of Avila is steeped in the rich Marian tradition of Carmel. She goes to Jesus as he came to us – by way of his blessed mother. Teresa is a child of Mary. For her, Carmel is Mary's own Order: it is 'her order,' she writes. 'She is our Lady and our Patroness.' The *Rule* which summons the Carmelite to pray unceasingly and to keep watch in prayer is Mary's rule: 'We observe the rule of our Lady of Mt. Carmel,' she reminds us. Teresa's foundations, she says, are Mary's houses: 'these monasteries of the Virgin, our Lady', or 'these little dovecotes of the Virgin, our Lady'. She urges her sisters to live 'as true daughters of the Blessed Virgin'.

Teresa's life-work of reform 'was begun,' she claims, 'through the agency of the most holy Virgin'. Jesus and Mary are inseparable in her prayer of intercession, for when she pleads for help it is 'for love of Our Lord and of His precious Mother'. Teresa cherishes the scapular as 'the habit of [Jesus'] glorious Mother', the badge of her protection and of Carmel's total commitment to Mary. But the mother of God is also the one who helped Teresa to stamp the *Rule* of Carmel with that gentle, compassionate, joyful and human touch so characteristic of the Teresian reform. Repeatedly, we hear these same lessons from Teresa: it is Mary's Order, Mary's habit, Mary's rule, Mary's service; the Blessed Virgin is our mother, our queen, our patroness, our intercessor with her Son, the woman at the foot of the cross, the model of every virtue that Teresa herself requires as a prerequisite for prayer. Yes, Teresa is her child.

Mary – Spirit-filled woman

John of the Cross speaks of Mary less frequently than Teresa, but his devotion to our Lady is no less tender and all-embracing. For him, she is the woman who is totally transparent, radiant with the light of God. He reminds us that 'the Angel Gabriel called the conception of the Son of God, that favor granted to the Virgin Mary, an overshadowing of the Holy Spirit' and explains: 'If an object...is transparent and delicate its shadow is transparent and delicate.' So it is with Mary who, in the words of Gerard Manley Hopkins, 'This one work has to do –/Let all God's glory through'. John, a man of prayer, is at one with the Mary he describes absorbed in contemplation of her new-born Son: 'The Mother gazed in sheer wonder'. Evoking the words of Jesus, 'Behold your mother!' (Jn 19:27), he invites us to accept Mary as our mother too. And in a few lines of simple beauty, he asks us to follow the example of the beloved disciple who 'took her to his own home' (Jn 19:27):

> The Virgin comes walking,
> the Word in her womb:
> could you not give her
> place in your room?

But John is not just a poet: he is also a theologian, with his trained mind firmly cast in the scholastic mould. His tributes to Mary are woven into the fabric of his superb synthesis of the whole spiritual life. 'The discreet lover does not care to ask for what she [herself] lacks and desires,' John writes, 'but only indicates this need so the Beloved may do what he pleases.' For the Mystical Doctor, Mary is the great model of this delicate form of prayer: 'When the Blessed Virgin spoke to her beloved Son at the wedding feast at Cana in Galilee, she did not ask directly for the wine, but merely remarked: *They have no wine*'.

As John wrestles with the problem of pain, his thoughts again turn instinctively to Mary: 'at certain periods, God allows [the soul] to feel things and suffer from them so she might…grow in the fervor of love…as he did with the Virgin Mother'. Indeed, John's description of the intense suffering experienced during the 'night of the spirit' may well be read as a portrait of Mary, Mother of Sorrows: '[Individuals in this state] remain in this condition until their spirit is humbled, softened, and purified, until it becomes so delicate, simple, and refined that it can be one with the Spirit of God'. And it is precisely in terms of her intimate union with the Spirit, in complete surrender to his action, that Mary is presented by John as an exemplar of those who have already reached the final

stage of transforming union: 'Raised from the beginning to this high
state, she never had the form of any creature impressed in her soul,
nor was she moved by any, for she was always moved by the Holy
Spirit.' This is John's variation on Paul's theme: 'All who are guided
by the Spirit of God are children of God' (Rm 8:14).

Mary – praise of glory

Elizabeth of the Trinity wrote her *Prayer to the Trinity* on the feast of
Mary's presentation in the temple, at the end of a retreat devoted to
the annunciation. As she penned this prayer, the angel's words to
Mary were still echoing in her ears: 'The Holy Spirit will come upon
you' (Lk 1:35). 'O consuming Fire, Spirit of Love,' writes Elizabeth,
'"come upon me," and create in my soul a kind of incarnation of the
Word: that I may be another humanity for Him in which He can
renew His whole Mystery.' Here, Elizabeth is also echoing the
Pauline theme of our identification with Christ. She sees herself
under the action of the Spirit who is transforming her into the
likeness of Mary and her Son, as a praise of God's glory. When
Elizabeth speaks of what it means to be a 'praise of glory', she gives
us a gospel portrait of Mary as the perfect reflection of her Son.
Mary, she writes, is 'the great praise of glory of the Holy Trinity',
and it is she who forms Elizabeth in the likeness of her Son: 'This
Mother of grace will form my soul so that her little child will be a
living, "striking" image of her first-born, the Son of the Eternal, He
who was the perfect praise of His Father's glory.'

For Elizabeth, the annunciation to Mary is closely linked with
the transfiguration. She writes: 'And You, O Father, bend lovingly
over Your poor little creature; "cover her with Your shadow," seeing
in her only the "Beloved in whom You are well pleased."' Mary,
overshadowed by the Spirit, is the woman of light, 'so pure, so
luminous that she seemed to be the Light itself' – a beacon always
pointing the way to Jesus, a glorious manifestation of her Son,
brightness made visible to us in his mother; as Hopkins expresses it:

'his light/Sifted to suit our sight.' Mary is also *the* woman of the indwelling. Elizabeth writes of the visitation: 'When I read in the Gospel "that Mary went in haste to the hill country of Judea"…I imagine her passing by so beautiful, so calm and so majestic, so absorbed in recollection of the Word of God within her.' For Elizabeth, Mary embodies perfectly the prayer of recollection: 'It was within her heart that she lived'.

Mary – companion beneath the cross

'[Mary] loves the souls who follow the Lord right up to beneath the cross,' wrote Edith Stein. That is what Edith herself did: carry the cross with Jesus and stand with Mary on Calvary. She invites every disciple of Jesus to do the same and distils the essence of her teaching on Mary into one single poem, written significantly on Good Friday, just a few years before her death: 'Today I stood with you beneath the cross…' It is like a summary of her Marian devotion, crushed into a few lines addressed to Mary herself. To explore the mystery of the mother of God, Edith, a Jewish convert, went back to her Old Testament roots: to Eve who is the prototype of Mary as *companion* and *mother*. At the beginning of her poem, Edith reminds us that Mary, 'beneath the cross, became our mother'. For Edith, Calvary is the scene of the new Adam on the cross, with the mother of God as the new Eve by his side. There, like Eve, Mary becomes 'mother of all the living' (cf. Gn 3:20), but in a profoundly spiritual sense. The poem continues: 'So you have taken his own into your heart/And with the heartblood of your bitter pains/Have purchased life that's new for every soul.'

For Edith, Mary is not just a mother who cares for, loves and cherishes her children, able to 'guide our steps with care', as the poem expresses it. She is also, as Edith once said, 'the first Christian to follow Christ' and 'the first and most perfect model of Christ'. In her poem, Edith explains how this is so: Mary's 'being and life were totally surrendered/To the Being and Life of the incarnate God.' So, to imitate Mary is to share her union and intimacy with her Son, just as Jesus himself was always at one with his Father. Jesus took flesh from Mary, with all that it means to be fully human, vulnerable and mortal, a companion who shares and understands our fragile nature. Edith addresses Mary: 'You know us all: our wounds, our weaknesses.' But for all our brokenness, we are still called to be companions with Jesus and Mary, extending the kingdom of God; to commune with Mary in her Son's work of redemption. So, Edith ends her poem:

> But those whom you have chosen as companions,
> Surrounding you one day at the eternal throne,
> They here must stand, with you, beneath the cross
> And purchase, with their heartblood's bitter pains
> The radiance of heaven for the priceless souls
> Whom God's own Son bequeaths to them, His heirs.

These concluding words of the poem are like a commentary on Paul's teaching: 'And if we are children, then we are heirs, heirs of God and joint-heirs with Christ, provided that we share his suffering, so as to share his glory' (Rm 8:17).

Mary — more mother than queen

'There is still one thing I have to do before I die,' Thérèse of Lisieux confided to her sister Céline: 'I have always dreamed of saying in a song to the Blessed Virgin everything I think about her.' She realised that dream in her final poem, 'Why I Love You, O Mary!' It was her swan song. Instinctively, she turned to the gospels for inspiration. There she found the real Mary whom she, and all of us, can imitate — not admire from a distance like a figure on a pedestal. On her deathbed, Thérèse would speak of Mary in this way: 'I must see her real life, not her imagined life. I'm sure that her real life was very simple. [Preachers] show her to us as unapproachable, but they should present her as imitable, bringing out her virtues, saying that she lived by faith just like ourselves, giving proofs of this from the

Gospel'. That is exactly what Thérèse does in her poem. She introduces us to the Mary she discovered in the gospels: a woman of faith – virtuous, simple and approachable.

There is no doubt that Mary provided Thérèse with a model for her 'Little Way' and a light for all who wish to follow what the saint calls '*my little* doctrine'. 'The number of little ones on earth is truly great,' Thérèse assures us in her poem to Mary. 'They can raise their eyes to you without trembling./It's by *the ordinary way*, incomparable Mother,/That you like to walk to guide them to Heaven.' In this same stanza, Thérèse exposes the ordinariness and radical poverty of Mary's hidden life, which speak volumes to us about spiritual childhood. 'Mother full of grace,' she writes, 'I know that in Nazareth/You live in poverty, wanting nothing more./*No rapture, miracle, or ecstasy/Embellish your life, O Queen of the Elect!...*' Thérèse is also inspired by Mary's deep and quiet communion with Jesus: 'Oh Mary!' she exclaims, 'how I love *your eloquent silence!*' In this same woman of faith, Thérèse also finds an exemplar for everyone who is tested by God in the darkness of his apparent absence: 'Mother, your sweet Child wants you to be the example/Of the soul searching for Him in the night of faith' – just as Mary herself sought 'anxiously' for her lost Son until she found him in the temple. But Thérèse turns to Mary especially for that lesson on love which gives her 'Little Way' its perennial value and which is so important for one who discovered her vocation as 'love in the heart of the Church': 'Mother, contemplating you, I joyfully immerse myself,/Discovering in your heart *abysses of love.*' Here, she is speaking of pure, unselfish love: '*To love is to give everything. It's to give oneself.*' For Thérèse, Mary is the woman who always said 'yes', who gave everything with her *fiat*. The last few simple words of the poem recall its title, explaining to Mary herself the 'why' of Thérèse's love for her: 'I am your child!' The mother of God is indeed Queen of Carmel – but always, as Thérèse once expressed it so well, 'more Mother than Queen'.